SPIKED BOOTS

Rivermen picking a log jam at the old Ledyard covered bridge between Hanover, New Hampshire, and Norwich, Vermont, around 1912.

SPIKED BOOTS

From New England's North Country,
true stories of yesteryear, when
men were rugged and rivers wild.

by Robert E. Pike

YANKEE BOOKS

A division of Yankee Publishing Incorporated
Dublin, New Hampshire

Some of the lively stories and folk songs in this book were
printed in the author's *Tall Trees, Tough Men* (W.W. Norton &
Co., New York, NY 1967), a profusely illustrated book that
was recently republished by Norton in paperback and that
has received acclaim from critics.

All photographs are courtesy of the author except as noted:
page 34 top, courtesy of John St. Croix; page 34 bottom,
courtesy of Victor Beaudoin; page 58 top, courtesy of Au-
brey P. Janion; page 120 bottom, courtesy of Prescott L.
Howard.

Designed by Jill Shaffer

Yankee Publishing Incorporated
Dublin, New Hampshire 03444
First Edition. Third Printing, 1988.
Copyright 1959, 1960, 1987 by Robert E. Pike

Library of Congress Cataloging-in-Publication Data

Pike, Robert E. (Robert Everding), 1905-
    Spiked boots.

    "From New England's North Country, true stories from
yesteryear, when men were rugged and rivers wild."
    1. Country life — New England — History — 20th
century. 2. New England — Social life and customs. I. Title.
F9.P57 1987   974'.009734   87-2053
ISBN 0-89909-137-7

To My Uncle
Harley Ellsworth Pike

By the Same Author

Granite Laughter & Marble Tears
Contes Intimes
Fighting Yankees
The Strangest Book in the World
Tall Trees, Tough Men
Laughter and Tears
Drama on the Connecticut

Contents

Preface

THIS BOOK is concerned with the history and mores of that part of New England known as the "North Country," that is, the northern part of Maine, New Hampshire, and Vermont. Dixville Notch, the Thirteen-Mile Woods, the Connecticut Lakes, the Androscoggin, Indian Stream, Umbagog, the Rangeleys, Big and Little Averill, the Stark Peaks, Parmachenee, and a hundred other famous names come to mind when one speaks of the "North Country."

It is a region well known to thousands of city "sports" (hunters and fishermen) and to many thousands more summer tourists who come for short stays or simply to drive through. They are attracted by the wild, rugged beauty of the forested mountains and beautiful drives along the winding rivers.

But most of these outlanders never see below the surface. They never see that the inhabitants, who earn a hard but comfortable living from their thin soil, form a race, or better, a "society" that is somewhat peculiar and well worth chronicling. For history has been made here, and here one finds bubbling close to the surface the elements of human nature that make for comedy and tragedy anywhere.

Some of the history and some of the drama I describe in the following pages. If it gives the reader pleasure, I shall have been amply rewarded.

Old Vern

ONE

Old Vern

THE MOUNTAIN road over which I had just jolted ended at a solitary white farmhouse. A thin, worn man clad in blue overalls stood in the yard and waited for me to speak.

"Where's Old Vern?" I asked.

"He ain't here no more, mister," replied the man, revealing a curious dental phenomenon when he spoke. His upper teeth on the left side were missing, as were the lower ones on the right side, which made the two remaining rows pass each other like a pair of scissor blades.

"He ain't here no more," the man repeated. "He sold out to me a year ago and went down to Maine to live. Bought a farm in Pittston and married the woman he bought it from. Or some say she married him."

He grinned at me in friendly fashion. I sat in the coupe, dumb with surprise, thinking of the many summers I had driven into that old dooryard, always sure of a booming welcome. It is true I had received only one letter from Old Vern, in all the years I had known him and had eaten his salt. But after all, I felt I should have been notified of such a cataclysmic change as this.

I thought of the first time I had ever come up Lyman Brook Valley, afoot, with a knapsack on my back. I had been tramping in the North Country, and I had turned off the main highway that followed the Connecticut River because the stream was so pretty and because the road, losing itself behind a steep turn, seemed attractive.

After a stiff climb through woods and past a few farms, the road ended at this white house covered with vines, though a dim cart-track led on across a field and into the woods.

The long-legged proprietor of this last farm was standing on one foot before the barn door. His other limb was furnishing motive power to a grindstone that was whirling madly as he pressed a scythe against it. I had never seen a grindstone turn so fast, but it was evidently hard work.

I slipped off my pack and called to the engrossed yeoman:

"Here, let me turn her for you."

He straightened up, fully six feet and three inches of him, and favored me with a long stare.

"Don't care if you do!" he exclaimed finally. "Take a holt!"

I took a "holt" and turned.

"Leetle faster, young feller," he requested, meanwhile bearing down with all his might. I set my teeth and bent to the task. Old Vern, for this I learned was his name (he lived alone except for a collie dog and a lonesome-looking hound), was apparently determined to get his money's worth.

Have you ever tried to turn a grindstone when a strong man is bearing a scythe down on it as hard as he can? Try it sometime and you will appreciate the fix I had gotten myself into. My arm began to ache. I shifted to the other hand, then back again, then tried both hands at once. At last, as I was about to drop on the grass and die, Vern removed the scythe. He ran his thumb along the edge — an operation that always makes me shiver — and announced that it "would do."

"You're a bear for punishment, all right," remarked this singular person. "I bore down on her pretty hard, but you stood it. Were you figgerin' on going some place over this way?" he went on. "For this is the end of the road. If you go any farther in that direction you'll walk thirty miles before you ever see another road, and if you get lost, which you probably would, you'd walk until you died and you'd never see any road at all."

In answer to his question, I disclaimed any desire to go farther than onto company land, which, according to my map, must lie just beyond his field.

"Hell!" he exclaimed violently, after I told him I intended to camp there and fish and see the scenery. "Hell! You can't camp down there. You might start a fire that would burn my house down!"

"Isn't it insured?" I inquired innocently.

"Insured, hell! And even if it was, I'm no damned Injun to be living in a wigwam until I collect the insurance and build a new one. If you just want to see the scenery, you'd better stay with me. You can sleep on the hay in the barn. It's better than the house, and you can use my stove to cook on, and you can go fishing all you damn please. In fact, I might go with you," he added, a pleased look spreading over his tanned features while he scratched the top of his big right ear reflectively.

So I stayed. I had more fun than a barrel of monkeys, to use one of Vern's phrases. We fished, we tramped through the woods, we called on neighbors, we played cards.

He was a loud-voiced, decisive-in-speech person, Old Vern; careless and quick in all he said and did. One of his neighbors told me that he had once shot a man for stealing his potatoes. When he learned that the fellow had a starving family, he not only paid the man's doctor bill, but kept the family alive all that fall and winter.

"You goddamned fool," Vern told him, "if you had only told

me your goddamned family didn't have anything to eat, I'd have given you all the potatoes you needed, if you'd only come and asked for them like a gentleman!"

Vern was a magnificent specimen of manhood. He was tall and wide beyond the average, and his fierce blue eyes glared out from beneath heavy white brows. A long, straight nose, and long arms ending in huge hands that had a grip like a blacksmith's vise completed his chief physical characteristics. I liked the man on sight.

Work did not seem to bother him much. "This damn grass ain't ripe enough to cut anyway," he rumbled. "It'll do it good to grow another week. And besides, living up here on this goddamned mountain top with only bears and bootleggers for company ain't very uplifting. It's a treat to meet a man who's read a book! In fact, it's unusual!"

Vern had lived in the North Country all his life. His grandfather had taken part in the Indian Stream War, and his own father had been a Baptist deacon.

"A hard hardshell one, too," Vern told me. "I had to go to church about three times a week, and sometimes twice on Sundays, and if I skipped, I got such a licking, by God, that I didn't skip the next week, now I can tell you! He was an awful good man, my father was, but he was too strict. When I got away from home, I swore I'd never go to church again, and I've stuck to it pretty well. I lived in Boston some years. Drove an express team."

"Oh, Boston," I said, trying to appear intelligent. "I suppose you've been to the Old Howard Theater, then?"

"Have I! By God, young feller, I've been there when if a man dropped his hat over the balcony he never saw it again, for it would float right down the aisle in the tobacco juice and out into the sewer!"

One day Vern went to town (North Stratford) and I rode along with him. He hitched a lank, sorrel horse into an open buggy and we set out. Our steed was an ungainly looking brute.

His hip bones stuck out, and his ribs showed plainly beneath the hide. But I noticed he didn't need any checkrein to keep his head up.

"Hosses still mean something in this neck of the woods," Vern observed as we jogged along. "Especially in the winter. We race 'em on the ice quite a lot. Now take this Ted hoss here. He ain't much to look at. He's a good deal like me that way. But he's built like I am, too — to cover a lot of ground in a short space of time."

And in truth the animal did walk faster than many a horse can trot.

"You'd think I didn't ever feed him, the pore dumb brute," Vern continued. "But it's a fact, I throw hay and grain into him something scandalous. But some hosses are like that. Just the least work and they're right down thin as a rail. I guess it's the nervous energy inside of 'em. At least I knew a doctor once who told me that was what ailed me — and I'm a good deal like a hoss."

"You don't mean that you race this awkward brute, do you?" I asked.

Vern chuckled. "He may be awkward," he replied, "but he's like the bedbug in that old song — he gits there just the same."

We were racking along over a level stretch when a man came from behind and passed us like the wind. He was driving a fiery, coal-black horse. A fancy, light buggy with brightly polished nickel on the harness, a tight checkrein, and a martingale all contributed to the impression that here was a *horse;* though to tell the truth all the accessories were unnecessary, for the horse *was* handsome, young, fast, and stepping high.

Vern called a word of greeting as this outfit rattled by us, but the driver gave merely a curt nod in reply.

"That's Charley Baker," said Vern placidly, "and that's a four-year-old colt he's driving. He thinks it's the best hoss in the North Country. It *is* a mighty fine critter, too. But a leetle mite too fancy to suit me."

We had come to the top of a long hill just as Baker passed us. As soon as he got by, he pulled his horse to a walk, for it is an axiom of good driving never to run a horse downhill. It ruins his forelegs. Our own steed kept racking stolidly along but taking about five feet in every stride. Halfway down the hill we caught up with the other. Vern was in no particular hurry, but his horse walked fast and he did not wish to hold him back.

"Git out of the way, Charley," he called.

But Charley, disregarding all the rules of driving etiquette, stuck obstinately to the middle of the road and would not let us by. Vern called again, louder, but Charley never budged. Of necessity, Vern pulled in his Ted hoss, forcing him to walk more slowly. But anger began to smolder in his blue eyes. We came to the foot of the hill, and a long "flat" lay before us. Baker's horse had been dancing to go, and now his driver let him loose. He shot away from us like an arrow. His owner turned around and thumbed his nose derisively.

The long, whiskery man beside me swore and spat out his whole chaw of tobacco, which meant he was thoroughly angry. He pulled sharply on the reins — once — and then let them fall slack again. The effect was magical. In a flash, the shambling, awkward gait of our horse was transformed into a marvelous, smooth-working pace. The light Concord buggy, with us in it, whirled through the air, and I hung onto the back of the seat for dear life.

Vern held a rein in each hand and talked to his "hoss" in a loud voice — meaningless words, but I'll swear the critter understood.

That flat was nearly half a mile long, and before we had covered half of it our Ted hoss had crept up behind Baker and was blowing in his ear. But the son of a gun wouldn't give us room to pass.

Vern swore again, and measuring his chances carelessly, he turned half out into the ditch. We were going fully thirty miles an hour, and we almost overturned, but at last we got by. Vern turned to swear at the discomfited Mr. Baker, but instead of cursing, the old pirate burst out laughing. He laughed loud and raucously. "Haw haw!" he chortled. "See him break! Did you see him break? He couldn't hold him! Haw, haw, haw!"

I looked back. Sure enough, Baker had not been able to hold his horse to its gait. The animal had "broken" and was coming after us at full gallop. Vern pulled in his own horse, and turned out. The other rig dashed by us, Baker sawing savagely on the reins, his face working with rage. Vern recounted the episode in half a dozen places in North Stratford, raising a hearty laugh of appreciation every time.

On our way home that afternoon we passed an isolated farmhouse. Beyond it, not far from the road (which it faced), was a backhouse, one of the little wooden cottages made famous by *The Specialist*. It had two doors, both of which were open. On one side sat an old man, on the other an old woman, both smoking corncob pipes and talking vociferously to each other.

Vern drew up with a startled oath. "What in hell does this mean?" he called.

The old lady eyed him for a moment. Then she removed the pipe from her mouth and answered: "This means, young man, that we're taking solid comfort!"

"Too bad you didn't have a camera," chuckled Vern as we rolled along.

In the course of time I departed from Lyman Brook. Old Vern gave my hand a tremendous shake. I was expecting it, and I gripped his with all my might. I might as well have squeezed a horse's hoof. But at least he shook his head approvingly.

"You've got a good grip, young feller," he boomed. "And I hain't no use for these damn fellers that you shake their hand and it's just like taking hold of a dead fish! Come again whenever you're up this way! Damn it all, I don't suppose you'll write to me, but if you do, I'll answer it. So long!"

17

I saw the old man once more that summer before I left the North Country. It was in a poolroom in Colebrook, at night. I saw him through the window and started to go in to speak to him, but just as I got to the door three men shoved me aside and entered first.

They were half-drunk and looking for Vern, which is the same as saying they were looking for trouble. They walked up to him, and one of them said something. They were able men, those three, and they weren't so drunk they couldn't have put up a battle. But they never had a chance. And I've never believed since that night that Vern was as old as he claimed to be — sixty-two.

His right fist came up like a blast of wrath and struck the nearest man under the jaw. The fellow flew up into the air as if he had been kicked by an elephant and landed with a sodden crash against the wall. The next one grabbed a cue and brought it down on the old warrior's skull with the same vigorous enthusiasm he would have displayed in splitting a block of wood. The cue broke, and Vern fell, but he rolled away from them and came up at the end of the table, blood running over his face and his eyes fairly shooting sparks.

He seized a pool ball off the table and hurled it with all his might. It missed the man it was intended for and went on through the heavy, plate glass window as slick as a rifle bullet, leaving a small, round hole. He seized a second one, but the trouble hunters had had enough. They ran for the door. The second ball grazed the last man's sleeve. Two inches more to the right and it would have smashed his shoulder like an eggshell.

Cautiously I straightened up from behind the next pool table, where I had crouched.

"Oh, it's you, is it?" growled Vern, unclenching a clublike fist. "Come on out and help me find a doctor to fix this cut."

I glanced at the man still lying in a crumpled heap against the wall.

"Him?" said Vern. "Oh, he'll be all right when he comes to — if he ever does. I hope I killed the ***!"

Other patrons came out of retirement and volunteered to take care of the unconscious man.

"That's what a little red-eye will do for you," Vern grumbled as we left in search of a doctor. "If those fellers had been sober, they'd have known better than to come in there and start a row!"

I thought privily of one night I had seen him tanked up on red-eye and looking for trouble in North Stratford, but I didn't mention it.

That winter Vern sent me a letter that I still cherish. It is rich in epithet and citation, and contains a history of all the folks on Lyman Brook. Now sitting there, looking blankly at the scissor-toothed stranger, I relived all the good times I had with Vern, heard again the stories he told me, and saw once more the North Country vistas he opened up to me . . .

TWO

The Brass Cannon

I WAS HELPING Vern mow grass by hand one hot, muggy July morning. For a man who was notably careless in most things, he insisted that the extensive hand mowing on his sidehill farm be done with a care and nicety that surprised me.

"I don't know why it is," he confessed as he stopped his rhythmic swinging, up-ended the snath, and wiped the long blade with a handful of wet grass before beginning to beat an energetic tattoo on it with a whetstone. "I don't know why it is, but I just can't bear to see hand mowin' poorly done. Just like I can't bear to see an axeman not leave a smooth scarf.

"I was goin' through the woods to Megantic one time and I come onto an English feller who'd taken up a homestead there and he was tryin' to clear the land. That feller'd been a clerk in a bank all his life and he'd never seen an axe before. Do you know what he was doin'? Honest to God, he was choppin' all the way around the trees, like a beaver!

" 'Great blushing geranium!' I said to him, 'May I ask do you do that for fun, or because you just don't know any better?'

"Well, sir, I stayed with that feller a week, and showed him how to handle an axe, and a few other things, and he was the most grateful cuss you ever saw. Every Christmas since then, he and his wife have sent me a big chunk of plum pudding they get from England. The English set great store by plum pudding at Christmas, I guess. I don't like it much, but I always write and tell 'em how pleased I am."

He laughed as a memory came into his mind. "His name was Mackay. He couldn't talk any Frenchy, but one day he went over to a French habitant's to buy a pig. The Frenchman wasn't at home, but his wife was. Mac tried to tell her what he wanted, but she no crompaw-paw. Then he thought he'd try sign language. He took out a roll of bills and showed it to her, and then he got down on his hands and knees and crawled around her skirts, gruntin' 'Oink! Oink!' like a hog."

"Did she understand?"

"Hell no!" said Vern, and chuckled delightedly. "She thought he was makin' improper advances to her, and she grabbed a besom and drove him out of the house! I had to go back with him and apologize."

"Can you talk French?"

"Sure! This Canuck kind, anyway. A feller's missed half his life up here on the border if he couldn't parley voo."

"Maybe you can teach me a little?"

"Sure. But the best way is to get a nice French girl and sleep with her all night."

"Is that how you learned?"

"Of course!"

"And you became fluent in one night?" I demanded.

"Well, some people learn faster'n others, I expect. 'Course you can always take more'n one lesson!"

"Look here," I said, as a sudden thought came to me. "If you've been to Megantic, maybe you've heard about a brass cannon up in Arnold's Bog?"

"Heard about it? Hell! Who hasn't heard about it?"

21

"Have you ever seen it?" I persisted.

"No, but I know fellers who claim they have."

"Do you believe them?"

"Of course I don't believe them! That bog is fourteen miles west of where Arnold went through to Megantic, even if it is named after him. Only a goddamn fool would believe such a story!"

"But there's a lot of men hunted for it. Even," I added courageously, "even me. I splashed around in that horrible swamp three days looking for it!"

The old man's laugh boomed out and echoed back from the woods beyond the field. "There's smarter men than you and me been taken in by that story," he said, "so you needn't feel bad. I'll tell you how it started. There's quite a story about that. But let's go over in the shade and set down."

We walked over to the stone wall, where, in the shade of a crab apple tree, reposed a tin pail full of a marvelous drink Vern used to concoct for haying. I generously pass along the recipe: first, have a pail of water with a chunk of ice in it; then put in ginger and maple sugar according to your taste. It's as simple as that, but it's the best drink for a hot day I ever tasted.

Having drunk mightily from the pail, Vern sat down with his back against the tree, and I sprawled beside him.

"There's a man, he must be most eighty years old, named Lewis Leavitt, lives over on the Magalloway. Maybe you've met him?"

"Yes, I met him once, but I never talked to him any."

"Well, you *want* to talk to him. Or let him talk to you. He's a licensed Maine guide, and he was one before I was hatched. And one time, before *you* were born, he was chosen as the best guide in Maine, which is saying something! Of course you've been to Parmachenee Lake? It's just below the border, and close to Arnold's Bog."

"Yes, I've been there."

Vern began his story:

Well, in the old days a man named Danforth ran a sporting camp there. And what I mean, it was a sporting camp! Millionaires came up there, men who had so much money they didn't know what to do with it, and Danforth saw they shot moose, and they thought nothing of leaving him a hundred-dollar bonus after paying his outrageous prices for accommodations and guides. Why, I've seen those fellers play poker with a hundred-dollar ante and the roof the limit, and in one jackpot — why, boy, you wouldn't believe it, so I sha'n't tell you.

But anyway, Lewis was Danforth's head guide, and one day he draws a potbellied, red-wattled sport who was kinda peeved because in two weeks, using all the guides at the camp, he hadn't even seen a moose.

"You damn lazy guides are all alike," says he to Lewis. "I could find just as many moose all by myself as I've been able to with your help. All you're good for is to take a man's money without doing anything to earn it!"

Lewis didn't like that talk very well, but he keeps his temper like a good guide should.

"We do the best we know how, Mr. Smith," he answers carefully. "I've been a guide in this country all my life, and I tell you I've never been so long as this without seeing game."

"Rats!" sneers the sport, or some such word. "You tell that story to all us city men. But you can't make *me* swallow it."

Lewis is a patient man, and as I said, he was known as the best guide in the woods, but at this remark he boils over.

"Do you mean, Mr. Smith," says he, "that I'm a liar?"

The sport looks up at him — and then he looks down again.

"No," he mumbles, "I don't know as I meant to call you a liar, Leavitt."

"It's a good thing you didn't," mutters Lewis.

But a moment later Smith starts again: "Listen, my man," says he. "You know I pay Danforth an awful lot of money to stay at his camp, and you guides are supposed to find us moose we can shoot. If we don't get a moose today I'm going to tell

Danforth to get a new crop of guides if he wants me to come back next year!"

Just then they hear a crashing in the brush and a big bull moose comes running straight across in front of them. Of course Lewis ups with his rifle, but he waits like a good guide should to give his sport the first shot. Smith raises his gun and shoots enough lead to cut a large tree in two. Then Lewis fires and the moose falls. And his bullet is the only one that struck the critter. Smith gets grouchier than ever. He orders the guide not to tell anyone who shot the moose.

The next day, pretty satisfied, he leaves camp, taking the head and a few pounds of meat with him.

A week later, old man Danforth is talking with his head guide and they mention Smith.

"Did he hand you anything extra for your services, Leavitt?" says the old man.

"Not a cent!" says Lewis. "Did he have enough money to pay *you?*"

Danforth grins. "I got two hundred dollars out of him, but it was pretty hard work. He's got scads of money but he's tighter than bark on a tree. It hurts him to part with money just like it hurts most people to have a tooth pulled."

"Yeah," says Lewis. "You know, Danforth," he says, "I shot that moose myself, after he'd missed five times — and he never as much as said thank you."

"Hmm," says Danforth, "but he knew very well that it's the custom to slip a guide a few dollars for such little helps. I'll tell you what, Lewis, he's coming again next fall. Charge him twice as much then!"

"If he comes, I'll charge him all right," Lewis promises. "You know," he goes on, "that feller gave me an idea, just the same. He told me the first day I was out with him that back about 1775 Benedict Arnold led an army up Dead River and over to Megantic in Quebec. I've never thought about it before, but that must be why that big swamp just north of here is called Arnold's Bog."

"Of course," says Danforth. "I supposed you knew that, having been in these parts so long."

"No," says Lewis, "it's one thing I never happened to hear about, or even to think about — but I'm going to think about it a while now. Smith told me quite a story about Arnold. Said he was trustee of some historical museum that owns a lot of Arnold relics. He told me all about them . . . You're sure he'll come back next fall?"

"He'll be here," says Danforth.

"All right then," says Lewis. "In that case you can count on me for next season, too. I'll even guide for you without pay."

Early the next November Mr. Smith comes to Parmachenee again. Age hasn't improved him any. Fat and sassy and bad-tempered, he makes life miserable for all the guides in camp. He asks for Lewis for his guide the first couple of days, but they don't have any luck, and then he tries two others. He's delivering his acrid opinion of guides to Danforth, who has to appear sympathetic, when Lewis comes into the office and asks to speak to the sport.

"I saw fresh tracks of a whopping big moose this afternoon, Mr. Smith," he begins, his blue eyes as free of guile as a little child's, "and I'd like to take you out tomorrow to see if we can find him."

"Huh!" says Smith through his nose. "Well, I suppose you can't be any worse than the others, and *if* you've seen tracks, that's more than any of them have done. I'll go with you."

Old man Danforth pulls his whiskers and looks his head guide over kinda doubtful. He smells trouble and he feels it incumbent on him to remind Lewis that he holds him responsible for Mr. Smith's valuable life and limbs.

"I'll take good care of him," says Lewis. "Don't forget I helped him to get that big moose last fall. And this one is twice as big!"

So the next morning the guide and his sport set out. Lewis leads him by devious ways all forenoon till about noon they stop for lunch. They're in a notch between two mountains and there's a little spring handy. Lewis builds a fire and boils the kettle. Then they rest for a while and smoke. Lewis points to the south.

"That's Dead River down there," he says, "and over this other way is Megantic."

Smith gets interested at once. "Why," says he, "then right here where we are now must be the Great Carrying Place."

"I don't know about that," says Lewis, "but this is where they portage canoes over from the Kennebec to the Megantic."

"Certainly," says Smith, "this is the very place that Arnold's army marched through! Let's see — where would Arnold's Bog be?"

"Right over there," says Lewis, pointing, "only you can't see it on account of the hill."

Smith starts a long speech on the trials and hardships endured by Arnold's men on that expedition. Lewis feels like saying that at least they didn't have any city sports to bother 'em, so it couldn't have been too bad, but he restrains himself.

He happens to turn over a flat stone lying between his feet at the foot of an old birch tree he was reclinin' against, and pokes idly at the dirt.

All at once he grunts with surprise. He'd picked something out of the ground. He rubs it on his sleeve and looks closer. It's an old lead bullet, run in a hand mould. He passes it to Smith, and digs up some more. There's a regular cache of those bullets. Pretty soon he's excavated nearly a peck of them.

"I guess you were right about an army coming through here, Mr. Smith," he says. "Some of them must have been so weak from hunger that they cached these bullets here — and never came back for them."

"They're genuine, all right," says Smith, "and they'll be worth a lot of money, too. I can sell them to the museum. Indeed, there's enough to sell to several places."

"Is that so?" says Lewis, all admiration. "Well now, Mr. Smith, don't you think you ought to give me a little something for finding them for you?"

"You're crazy," says Smith with a sneer. "Why should I give you anything? You're working for me, ain't you? You found them on my time, didn't you? I'll pay you to carry them back to camp, but that's all!"

Lewis wants to punch him on the snoot, but he remembers he's the best guide in Maine, so he acts polite, like a bear meetin' a skunk. He puts the bullets in the canvas lunch sack and they head for camp. Smith is so elated he's forgotten all about moose hunting.

Some time after they've left the Great Carrying Place, they stop on the brow of a hill and Lewis points to the landscape below. It's a tremendous swamp, stretching out for miles — a horrible tangle of dead tree trunks and bushes on low, hummocky islands that are surrounded by dismal, icy-looking black water.

"You must have been there," I said.

"Of course I've been there," said Vern, and swore feelingly. "I was there more than forty years ago, and years after that a city feller paid me seven dollars and a half a day to guide him in there while he hunted for the brass cannon all one summer."

Then Vern continued:

"That's Arnold's Bog," says Lewis. "I've known three men, all good woodsmen, to get lost and die in there. I was on each of the searching parties that found them. That swamp is bad medicine for any stranger. I ran a trap line through it one winter, so I got to know it pretty well. And I can tell you a curious thing about that swamp, Mr. Smith. When Arnold's men came through there they left a brass cannon — it must have been Arnold's, for no other army was ever in this region — that they couldn't drag any farther. I found it there last

27

winter. The undercarriage is all rotted away, but the cannon is as good as ever, only it's sunk down some into the swamp, so the muzzle sticks up into the air sort of slanting-ways."

Smith gets tremendously excited. His red wattles quiver like an old turkey cock's.

"Why," he exclaims, "such a relic would be worth a thousand dollars! You must take me to it!"

"I'd look pretty taking you cannon hunting," says Lewis. "As you said a while ago, I'm paid to guide you *moose* hunting. I charge special rates to guide cannon-hunters."

"Well," says Smith, who sees he's licked, "how much do you want?"

"Seeing as you mentioned a thousand dollars," says the honest guide, "I'll take just five hundred, payable in advance!"

The cannon enthusiast pleads and swears, but it's no use. They get to camp, but Lewis doesn't yield. After supper that night Danforth calls his head guide into the office. There was half a dozen fat sports sitting around a table playing poker and drinking rum. Damn good fellers, too, every one of 'em. Except Smith. But all business is suspended while Danforth interrogates the guide.

"Leavitt," he begins, "Mr. Smith says you know of a brass cannon up in Arnold's Bog?"

"That's right," says Lewis without a quiver.

"He wants you to guide him to it."

"I know it."

"But you refused to do so?"

"I told Mr. Smith that I charged special rates for cannon-hunting. *He* refused. I didn't."

"But five hundred dollars!" breaks in Smith. "That's highway robbery!"

"Well," says Lewis, "you said yourself it was worth a thousand. Besides, look at all those bullets I found and you're going to sell."

"He showed us the bullets," interrupts one of the other

sports, who was a railroad president named — oh, I forget his name. Let's call him Jones. "He showed us the bullets," says Jones, "but he didn't say *you* found 'em."

Smith proceeds to explain how the treasure had been discovered.

"And you aren't going to give the guide anything for his share?" asks Jones. Smith shakes his head. "You *are* a cheapskate, Smith," he says.

"But how about the cannon?" asks Danforth.

"I told him my terms," says Lewis. "Five hundred dollars, paid in advance."

"But how can I trust you?" protests Smith. "I haven't even *seen* the cannon."

Lewis compromises. "I'll guide you to it," says he, "and then you can pay me after you're satisfied."

"That's fair," says Jones. "You couldn't ask for anything fairer than that, Smith."

So the next morning Smith and Lewis and Jones, who was curious to see the old cannon, start out. Lewis led 'em over the roughest country he could find, through windfalls, up hills, across swamps. Finally, when they was good and lost, he stopped in the middle of a bog and points:

"There's your cannon," he says, and the sports look across a hundred feet of icy black water to a little hummocky island. Projecting up out of the brush on one of the hummocks was a thing that might have been a cannon. That was what Lewis was pointing at.

"Maybe it's an old stub," suggests Jones, who has been entertaining some private doubts about the age of those bullets Smith had claimed were genuine. He looks Danforth's head guide right in the eye.

"Nope," says Lewis, looking right back at him. "It's a cannon. Look!" He throws up his rifle and fires. You couldn't mistake the "spang!" when the bullet hit metal.

"But we can't get it now," says Smith, shivering as he looks at the skim ice on that dirty water.

"No," says Lewis, "you'll have to come in the winter, when everything is frozen up tight. The best way would be to come to Woburn, in Quebec, and hire some Frenchman to go in with a yoke of oxen and drag it out. I'll make you a map of this place so anyone can find it for you. Well, are you satisfied?"

Mr. Smith isn't very cheerful, but he agrees he is. When they get back to camp, Lewis draws the map and Smith gives him the money — in cash. Smith leaves the next day, mooseless, but happy with his bullets.

"That winter," Vern continued, after an appropriate pause, "Lewis and I run a trap line over east of Kennebago Lake, and one day we happened to pass close to the Great Carrying Place, and he took me up into the notch to show me the exact spot where he'd found those bullets.

"I looked him in the eye and I grinned, and to save his soul from hell he couldn't help busting out laughing. Then he says to me: 'Do you know what that cannon really was?'

" 'Why no,' says I. 'I supposed *that* was genuine, wasn't it?'

" 'Nope!' says Maine's best guide. 'It was an iron boundary post. All along the border here the boundary is cut out forty feet wide, except in bad swamps like Arnold's Bog — which is the only place in many miles where you'd fail to see you were on the line.'

" 'I know that,' I says. 'Those posts are hollow iron pipes set in a base, put up every so often for markers. And it's lucky for you,' I told him, 'that that particular post should have fallen over sideways like that, so it looked like a cannon muzzle pointing away from you.'

" 'It wasn't all luck,' says Lewis, grinning. 'There's a way onto that island from the other side. I went and pushed that post over the same day I buried the bullets!' "

THREE

George Van Dyke and the CVL

"ONE OF MY sad pleasures," said Vern, the second year I had known him, "is huntin' bobcats. Not *Felis rubor,* either, but *Felis gigantea.*"

He grinned widely at my bewildered look. "You ain't the only man who ever read a book," he said. "But to stick to the cats — I hunt 'em in the winter. Me and old Trailer" (and he scratched the floppy ears of the sad-faced hound) "go out and git quite a few every season. There's a bounty on 'em, you know. Twenty dollars. Maine has a bounty, too, and so does Vermont."

"In the old days a bobcat hunter could earn a pretty decent living. Turn in the nose in one state, the ears in another, and the tail in the third. Now you have to hand over the whole damned carcass. But twenty dollars ain't to be sneezed at. Now if you could come up at Christmas time, or New Year's, I'd like to have you go with me."

I went. It was the 21st of December when I dropped off the train at North Stratford. Vern was waiting for me, his Ted hoss hitched into an old pung sleigh. Snow was banked everywhere. The day was cold and clear and still.

"Git in," said Vern, "and wrap this buffalo robe around you. I've got a freeze-stone in the bottom for your feet. I suppose you knew enough to wear long underwear?"

"Yes. I've got on two pair."

"That's the stuff. It's what you need up here. The Frenchmen don't take it off even in the summer. There's old Pete Emory. He's on the town, has been for years. They pay Hat Hurlbutt to keep him. Pete never takes a bath but once a year. When the tax assessors come around they strip him and put him in a tub and curry him just like you would a hoss. They always find three or four suits of underwear on him."

"This is a nice robe," I told him.

"It is so. My father bought it, back in 1879. I had a new lining put on it five years ago. It'll last fifty more years, I don't doubt. When it wears out for a robe, I'll take and make it into a fur coat. That's how we poor cusses have to scrimp up in this country!"

There is nothing less exhilarating than to get out of bed in the black cold of a northern New England winter morning and build a fire. Vern slept in the kitchen in winter. The next morning, long before daylight, I heard him rattling cold things over at the stove. I shivered comfortably and pretended to be asleep.

Having built a roaring fire, the old man took a lantern and a milk pail and, hatless and coatless, went off to the barn. I heard the snow crunch coldly under his boots as he went down the path. Then he began to sing.

"The old devil!" I thought. "He knows I can't stay in here while I know he's out there working." Reluctantly I crawled out of the blankets and put on my second suit of long underwear (I had slept in the other) and my outer garments and went down to the barn to help milk.

"It smells like a storm," he informed me. "I'll have to tell

Hinman to come over and do my chores, in case we git waylaid tonight."

"Do you mean we may have to sleep out in the woods, in a blizzard?"

"Sure. Why not?"

We went up over the height of land and down the other side. Trailer got on the track of a cat near the head of the Devil's Washbowl and chased him over the ridge and down toward Bragg Pond, where Vern shot him, spitting and squalling, from the branches of a spruce tree. It was too late to get home, and it had begun to storm, so we stayed at the office at Camp Seven. The men in charge knew Old Vern, who had himself been a woods boss in his time.

We sat there after supper talking. The long box stove glowed red-hot. A Coleman lamp shed its soft white radiance over the men who sat at ease in comfortable chairs or sprawled luxuriously in the double bunks. One and all they smoked rank-smelling pipes, and one and all they had tanned, clean faces and clear, bright eyes, for they were the elite of the woods — scalers, stumpage inspectors, a clerk, a walking boss — and two stray bobcat hunters.

Outside, the wind roared and howled and shrieked like a million lost souls crying out of hell. In the forest in back of the camp the interlocked arms of the bare hardwoods wrestled with each other as the gale swept them back and forth. But in the camp we were snug and warm. The sight of the glowing stove and the knowledge of our security from the raging elements made us feel more deliciously and lazily comfortable than ever.

There being a lull in the conversation, I asked the walking boss a favorite question of mine, to wit: what was the strangest thing he had ever seen in the woods?

After due deliberation and hearty expectoration — quite oblivious to the large printed sign above his head that in five languages forbade him to spit — he looked upon the assembly

ABOVE: *Connecticut Valley Lumber Company log drive in the Connecticut River, just below White River Junction, Vermont, in 1898. In the background is the "Mary Ann" (the cook raft).* BELOW: *Lumberjacks playing poker in the "ram pasture."*

34

from beneath his thin gray eyebrows and spoke as follows:

"The most unusual thing I ever saw was a dam that blew upstream."

At this terrible lie, the smoking ceased for a moment, but though every man present knew that no dam ever did or ever could blow upstream they prudently refrained from saying so, for the boss was a man of uncertain temper. But by their loud silence they condemned him. I, too, thought he was prevaricating, but I wanted the story, so I asked innocently:

"Is that so unusual?"

Then the men released their disapproval of the boss in a burst of laughter at my ignorance and informed me that a good dam-builder's boast is that his dams never "blow," that is, spring a leak and consequently are torn away by the stream — always *down*-stream.

"There are many good dam-builders in this North Country," said the gray-haired boss, "and most of them will tell you they never built a dam that blew — and most of them are liars. I never knew but one man, and I have known them all, who could make that boast and make it good."

"And he," said Old Vern promptly, "was Grinner Schoppe."

"Aye," said the boss. "It was old Win."

And so he sat for a space, his mind busy with God knows what memories of other days, until I ventured to ask him how it was the dam had blown upstream. Then he grinned a little with his thin, smooth-shaven lips, eyed the men he knew believed he was telling a lie, and said:

"Have any of you ever been to Success Pond?"

Several of us had, though it is a pond miles in the woods, at the foot of Goose High, and no roads lead to it.

"There is a beaver dam there," I said, "the largest beaver dam ever found in the North Country, across the outlet of that pond."

The boss looked at me with interest.

"Are you sure?"

35

"Quite sure."

"I'm glad to learn it," he said. "I've been in the woods all my life and I've seen hundreds of beaver dams, but it never occurred to me that that embankment had been put up by beaver. I remember we wondered how it came there. Why, it's three-quarters of a mile long and you could make a two-sled road on top of it. Now I can understand some things I couldn't understand before.

"You see, the part of the beaver dam right at the outlet had gone out, but the rest of the embankment was still there, so all we had to do was to build a piece to fit in the hole, which we did. Now there's a stream called Silver Brook comes down the mountain and flows along beside the foot of the embankment and empties into the outlet just below our new piece of dam, and it comes in at such an angle that it's headed right toward the dam.

"We were driving Silver Brook the next spring, and the first time a head of water was let loose from our driving dams, it came smashing down there so fast that it swept right up against our new section of dam and pushed it way back into the lake — *upstream!* We got some bateaux and towed it back, the whole damn thing, all in one piece, and made it more solid, and it's there today, and half of you fellows have seen it. But she blew upstream, just as I said."

He looked around the room from beneath his gray eyebrows, the shadow of a grin on his thin lips. The men nodded their heads solemnly.

"Who was this man Schoppe?" I asked.

"He was Van Dyke's right arm," said the boss.

"He was the best goddamned man who ever went down the river!" said Vern. "Except maybe Van Dyke himself," he added.

"Well, then," I said, "maybe you'll tell me who Van Dyke was?"

"Van Dyke!" repeated Vern, perplexed. "Why, hell, he was

36

— he was George Van Dyke. The old lumber king. Didn't you ever hear of him?"

"George Van Dyke," said the walking boss slowly, "was the greatest man the North Country ever produced — bar none."

"That's a pretty strong statement," protested a little old man mildly. His name was McKelvie, and he was a scaler.

"You've known 'em all, Mac," said the boss tolerantly. "Do you recollect anyone who ever got the better of him?"

"Well," said Mac, grinning, "there was a man named Higgins . . . "

The boss laughed, a single explosive chuckle, immediately repressed as if unbefitting his dignity.

"What's the story?" I asked.

Mac looked at Vern. "You were at the office that day," he said. "Why don't you tell it?"

Vern spat hugely at the stove, and his laugh boomed out.

"Van Dyke," he began, "was going to log the spruce off a mountain in Lemington. He was going to land it on the Connecticut, and the best place for his two-sled road was right across an old, abandoned farm — that is, it *had* been abandoned. He sent a crew down to build camps and swamp roads; and the boss laid out the main road right across the fields of that farm, breaking down fences regardless.

"The next day Van Dyke was sitting in his private office in Stewartstown when a tall, lean, raw-boned cuss with a handlebar moustache came busting in, herding the bookkeeper in front of him by the persuasion of a double-barrelled shotgun.

" 'I t-t-told him not to come in, Mr. Van Dyke,' stuttered the bookkeeper, 'but he — he's bloodthirsty. He said he'd blow a h-hole through me I c-could jump a goat through!'

" 'What in hell do you mean by such actions!' roars old George, jumping up from his chair, but the stranger reaches around the bookkeeper and pokes his shotgun in George's belly and the old warrior sits down again.

" 'I'm runnin' this show!' Moustache says, and the cocked

hammers on that weapon of his were mighty convincin'. 'Now you shut up and listen to me. My name's Higgins, and I live down on the old Nugent farm in Lemington. I came up from Maine and bought that place a week ago, and it's mine! Yesterday your damn foreman came there and broke down my fences and laid out a road right across my fields! I told him to quit, and he said to come to you. Here I am! My neighbors told me what kind of a crooked old skinflint you are, but you won't put over any guff on me, Mister Van Dyke! I came prepared!' With that he shakes that old blunderbuss, both barrels of it cocked, in George's face.

"But the old man didn't scare very easy. He says to him:

" 'Why, Mr. Higgins, I'm sure we can fix this up all right. I didn't know you was living on the old Nugent place. My foreman didn't, either. If he had, I'm sure he wouldn't have acted that way.'

" 'The hell he wouldn't!' growls Higgins, his eye never wavering.

" 'Have a cigar, Mr. Higgins,' says Van Dyke, shoving up a boxful, 'and sit down and we'll talk this over like gentlemen. Now I don't want any trouble with you,' he says, after Higgins had finally decided to take a cigar and sit down. 'As you see, it was a mistake, and I shall not only speak to my foreman — ' " Vern broke off to grin at the walking boss, who grinned faintly back.

"He spoke to me all right," he admitted.

" '. . . and I shall not only speak to my foreman,' " repeated Vern, " 'but I'll make it right with you, Mr. Higgins. Nobody could do more than that, could they?'

"By then the raw-boned gent from Maine was beginning to think he'd been barking up the wrong tree. He still kept the shotgun cocked, but he'd turned the muzzle away and was sitting there opposite Van Dyke puffing away on the best cigar he'd ever had in his mouth.

" 'So you've just bought that old Nugent place,' says George.

38

'and there I supposed it was abandoned. I suppose,' he says, 'the fences ain't in very good condition?'

" 'No,' says Higgins, 'they ain't. Next spring I figure I'll have to lay out a hundred dollars on fence posts.'

" 'Hmm,' says George, 'that's quite a lot of money. Look here, Mr. Higgins,' he says all at once, as if struck by a bright idea — as indeed he was. 'You know I've got a cedar swamp up back of that mountain. Now you need fence posts and I need a road. I'll tell you what — you let me use that road this winter, and I'll *give* you all the cedar in that swamp. It ain't worth anything to me. I only want the spruce. What you don't need yourself, you can sell. How's that?'

"Well, Higgins, he thought that was just dandy. He took another cigar and went home, thinking what a good, kind man Van Dyke was."

Vern ceased his tale. With his big stockinged feet on the table, he took his empty pipe from his mouth and rolled it slowly to and fro in his hands, staring at it attentively. Outside, the wind had died down. The camp was very quiet. "Then Mac was right," said the clerk. "At least one man got the better of the great Van Dyke."

The way he said it, it was a sneer at the walking boss. Strangely, the latter took no offense. He even smiled gently at the clerk.

"You see," he said softly, "when Higgins went up there in the spring to get his posts, he found a swamp all right — but there wasn't a cedar tree in it!"

"Then there was the time he built the hay scales," another man took up the tale. "They'd just had an epidemic of hog cholera in Stewartstown and over two hundred hogs had been buried in one hole. About a month later Van Dyke wants some scales built, so he takes a crew out and says: 'Dig there.' 'But, Mr. Van Dyke,' says one of the men, 'that's where they buried the hogs.' 'I don't care a goddamn,' says George. 'I said dig there!' And they dug there. They dug down into those hogs and they built the scales and there they stand today."

"Remember the time," chuckled the boss, quite forgetting decorum in the flood of memories that rushed over him, "remember the time that fellow told him he didn't use tobacco? It was when the men were being paid off in the spring, at the office," he explained to the rest of us. "The men walked past the pay window and the bookkeeper gave them their winter's wages. George stood beside him watching things. Supplies the men had bought at the wanigan* during the winter were deducted, of course. This fellow read his wanigan slip and saw ten dollars taken off for tobacco. 'But Mr. Van Dyke,' he says, 'I don't use tobacco. I never have. Any of the men will tell you so.' 'Can't help it,' says George. 'It was there for you if you'd wanted it. Next man!' "

"Ayuh," said McKelvie, "but don't forget what Bill Bacon did the same morning."

"That's right, too," assented the boss. "He was a tough nut to crack, Bill was. He and Van Dyke were cut out of the same piece of goods."

"What did he do?" I asked.

"He'd figured out just what was coming to him," said Mac, "and when he got to the window and didn't receive that much money, he pulled a revolver out of his pants and held it against Van Dyke's Adam's apple until the old gentleman decided to hand over the rest."

"Do you think he would really have shot him?"

"He would!" said Vern, Mac, and the boss simultaneously and with conviction.

"Of course," Vern explained, "George said it was the bookkeeper's mistake, and he would never think of cheating one of his men. The next winter he made Bill a straw boss."

* The outfit that accompanies rivermen "on drive" — tents, cooking equipment, bedding, etc. — is called the "wanigan." The term also designates the company store in the logging camps.

"He bought a trotting horse once named Esperanza for ten thousand dollars," said another man, "and bet ten thousand dollars on her first race. And she won it."

"He must have made some money," I said.

"He was born a pauper and died a millionaire, and in between he went broke three times," said the walking boss. "If you are really interested," he added slowly, "I can tell you all about him. Or at least as much as anyone here, I guess.

"He was born at Stanbridge, Quebec, in 1846. He was the fifth child in a family of eight children. His father was a native of Highgate, Vermont, and the family came originally from Kinderhook, New York. George's father was poor as hell. Naturally, with eight kids. They lived in a log cabin, and George never owned a pair of shoes till he was eleven years old. He went to school though, when he was a kid, and he happened to have a teacher who saw he had stuff in him and she took a lot of pains with him.

"But when he was eleven, he left home to support himself. When he was fourteen, he was an axeman over on the Androscoggin. For ten years or more he worked in the woods and on the river, carrying a cant dog on his back like any ordinary riverman. But he was different from the ordinary lumberjack. He was strong in the back, but he wasn't weak in the head.

"When he was twenty-six, he was partner in a sawmill at Guildhall, Vermont, and in 1878 he bought a lot in Hereford, Quebec, for one hundred dollars. He cut a million feet of logs off that lot ("Which means," interpolated Vern, "that he cut all the adjacent timber, too.") and drove them down the river to South Lancaster, where he had agreed to deliver them to the man he sold them to.

"But just as the drive was coming into the booms, his prospective purchaser went into bankruptcy, and Van Dyke was left with a million feet of logs in the river. There he was, stuck. He hadn't paid his winter crew, but hired them to bring down the drive, telling them he'd pay them when he got his own money. He'd done the winter's work on credit, and now his credit was all shot. But 'Never say die' was George's motto.

"The mill men were on strike, so he took over the mill, put in enough of his rivermen to run it, and proceeded to saw out and sell his own lumber, the remainder of the men living meanwhile at the wanigan."

"The price of lumber jumped three dollars a thousand, and Van Dyke cleared ten thousand dollars on the deal. With that to start on, he began to acquire timberland in the North Country.

"Van Dyke's history is so bound up with the history of lumbering and especially of the Connecticut Valley Lumber Company (CVL)," the walking boss in his slow, careful voice went on, "that we sort of have to consider them together. The first drive from the upper Connecticut was in the spring of 1868, the logs being cut by Eli Hanson on the lower end of Indian Stream and driven to Holyoke, Massachusetts, where they were sawed out.

"After that, there were considerable cuttings on Cedar Stream and Deadwater Brook, and in 1873 the Schoppe brothers, Harvey and Winfield — Win was the dam-builder, the one they called "Grinner" — took a logging job on South Bay at First Lake. About that same time a New Jersey millionaire named Isaac Homans was busy buying up "State Lands" from the state of New Hampshire — he got 'em for around forty cents an acre, I think — and he logged 'em a little before he finally sold out his holdings to the Connecticut River Lumber Company in 1879.

"That company was chartered in 1879 under the laws of the state of Connecticut, and was composed mostly of a group of Connecticut capitalists intending to exploit the vast timber resources of this region. The first president, and the man who organized the firm, was named George S. Scott. We never heard much about him, but Asa Smith, who was general manager of the company from 1880 to 1884, was an unusually fine man. A square shooter if ever there was one.

"Eighteen seventy-six was called the 'Ross year,' after John Ross, the great riverman of the Penobscot, who they hired to come over and take the drive down the Connecticut that spring. He came, bringing his double-ended bateaux and his Indian rivermen — the best rivermen in the world — but even John Ross couldn't lick nature. In 1876 there was the highest and the lowest water ever known on the Connecticut.

"Of course a drive starts in the spring, as soon as the ice goes out, the idea being to get the logs to their destination while the water is high, so they won't be held up and jammed on sandbars and rocks. But that year Ross had only got to the Fifteen-Mile Falls by the Fourth of July. So his entire drive was hung up in the river all that summer and in the ice all the next winter. Took him two years to go through to Hartford!"

"That was one year," interpolated Mac, "that Ike Homans' suggestion for logging the North Country didn't seem quite so foolish — 'When the logs are once loaded on the sleds, why not haul them right through to Hartford, instead of waiting for the spring to drive them?' It's over three hundred miles from Indian Stream to Hartford."

The walking boss continued his story: "Asa Smith logged on Indian Stream and Perry Stream and around First and Second Lakes. In 1884 he resigned, and George Van Dyke succeeded him. In 1886 Van Dyke sold his own holdings to the Connecticut River Lumber Company (CRL) and became its president. Van Dyke had owned mills at Guildhall and at McIndoes Falls, Vermont, but from 1887 on, the company took out all their logs at Mount Tom, Massachusetts, just north of Holyoke.

"An odd thing happened in the summer of 1897, when the boom at Mount Tom broke, and many of the logs went down the river and out into Long Island Sound. Van Dyke paid a dime apiece for all logs salvaged and landed on the shore of the Sound near the mouth of the river, and the fishing schooners did salvage a lot. They were all towed back up the river to

George Van Dyke, the old
lumber king and (below) his
smashed Stevens-Duryea car.
Van Dyke and his chauffeur
were killed when the car
slipped off the riverbank
opposite Turners Falls,
Massachusetts, on
August 9, 1908.

Hartford, where the company set up a portable mill to saw them out.

"In 1902 the CRL changed its name to the Connecticut Valley Lumber Company (the CVL), and in 1908 Van Dyke was killed. He had a drive of fifty-three million feet of logs in the river and at Turners Falls, Massachusetts, there was a big dam. On the west bank at the village of Gill (also known as Riverside) on the eighth of August, 1908, his crew of rivermen were up at four in the morning guiding the logs through the sluice in the dam. From four o'clock until seven Van Dyke watched them, sitting in the rear seat of his new Stevens-Duryea automobile which was driven by his longtime chauffeur, Shorty Hogdon. In Van Dyke fashion he had told Shorty to drive out onto the extreme edge of the seventy-foot precipice. As they started to leave, the shaley top of the cliff slid off into the river, and the car overturned as it fell to the bare rocks below. Both men died before night."

For a space the men were silent, the old-timers out of respect for the long-dead man who had been their master; the young ones because they sensed how the others felt. The clerk was a thickset, aggressive man, with black hair, who seemed out of place in that company. He broke the silence.

"Isn't it true," he demanded, and managed somehow to make the question offensive, "that when a man working on a jam fell into the river, old Van Dyke used to yell: 'To hell with the man! Save the cant dog!'?"

"It's true," said the walking boss. "And a damned good reason for it, too. A lot of rivermen were just like you, Chadwick! They weren't worth as much per board foot as good sound hickory!"

The clerk flared up. "I don't care! From what you say yourselves, Van Dyke was a lying, cheating, grasping scoundrel who ground down the workingman to fatten his own pocketbook. . . ."

"Listen, Chadwick," broke in Vern, removing his feet from the table and transfixing the clerk with a fierce stare. "I've heard guys like you. They stand around on Boston Common, too goddamned lazy to work, yelling how they're being downtrodden by the rotten capitalists. Why, you greasy swine, if it wasn't for the capitalists, you wouldn't have a job today nor anything else! Why in hell don't you go back to Russia, where there ain't any capitalists? I'll bet your folks were damned glad to get away from there to come here!"

"I've heard how Van Dyke used to go into a train and pull the very boots of rivermen," growled the clerk, ignoring the epithet Vern had hurled at him.

"Yes!" boomed Vern. "And they was his boots, too!" He'd worked and earned the money to buy 'em and he'd paid for 'em! You and the scum like you, you want other people to work and then *give* you a living while you sit around and yelp for more! Goddamn your ignorant soul! You've got a nerve to criticize a man like Van Dyke! You was never so poor in all your life as Van Dyke was! You've had a lot better schoolin' than he ever did! You never went out from home when you was eleven years old, to support yourself. Today you and the likes of you can get shoes and clothes and food and everything else you need — free! — which is more than you can do in any other country in the world. Why? Goddamn you, tell me why! I'll tell *you* why! Because capitalists like Van Dyke and taxpayers like me who *earned* what they got, *give* it to the likes of you! Hell! If I was boss of this camp I'd put you out in the road tonight! You're no benefit to a sufferin' humanity!"

"Calm down, Vern," said the boss. "You aren't running this camp. And you, Chadwick, I'll tell you now, and I'll not bother to tell you again, that you'd better watch your tongue if you want to stay here.

"To hear us talk," he continued after a moment, addressing himself particularly to me, "you'd think Van Dyke was a pretty bad egg. For what we've said is true, and I could tell you other stories of the same nature. But that's only one side of the story. A man as big as Van Dyke was bound to have enemies, and you

46

know how much faster evil stories circulate than good ones. He may have stolen a little timber off government land, but everyone did that. The very people who criticize him — like Chadwick here," (and he waved a scornful hand toward the clerk) "would do the same thing if they had the chance. And when they talk of how hard he was on his men, that's nonsense. He was an axeman and a teamster and he could go out and pick a jam with the best of them. He never asked a man to do something he wouldn't do himself.

"He was generous, too, and public spirited. I could tell you of plenty of kind things old George did. And personally he was a man of clean habits. Even his enemies won't say anything about him that way. Another thing they'll all tell you is that he had a lot of common sense, he had good judgment in practical matters, and he was a born executive.

"He had a wonderful memory. One time — it was in the fall of 1901 — I was in New York with him and we saw a pair of black horses on an express wagon. He stopped like a shot when he saw them. 'Those horses were at Charlie Layton's camp on Teapot Brook,' he said. 'And they got on the horse raft at the Narrows that spring. You look and see!' The rig was standing in front of a building. I went over to see, and sure enough, there was our mark on their front hoofs.

"George's big weakness was stock-market gambling. He went broke three times speculating in stocks, but he always pitched in here harder than ever and made it up.

"The businessmen up here," said the boss slowly, "have always talked a lot about the lumber being shipped down the river and out of the state to 'foreign' mills, instead of being worked up in local plants giving work to local men. The Brown Company has its big mills on the Androscoggin at Berlin, and before he died Van Dyke saw the handwriting on the wall and he knew saw logs would give way to pulp. He was planning to put up a paper mill at North Stratford when he got killed. And no man came after him with enough vision and guts to carry out the scheme.

"His family? They all died. He had no wife, no children, and his brothers Tom and Philo and all their children died. There's not one left in the North Country today.

"But the CVL kept going. In 1912 the company was bought by Stone & Webster of Boston. Stone & Webster aren't lumbermen, but they were interested in waterpower. So they bought the holdings of the company in order to control the flow of the Connecticut River by owning all the headwaters.

"But they went in for lumbering on a large scale. In 1915, the largest drive that ever went down the river — sixty-five million feet — was also the last of the long-log drives. There'll never be another. From then till 1921 the company cut and drove pulpwood in four-foot bolts, delivering it all the way along the river from South Lancaster to Bellows Falls. In 1918 the war was on, and pulpwood brought fabulous prices. We drove a hundred thousand cords down the river that spring.

"After 1921 they stopped logging themselves, but they began to sell stumpage licenses to other companies or to individuals. By this arrangement the pulp is sold "on the stump" at so much per cord — say $4.00. Back in 1914 the Brown Company had bought 46,000 acres of stumpage in one block from the CVL — all the softwood they owned on the Diamonds and the Magalloway.

"The CVL was in its glory while Stone & Webster owned it. It was a compact little unit, a subsidiary of the corporation, and they liked to come up to their 'northern office' (the main office was in Boston, of course) on weekend trips and go fishing or hunting. They owned half a million acres of land up here, but that was just a drop in their bucket.

"They fixed up Idlewild on Second Lake and built a decent road to it and put a man and his wife in charge. They bought a big new motorboat for the camp, and a big new flag. Oh, nothing was too good for our 'northern office.'

"They put two genuine foresters on the staff, who used to rival one another writing treatises on *Dendroctinus piceaperda* — which is what fellows like that call the spruce budworm. They got a man who had been an officer in the Engineering Corps of the Army and appointed him resident engineer, and he went around surveying for dam sites and logging railroads and such things."

"That's Orton Newhall," interrupted Vern, "and a mighty fine little man he is, too. I've worked for him."

"Newhall's a good man," the boss agreed. "Well, Stone & Webster treated everybody fine. A lot of poor devils who had worked all their lives for the company and maybe lost a leg or an arm in service, as you might say, were given pensions. So everybody was happy.

"Then the blow fell. In 1927 Stone & Webster sold the CVL for about twice what it was worth to two other corporations, the St. Regis Paper Company and International Paper and Power. They juggled the stock around until the timber finally came into possession of the St. Regis, while The New England Power Co. owns all the waterpower rights.

"Well, the 'golden age' was at an end. The St. Regis came in and slashed right and left. They fired the manager, they fired the walking boss, they looked at the list of pensioners and tore it up.

" 'Is this a lumber company or an old ladies' home you're running?' they sneered.

"They made John Locke manager. John had been chief forester and he was a native of the North Country."

"And he never had an enemy in the world," said old Mac feelingly.

"He had one," the boss corrected him, "and that was enough. Well, they painted a new sign and hung it over the office door in Stewartstown in place of the old CVL. It's now the New Hampshire–Vermont Lumber Company. The CVL had been forced to take over the property of the New Hampshire Stave and Heading Company at North Stratford, and the St. Regis put a man named George Kezar in charge of that plant. Kezar had been a horse-trader and a cattle-dealer all his life. Lived in Canaan. How did he suddenly get to be superintendent of a large and active hardwood mill? I could tell you," said the boss grimly.

"I could also tell you how pretty soon John Locke got a notice from the New York office that he was fired. And when he went out, Mr. Kezar stepped in."

"So," concluded Mac, "all that's left of the old CVL is Newhall and Cozzie."

"That's right," said the boss. "I'd forgotten Cozzie. He's Newhall's right-hand man," he added.

"And," came Vern's loud voice, "he came from Russia just like your parents did, *Chadwick,* only Tom Cozzie was poor. He'd never been to school and he couldn't read nor write. He couldn't even speak English. He didn't know anybody here. He didn't have any friends. Today he owns his own home and he's got a wife and children and money in the bank. Furthermore he's become a citizen of the United States, and he don't go around yelling how the rotten capitalists like me and old George Van Dyke grind down the honest workingman!"

He glared at the clerk, but the latter dropped his eyes and kept his mouth shut.

FOUR

Spiked Boots

V ERN HAD gone up to the attic to hunt for a fish pole, and I trailed along after him. The attic was just like that of any other North Country farmhouse — cobwebby rafters from which hung mysterious bags, braided traces of corn, and old clothes; corners piled full of haircloth trunks, boxes, and dead furniture. I saw a homemade cradle, an ancient spinning wheel, a flax-carder, piles of books and magazines, and then, suspended from a nail, two pair of rivermen's boots.

The one-inch calks were sharp as needles and looked like new. The leather had been recently oiled and shone dully in the sunlight that filtered through the dusty windows.

"Ice going out?" I joked. "I see you've got your boots greased."

Vern turned from tossing in-the-way objects aside and stalked over to the boots. The great size of one pair attested that they belonged to him. The others were much smaller. He took them in one huge hand and held them almost tenderly.

"Those boots, young feller," he said, "may be said to mark the passing of an era, if you know what I mean. There's no fool like an old fool," he went on. "Every spring I take these boots out and file off the rust, and grease 'em. And I know I'll never use 'em again. Not ever."

I had seen the old man in many moods, and once I saw him stand grimly over the grave of the woman he loved, a grave he had dug himself, but this was the only time I ever caught a note of sadness in him.

"You want a story?" he asked. "Well, I'll give you one. One spring, quite a few years ago, I was a woods foreman for the Brown Company, and I had fifty or sixty men up on the Little Magalloway River, breaking out rollways. The ice had just gone out, and we were rolling the logs down into the river over a steep bank fifteen or twenty feet high.

"The water was high and fast, of course. Below one rollway was an eddy that kept the logs inshore instead of letting them float down with the current. They got piled up pretty deep there, so I told the men to wait while I took two men and went down to pole them out into the river.

"We were working away, and had got them pretty well cleared out, when there came a yell from the men on the bank. We looked up, and there all the logs on that rollway had got loose and were starting to roll down on top of us. We turned and ran over the floating logs for the middle of the river. The other two men made it safely, but I didn't.

"My first jump, I landed on my left foot on a big spruce, but before I could bring up my right foot, another log bobbed out of the water and caught it between the two logs. I stuck my peavey into the log and pulled for all I was worth, but I was stuck there as if I was in a bear trap. I caught a glimpse of those logs just leaping over the bank, and I knew my time had come — and by God, mister, it would have come, right there and then, if pretty near a miracle hadn't happened.

52

"There was a riverman named Dan Bosse* working up on that rollway. Dan was the best man on logs I ever saw in my life. I've seen him do things I'd never have believed if I hadn't seen 'em myself. Well, he seen what a fix I was in, and even before the logs came thundering down off the skids, he run out and jumped. So help me, he jumped fifteen feet straight down, and landed on that log behind me and drove one end of it deep into the water. The other end snapped up past my head like a flash of light, but that didn't bother me.

"My foot was free then, and I sailed out of there on my other log as quick and easy as if I were on a feather bed. And not one second later that rollway landed kerplunk where I had been standing, and filled the river ten feet deep with logs. Bosse? He was right behind me, on the same big spruce.

"He wasn't a big man. He wouldn't have weighed more than a hundred and sixty," Vern went on slowly, his eyes fixed on the smaller pair of boots. "But he had an unnatural sense of balance. I saw him one day down to Berlin, in the Brown Company railroad yards. They were building a pulp-hauler to take the pulpwood out of the river, and they had a pole that was two feet and a half through at the butt and forty-five feet high.

"That pole stood right straight up in the air, and Dan Bosse hung onto the hook of the derrick and let them hoist him up onto the top of that pole, and I'll swear before God, and get a dozen witnesses to swear with me, that he *stood* on top of that pole with a sledge hammer in both hands and drove bolts into the pole beneath his feet! There was a man named Haines working in the yard office and he saw him hammering there, and Haines just laid right down on his belly and clawed at the grass with both hands.

"I've seen Bosse in his stocking feet go out in the river on a big four-foot stick of pulp and play with it till he had it on end, and he'd *keep* it standing on end. A lot of people don't believe

* Pronounced "Bossy" but properly spelled Bosse.

53

that. Nobody who'd never seen it *would* believe it — unless they knew Bosse. I've seen him light a fuse on two sticks of dynamite and swim in under a log jam and place it and swim out and be picked up by a bateau before the powder exploded.

"One summer the company sent him up to Windigo on the St. Maurice, to drive team. Ralph Sawyer had charge there. They'd just strung an inch-and-a-half steel cable across the river. It was four hundred and two feet long, and of course it sagged in the middle. The men used to amuse themselves trying to walk across it.

"With a pike pole to balance themselves, they could get halfway across, but when they started up the other slope, they always fell in. It wasn't because of the upward incline but because a peculiar sway got into the cable then and they couldn't keep their balance. One Sunday, after Dan arrived, the boys got him down to walk the cable. They tried it and they fell in. He swam back across the river and took off all his clothes except his underwear and socks."

With the skill of the true storyteller, Vern paused.

"Well?" I demanded impatiently.

"Well, Dan walked across that cable, turned around, and walked all the way back!"

"I suppose these are his boots?"

"Yes, they're Dan's boots," said the big old man, and the sad note sounded in his voice again. "Dan was a terrible booze-fighter. A lot of these old unmarried woodchucks up here are. Well, one day the Brown Company had a woodsmen's jubilee in Berlin, and of course logrolling was one of the principal events. All the big lumber companies in New England sent their best bearcat to cop the prize. The old CVL thought I might have a chance, so they sent me."

Vern stared at the gleaming boots and ran a horny thumb caressingly over their needle points.

"It would have been a contest between me and Bosse. Everybody knew that. I don't know whether he could have licked me.

He probably could, though I'd have got a lunch while he was getting a feast. Anyway, the Brown Company brought Dan down to Berlin and kept him locked up in jail overnight so's he'd be sober for the logrolling. But the damn fools let him loose an hour before the contest started, and he was so drunk by eleven o'clock that he couldn't have stood on a log.

"I'd watched the other contestants, and they weren't anything to brag about. Dan came up to the pool, but he was noisy drunk and finally the police had to lead him away. He gave me his spiked boots to keep till he came back. The last I saw of him he was going down Main Street in Berlin in his stocking feet with a big policeman in front and one behind and he was kicking the one in front in the tail at every step."

"So you won the prize?"

"Hell no! If I couldn't roll against a good man I wasn't going to roll at all, so I didn't compete."

"How come Dan never came back for his shoes?"

"The red-eye was too much for him at last. He went crazy. They took him down to Concord to the bughouse. He'll die there, I suppose, if he hasn't already."

He blew his long nose violently on the floor and hung the boots back on the nail.

"I'll never wear 'em again," he repeated. Having stared fiercely at the boots for some moments he turned to me and continued:

"I've often thought of how the boss there at Camp Seven exposed to you the history of the old CVL and what he said about driving the Connecticut. And how dry he made his account. He gave you the bones, dry bones, but no blood and red meat. When I was polishing up these old boots the last time, I got to thinking about the last long-log drive down the Connecticut, and how I wished someone could write it up so's it would be remembered.

"You know, the Connecticut River drive was more than an ordinary log drive. It was an institution. It had existed for more than forty years and was the biggest annual event in the North Country. The people couldn't imagine a spring without a drive any more than you could imagine a winter without Christmas.

"Practically every man in this region is a farmer, and practically every one of them works in the woods in the winter. But driving logs ain't like cutting logs. Most anybody can learn to handle an axe, but when it comes to breaking jams and riding logs in fast water and working in ice water up to your belly button sixteen hours a day, it takes a special sort of a man. Of course it's evident he's got to be sort of thick in the head, but he's also just got to have physical stamina."

"I should think," I interrupted him, "that every riverman in the world would have permanent pneumonia."

"You're wrong there, sonny. The only man on drive I ever knew to catch pneumonia was a cook — and he never went near the water. What does happen, though — when those river drivers get old you'll find most of 'em all crippled and twisted with rheumatism. And I reckon those cold baths are a sort of contributing factor.

"A lot of fellers would start out on the drive and not be able to finish. They'd quit after a couple of weeks and walk back home. But the fellers who went down 'all the way,' as we used to say, were somebody. A man who'd gone down all the way on the Connecticut River drive could get a job on any drive in New England and at top wages.

"It was dangerous work. The women up here who kissed their men good-bye in the spring never knew whether they'd see 'em alive and whole again.

"Well, it came along to 1914 and 1915, and the CVL had 'most a thousand men in the woods that winter, but before spring the whisper went abroad that there'd never be another long-log drive down the Connecticut. The whisper grew and grew until it became a roar, and all you'd hear men talking about on street corners and in barrooms and in country stores

56

was this incredible thing that couldn't be true, that just couldn't be true.

"It was the most exciting news that had hit the North Country since the Indian Stream War. They argued and swore and fought about it, and there was a lot of 'em who maintained that logs would be driven down the Connecticut till the end of time. But before the ice went out, the rumor received official confirmation. The CVL said there'd never be another sawlog rolled into the Upper Connecticut.

"Then when the people had recovered their breath, it became a scramble to get onto the drive. It was the last chance the young men would have to carve their names on the North Country totem-pole of glory, while the old-timers wanted to give her one more whirl and be in at the death of the greatest thing in their lives. And there were men alive then — there's only one left now — old Rube Leonard in Colebrook — who had gone down all the way with every drive since 1868.

"The CVL did it up in style. Over two hundred men on the drive, the damnedest gang of rivermen who ever went down a river. The ice went out in the middle of March, and the next day they were rolling in the logs at Second Lake. Forty million feet went down over the falls there and came bobbing down onto First Lake. Then they towed 'em across to the outlet in booms at night when the wind was quiet. Ten million more came out of Perry Stream, and six from Deadwater Brook, and so the drive grew like a snowball until when it hit North Stratford there were sixty-five million feet of logs in the river — the greatest drive that ever went down the Connecticut.

"Two men were killed on Perry Falls that spring. I saw one of them die. There was a wing jam on both sides and he was walking across the stream on a log wedged about a foot under water. He held his peavey dangling from his hand, on the upstream side, and the current hit it just enough to throw him off balance. He fell into the middle of the stream, where the water was fast as a mill race. He could swim some, and a log

ABOVE: *Covered bridge over the Ammonoosuc River between Woods-ville and Bath, New Hampshire. Note the riverman tending out at upper right.* BELOW: *The Connecticut Valley Lumber Company's spring drive in 1897 took out two sections of the Boston & Maine railroad bridge over the Connecticut River in Windsor, Vermont.*

came along and he grabbed it by the middle and tried to hoist himself on top.

"If he'd only used his head and taken the log at one end, he could have held himself up until we'd pulled him out; but I suppose he was too scared to think, and he kept trying to wrestle that log and it kept rolling out of his hands.

"The jam stuck out into the stream a few rods below and the current set in against it. I ran to beat hell over those logs and got out on the point and was all ready to pull him in when the cold water and the shock was too much for him, and he let go of the log and went under. I looked down between the logs and he was swept right under me. One of his hands came up as if he was waving good-bye — and that was the last of him. His name was George Anderson, if I remember rightly. He came from up in New Brunswick, near Houlton, Maine.

"Well, after we'd lost a couple of men there, everything went merry as a wedding bell until we got to North Stratford. And there, between ice and logs, we got the goddamnedest log jam that was ever conceived by mortal man. Even old Rube Leonard said he'd never seen nothing like it. For there was thirty-five million feet of logs in one bunch, sticking straight up and sideways and every other way, the most intriguing and diabolical and inextricable mass of logs I ever gazed upon.

"They kept piling up and piling up and they backed up a flood and the Grand Trunk tracks were torn up and the Grand Trunk started a lawsuit and there was hell to pay. Phonse Roby had charge of the drive that year, and Win Schoppe bossed the rear. They got all the men down there and we worked by day and we worked by night by the light of flares, and we picked those logs and we dynamited them and at last after many days we got 'em loose and floating off down the black, sullen river.

"I saw a funny thing while we were breaking that jam. The dynamite had frozen, so they built a fire to thaw it out. They shoveled up a bank of earth all around the fire, a foot or two away, and stood the sticks of powder up against the inside of the bank. They left a young feller in charge of it who didn't know much about the vagaries of dynamite. One of the sticks happened to slip and fall towards the fire, and he reached over to pull it out. Probably someone had told him dynamite had to be jarred to explode. Just at that precise moment, old Win came striding up to see if the powder was ready, and just as the youngster reached over the embankment, Win reached out one paw and wrapped it around his short ribs and flattened him on the ground like you would a doll.

"Boom! And that stick of dynamite exploded all over the adjacent territory. But nobody was hurt. Win got up and brushed himself and says to the lad: 'G'acious! G'acious, sonny, you must learn to be more careful!'

"They had Dan Bosse that I've just told you about doing the shooting. He was a good man with powder. He put in one blast and it didn't do any good. It sort of bothered him, and he made up his mind that the next time something would give. So he wrapped his dynamite around the end of a pole about fifteen feet long and skipped out onto the jam, pushed it into the hole he'd selected, and stood there watching to see what would happen. It happened all right. The whole front of the jam came loose, and I'll swear it looked as if Dan went up into the air more than ten feet. But when he came down he was standing on both feet on a log and headed downstream.

"We got down past Fitzdale dam and through the Horse-Race, and over the Fifteen-Mile Falls. Sam Martin got drunk and got into a bateau all alone and started down through the Horse-Race. Halfway through, the bateau hit a rock and turned over, and left Sammy out there in the middle of the rapids, clinging to a slippery boulder and sober as a preacher.

"While they were wondering what to do about him, someone bet Bill Bacon ten dollars he couldn't ride a log down past Sam and pick him off the rock. He was a tough nut, Bill was. He jumped on a log and rode down into that white water and when

60

the log surged past the rock he grabbed Sam by the collar and hauled him clear. And brought him safe through, too. And if that don't beat some of the feats of knightly daring I've read about, nothing ever could."

"How come you didn't do it yourself, instead of letting Bill?" I asked.

"I would have," he answered simply. "But I was working farther up the river, and by the time I got down there, he was on his way. I'm no hero. I'll tell you frankly it was a chore I didn't crave. And Bill Bacon is the only man I ever knew who rode a log through the Horse-Race.

"The water was high and fast, and the logs chucked along like race horses. The wanigan could hardly keep up with us. The wanigan — the tents and blankets and cooking-stuff and so on — was transported in high-wheeled wagons drawn by eight horses. Next to rivermen, teamsters are the highest paid men in the woods, you know.

"Wherever we camped, near those little country villages, all the kids would come down and stand around the cook tent and watch the cook mix his biscuits in a pan as big as a bushel basket, and he'd give 'em cookies to eat, and they'd fairly worship him. Every one of 'em firmly determined to grow up and be a riverman some day.

"Well, the drive went down and down. Over Mulliken's Pitch, and past the Twenty-six Islands where Van Dyke used to have such scraps with the farmers, and it came to the Narrows at Woodsville. It's the last time they ever put the old Mary Ann (the raft that carried the cook's equipment from Woodsville down) into the water. And the last time the horse raft was ever built. Bill Bacon had charge of the horse raft. He knew it would be the last one, and he did a handsome job. I've often thought it was a pity nobody was around to take pictures. What was the horse raft? Just a big log raft onto which we loaded the horses we might need to haul stranded logs into the water. The horses were sold when we got to Holyoke.

"Woodsville was the first real town we struck since leaving North Stratford. Woodsville, White River, Bellows Falls, Holyoke — Christ! What stories I could tell you of what I've seen rivermen do in those towns! They'd been working in the woods all winter and then gone straight onto the drive, and it was their first chance for a little fun.

" 'Git your rosin, girls! The drive's coming!' is the cry that used to go through the fancy houses. One time in Woodsville I saw a riverman who was drunk and feelin' his oats, and he saw a woman's head and bust in a clothing store window and he gave a whoop and jumped right through the plate glass, spiked boots first, and grabbed that female figger and tried to ravish it.

"Win Schoppe was getting on in years that spring, but he was still able to show the young bucks a thing or two. Win was the most powerful man I ever saw, and I've seen some pretty husky gents. But he'd never had a fight in his life. He was always good-natured, and they nicknamed him "Grinner." His strongest oath was 'G'acious!' "

"Of course the men who knew Win knew better than to tangle with him, either because they liked him or because they thought it was healthier, but that year there was a mean-tempered, red-headed bruiser working on the rear who somehow got it in for the old man. He used to talk pretty loud to the boys about what he would do to Schoppe if the old man ever tried to ride him. They just stuck their tongues in their cheeks and listened.

"This feller came in drunk and noisy one night at Windsor, and Win told him to shut up. He called Win a son of a bitch and proposed to give him a licking. He made a pass at him, but Win reached out one hand and took him by the throat and laid him on the ground and bore down.

"When the feller came to, Win said: 'G'acious, I hope I haven't hurt you. But really, you shouldn't go around calling people sons of bitches.' The feller took his turkey and got out of there as fast as he could caper.

"We came to Mount Tom at last. When the drive was in the booms, they paid us off and let us go. I had between seven and eight hundred dollars coming to me. I gave half of it to Win and told him to keep it for me. 'This is the last drive,' I told him, 'and I'm going to celebrate it proper.'

"I took the rest and went to Boston. I had one great and glorious time. The first thing I did was to buy a ticket for North Stratford, and the next was to go over to the Adams House and get a room. Then I got all cleaned up — shave, shine, shower, shampoo — even a manicure. I bought a new suit of clothes at Filene's, and then I started out to paint the town red.

"As I told you once, I lived in Boston some years, and I knew my way around. I still had a lot of friends down there. It was wine, women, and song for two weeks. I never went on such a tear before, and I never will again. But I'll bet you there are still people in Boston who remember it! They had to lay new floors in some of their swankiest ball rooms after I, in a festive mood, had led my Kitty out in the mazes of a waltz."

The old pirate patted the spiked boots fondly and his booming laugh rang out. All his sadness forgotten, he resumed his hunt for the fishing pole.

FIVE

The Golden Trout

THE TIME to fish up in this country is before the first of June," Vern told me. "Now if you come then, I'll show you some damn *good* fishin'."

So the next May found me driving up the Connecticut River all the way from Hartford, marvelling more and more at each new vista that unfolded to me. Especially at the Fifteen-Mile Falls and beyond. There, every curve in the road heralds something worth seeing: a hillside covered with the soft wide green of maples, or littered with a terrific landslide of gigantic boulders; a lane through clean white birches; a weather-beaten sugarhouse peeping out from the edge of the trees on a distant hillside; wide lush meadows through which the river loops and twists; groves of cathedral pines, whose brown needles form a soft carpet beneath your feet; intriguing side roads twisting mysteriously out of sight up unknown mountains; brightly painted farm buildings making splotches of color beside the road, or set far up in the middle of green fields; the fields themselves bright islands dropped in the immensity of forest;

sawmills with their pleasant smell of freshly sawed lumber and the screech and whirr of the saws; waterfalls leaping down over ledges to fall almost into the road; romantic covered bridges ("which are only good for one thing, that I know of," a lass from Groveton once told me, and then, at my continued ignorance, proceeded to demonstrate). There are the granite cones of the Stratford Peaks rising majestically above timber line; the once celebrated (but now forgotten) Brunswick Mineral Springs that you can smell for rods before you can see them; attractive tourist cabins; little white villages set around a village green — oh, ever so many things that are a pleasure to the eye and a delight to the soul.

As the librarian in Stark once told me: "We may be short of money but we're long on scenery, and though you can't eat it, it does help the digestion!"

Such were the sights I saw that May day on my way to Vern's mountain farm. He was laboriously planting corn with a hand-planter, but even from a distance it seemed to me that his usual vim and vigor were lacking. He came over to the wall and greeted me heartily when I honked the horn.

"I was hopin' you'd come," he said. "I'm just achin' for an excuse to leave this damn corn plantin'. I'm only halfhearted about it anyway, 'cause I was down to the Falls last week and met an old friend of mine who used to work in the woods, and now he's retired and gone to farming.

"He says he only keeps two cows 'cause he loves ice cream, and they supply him with cream for that, and in the winter he can make it without ever turnin' a freezer. Just sticks it into a pail out in a snowdrift, and it freezes itself. He calls it 'moose.' I'd never heard of it, but he claims it's better than real ice cream.

"Now I'm awful fond of ice cream, and I'm old enough to retire from hard and debilitatin' work like milkin' cows. Cows ain't nothing but chains of slavery anyhow. So I'm debatin' whether to sell all my cows but two, or not. At least that would save me plantin' so much damn corn!"

The next day he proposed that we go over to Little Averill Lake for a couple of days' fishing.

"I always go about this time of year," he said. "Hinman will take care of my stock. He always does when I'm away. We'll pick up Uncle Sammy Martin in Canaan. Sammy and I generally go there together. Sam ain't no great use to a sufferin' humanity, take him on the whole, but he's good company."

So we got into my car and drove through Colebrook to Canaan, which is where Vermont and New Hampshire and Canada come together. As we drove down the main street of Colebrook, Vern saw a short, bare-headed man standing in front of the post office.

"Jigger!" he shouted.

The man glanced up swiftly, saw Vern's grinning face, and shouted a humorous and obscene greeting that could have been heard two blocks away.

"That's Jigger Johnson," Vern explained. "I've heard he's become a fire warden somewheres. He and me were straw bosses for George Van Dyke, years ago. Quite a quaint character, too. I remember one spring we came back from the drive, and him and me and Phonse Roby, who was walking boss, and another feller rented a two-hoss, two-seated surrey with a fringed top at North Stratford and we were goin' over onto the Diamonds fishin'. Christ! What I'd give for a picture of us fellers that morning! Jigger was shaved clean, but I had a handlebar moustache, and Phonse wore a big black beard . . .

"Well, we stopped at Beecher Falls to get a couple of gallons of Canadian high wines . . . "

"What's that?" I interrupted.

"It's pure alcohol — 190 proof. And that Jigger is the only man I ever knew who could drink the stuff straight. I've seen others try it, but they never lived to tell about it. You know where Cold Spring is?"

"Yes, I know. It's down below the road in the river bank, a couple of miles above Beecher Falls."

"That's the place. Well, we stopped there to cut the alcohol. We tied the team to a tree and we skittered down the bank and cut the liquor and had us a drink or two. It was pretty warm and we'd all left our coats in the surrey. Jigger had on a vest, with his whole winter's wages, more than five hundred dollars, in bills in one pocket. But it was warm, so he took off his vest and hung it on a limb.

"We sat there a while and had a couple more drinks and finally we started north again. We rolled along for more than fifteen miles — clear up to First Lake — before we noticed Jigger didn't have his vest. Phonse and I wanted to go back and get it, but Jigger says, 'Ah, to hell with it! We're goin' fishin'!' So we go on over to the East Branch and stay ten days until our bait is all gone and then we come back to the lake and get our team and start back to North Stratford.

"When we come to the Spring, Jigger says: 'Just stop a minute while I go down and get my vest.' And so help me, there it was, still on the limb where he'd left it, and all the money still in the pocket."

We arrived in Canaan just in time to witness an unusual sight — unusual even for Canaan, where murder and sudden death were more a rule than an exception in those days. A handsome girl walking along the board sidewalk suddenly stooped and picked up a good-sized rock with which she struck an elderly pedestrian between the eyes, knocking him flat on his back. Then she danced upon his prostrate frame and shrieked at him.

"Goddamn you!" she shouted. "Don't you dare to call my mother a whore! You're nothing but a damned whoremaster yourself!"

Her victim sat up and tenderly felt his forehead, where blood was running in copious streamlets.

"All right, Clarice," he mumbled placatingly. "All right. I guess you're all right — but I'm not sure," he added under his breath. Several citizens had now come up, and the girl retreated into a house.

67

I laughed, but to my surprise the big man beside me only frowned.

"That's Henry S——," he said. "He's been runnin' Clarice's mother, who's a widow, quite a spell. But the old lady takes in washings for a living and she's tried to bring Clarice up to be decent. She's a clever girl and it's too bad. I don't mind a man whorin' a little, but he shouldn't go around talkin' about it."

"If that's the way your nice girls talk," I said, "I don't know as I'd want to meet one of the baser sort."

Just then Vern saw a man coming down the street, and he laughed. "There's Sammy now," he said. "Hello, Sam! This man's a friend of mine, Bob Pike. He's goin' fishing with us. He wants to meet some of the baser maidens around here, and I know you're just the man who can show 'em to him!"

Sam was a short, roly-poly man with scant gray hair and a bulbous red nose set between constantly twinkling blue eyes. He chuckled as he shook my hand.

"Don't pay any attention to him," he said. "He's the most notorious liar in the North Country — though some misinformed people say I am."

"Sam is old and he's lazy and he's no 'count," said Vern, "but he can always get a job for he tells such god-awful lies that it amuses people that don't know any better."

At which the two old friends shook hands.

"I saw Jigger Johnson just now," Vern went on. "I should have stopped to talk with him, but I'd said I'd see you at ten o'clock and when I tell a man I'll meet him I don't like to be late. I haven't seen Jigger for some years. What's he doing now?"

"He's a fire warden over in Gorham," Sam answered. "He should be there right now, but he got someone to take his place while he came over here on business.

"Remember the winter he logged at Dennis Pond?" Sam added. "The year Pat Monahan built the million-dollar two-sled road up Wheeler Brook to get out Jigger's winter cut?"

"Yes, I remember. The next spring was the last long-log drive. I guess I won't forget it."

"You don't mean that the road really cost a million dollars, do you?" I asked.

"It happened this way," Vern explained. "Stone & Webster had just bought the CVL, and they brought in a man named McDonald to be manager. I think he came from Massachusetts. Anyway, he didn't know much about the woods. They had two camps on Wheeler Brook that winter, one at the head of Deep Dennis Pond, and Jigger had charge of that camp. The other was about halfway down to the river. Mike Foy ran it. McDonald hired Pat Monahan, down in Lancaster, to build the two-sled road from Jigger's camp to the river. The ground was so steep and rocky on the north side of the pond, he decided to build it on the south side, which wasn't much better, being as low and swampy as the other side was high and steep.

"Monahan* built a road wide enough so that two teams could easily pass each other, and he filled in the boggy places with gravel. All in all it was quite a road, and it cost quite a lot of money. Well, the snow was late in coming that year, and there were thaws all through the month of January, and it was February before they got started to two-sled, about a million feet, and then they had to keep the sprinklers running all night and get started hauling at three in the morning and quit again at noon.

"McDonald was pretty mad and threatened to fire Monahan, but thought better of it when he saw they wouldn't have been able to get out the logs if there hadn't been a good road. I was scaling on the river that winter and I remember that road well."

"Yes," agreed Sam. "It was the last long-log drive. That was what broke Jigger all up, no more long logs. He didn't take kindly to four-foot pulpwood."

* *New Hampshire Profiles* (April 1957) has a nostalgic biography of Jigger Johnson by Robert Monahan. I wonder whether he wasn't a son or nephew of old Pat.

"That's right. I recall he had a camp at the head of Scott's Bog the next winter and cut about seven hundred cords, but as soon as he had landed his wood on the bog he quit and went down to Maine. He didn't like pulping."

We went to Sam's boardinghouse, collected his equipment, and headed west out of Canaan. As we passed the Canaan House, Vern waved to a man fitted comfortably into a rocking chair on the piazza.

"B' Jesus! Vern, I'm glad to see ye!" called the man.

"That's Bill Buck. He owns the hotel," Vern told me. "His byword is 'b' Jesus!' They know him all over the North Country. One day down in Lancaster a Frenchman came into the railroad station and wanted to buy a ticket for Stewartstown (that's Canaan's railroad station), but he couldn't remember the name of the place.

" 'Hotel d'ere — b' Jesus!' he says to the ticket agent.

" 'Oh!' says the agent. 'You want to go to Stewartstown!'

"Of course he has a livery stable connected with his hotel, and one day a drummer sold him an order for a gross of whips.

" 'What name would you like to have stamped on the handle?' the drummer asks.

" 'Buck, b' Jesus!' Bill says.

"And damned if they didn't arrive, every one of 'em stamped 'Buck, by Jesus!' "

We crossed into Canada and out again, passing Wallis Pond, where Sam told us a plausible but highly improbable story of being blown up in a rowboat by two drunken Frenchmen dynamiting fish. Then, having passed by the lower end of Big Averill Lake, we angled back into the woods.

There were no more farms or houses. We paused at a spring beside the road and got a drink of the best water I had tasted for a long time in a country where all spring water is good. Vern grumbled at the delay, but Uncle Sammy remained unmoved.

"My dear boy," he chided him, "when you get to be as old as I am, you'll learn to take your blessings as they come."

We drove a mile or two down this wild forest road until we saw a sparkle of water through the trees and turned into a sort of private driveway around a pretty little lake.

"That's Forest Lake," Sam said. "It used to be called Leach Pond. The water goes into the Connecticut, but the Averill Lakes drain off into the St. Lawrence."

"It isn't much of a lake," I said.

"Mister," said Sam earnestly, "It don't look big, but it's deeper than it is wide, and it's half a mile wide. And there's trout in there, brook trout, millions of them."

"Surely you don't mean millions, Sam," I protested.

"Well, of course I never counted them, but I was here the day Charles Quimby opened his Cold Spring Camp thirty years and more ago, and we caught over a thousand trout out of that Forest Lake. And what's more, I can show you a photograph to prove it."

Which he did when we got back to Canaan. Some twenty sportsmen are grouped before the new camp, each one holding his day's catch. And a thousand trout does not complete the tally of that catch.

"Charles Quimby," Sam went on, "was a man of very strong ideas. He didn't have very many, but those he did have were very tenacious."

"What does 'tenacious' mean?" Vern asked suspiciously.

"Don't interrupt your elders, Vern," Sam answered severely.

"As I was saying, Charles had a corn on his little toe that bothered him, and one night after he and the boys had been drinking some he took an axe and cut off that toe as slick as a whistle. He kept it for a long time, and got a lot of pleasure looking at it and thinking how it couldn't hurt him any more."

But today, Charles Quimby's camp, consisting of one building, has become the best sporting camp in the North Country, if not in all of New England. At least Vern said so, and he knows that region better than any other man I'm acquainted with.

"It's all due to Hortense," Vern said. "She's Charles's daugh-

71

ter, and she's red-haired and she's good-looking and she hates men. I mean she never seemed to want to get married."

"She was left a poor orphan," said Sammy, "and she pitched in and built this place up all alone without help or encouragement from anyone. With all the cottages and tennis courts and boats and saddle horses and one thing and another, the place must be worth a hundred thousand dollars."

"That's probably the only time in your life you ever told the truth," grunted Vern. "I'm glad to see you reforming in your old age.

"It's hard work, though," he went on. "It must have near broke her heart more than once, but the tougher the sledding, the harder she pulled. She never quit."

He laughed. "Remember that clerk at Camp Seven? He's the kind that would say because Hortense had started with nothing and had the guts and the brains and the will to work hard to build this place up, she's a bloated capitalist treading down the poor. All those bastards like him ought to be put on an island together where they couldn't bother people who are willing to work for a living. Wouldn't that be rich, though, to watch 'em? Not one of 'em willing to do a damn thing! By God, I'd give the best five years of my life to see it!"

Sam talked with Miss Quimby's majordomo, a man named Hall, and then we drove the car under a shed, took our camp on our backs, and strode away through the primeval forest on a wide and much used trail. We came to the spring that gives the Cold Spring Club its name, and paused to drink. The water was pure and cold as ice. Ten minutes later we had crossed over onto the St. Lawrence watershed and so came to Big Averill, about a mile from its lower end.

Several boats were drawn up on the shore. Vern and Sam had made arrangements for the use of one, so we shoved it into the water and rowed straight across the lake to the beginning of another trail on the west side. This path was not so good as the first one.

"But I can remember when she was knee-deep in mud," said Uncle Sammy. "And we used to walk out in the brush instead of on the trail. They had a pole trail along here when Hub Hall logged Averill Mountain. He was hell on wheels, Hub was. That Hall at the Cold Spring Club is his grandson. He ain't much like his grandsir."

"I've never seen a pole trail," grunted Vern. "I don't think you have, either, Sam."

"Don't you believe it," Sam retorted. "They were never very common in this part of the country, for as a rule we have plenty of high ground so we manage to circumambulate the swamps . . ."

"What does 'circumambulate' mean?" interrupted Vern, shifting his pack and brushing a mosquito off his nose.

"Never mind what it means. We're talking about pole trails now, and I tell you there was one coming right down past here. It was a one-log-wide affair put on 'horses' about five feet from the ground."

"One log wide!" I exclaimed. "How could a man stay on it?"

"My boy," answered Sam impressively, "woodsmen in those days were born on a log. Why, when we used to pick men for the log-rolling contests, we first put them out on a log with a squirrel, and if they couldn't roll the squirrel into the water they were just naturally eliminated right then. The best rivermen in the world used to come up from Bangor to work in this North Country. I've seen them run the falls at Pittsburg in canoes — Faugh! The rivermen you find today wouldn't go over those falls in a double-ended bateau!"

"Neither would you," said Vern.

"Maybe I wouldn't, and maybe I would," Sam retorted, "but even as dull a clod as you are may have heard that Uncle Sammy is the only riverman in the North Country who ever took a bateau over Mulliken's Pitch."

"Yes," agreed Vern, "but you were so drunk at the time you

73

didn't know what you were doing, else you'd have been scared to death."

Amid such pleasant repartee we made our perspiring way through the woods, pausing at intervals to rest, until at last we came to the shore of Little Averill Lake.

This beautiful sheet of water, a mile and a half long and three-quarters of a mile wide, and no one knows how deep (sounding-lines let down to a depth of three hundred feet fail to touch bottom), nestles in a great triangular bowl hemmed in by lofty, forest-covered mountains. No road leads to it. No outboard motor disturbs its calm. It is as wild and remote a spot as one can wish.

The trail we had come in on follows more or less closely the outlet of Little Averill that flows into the larger lake. We had debouched at a dam across this outlet. Here were boats and canoes, but my companions turned to the left and we continued for some distance around the lake before Sam, who was in the lead, sighed with relief and dumped his pack onto the ground.

A small spring bubbled up and trickled down into the lake, and here we made our camp. We had a small green silk tent for shelter, and all the other necessities of a fisherman's life, including the concomitant and inevitable bottle of rum.

This last, jocosely referred to as "liquid bait," is even more necessary to a successful fishing trip than is real bait. Over on the Magalloway I once met a party of four fishermen who had lugged two whole cases of whiskey into their camp — and that was all the supplies or outfit they had.

I came upon them just after one of them had "got the horrors," as the other expressed it, and was fleeing into the woods. He was a tall, thin citizen with a big, black moustache, and he ran like a fox through the brush and down to the river. He waded across and disappeared into the woods on the other side, shouting like mad (which in a way he was) and striking at imaginary enemies.

I met him again several weeks later after he had been captured and sobered up. Two men had found him, standing in a tote road and clad only in his underdrawers, three days and three nights after I had witnessed his melodramatic departure through the woods of Skilling's Gore. With some difficulty they persuaded him to accompany them. Later, when he had recovered, he went back into the forest and got his watch where he had left it hanging on a bush, but his clothes he never could find.

Since I had seen him fleeing and crying in the wilderness I ventured to speak to him of the matter.

"Goddamn it, yes," he assented. "There was a little green man about a foot high, and I kept trying to strike him but I never could reach him."

But to return to Little Averill. We caught fourteen "squaretails" the first afternoon. Ask anyone what a "squaretail" trout is, and I'll bet he can't tell you. And if he can, I'll bet the next man you ask will tell you something entirely different. Some people say they are merely big brook trout. I have caught squaretails in Third Connecticut Lake. Over in that country it is opined that the squaretail is a small laker! At any rate, they are good to catch and good to eat.

The lake trout I (almost) caught was the high point of the trip. I had rowed out onto the lake after supper to watch the sunset and to practice fly casting. I was the most surprised fly-caster in the world when that twenty pounds (oh, he must have weighed *at least* twenty pounds!) of gray fury grabbed the fly. He hooked himself hard and fast, and there we were with a lake three hundred feet deep and a couple of miles long to maneuver in.

I thought I was going to need all of that room, for with his first rush he went over fifty yards, straight away from the boat, and the line shot off the bobbin and along the pole as though an elephant had hold of it.

Then he turned and headed back just as fast as he had left, and I reeled in with all my might, desperately wondering what

75

kind of whale I had hooked and praying fervently that he wouldn't get away. The creature kept rushing back and forth like that, scaring me every time lest all the line should run out and then it would have been good-bye.

If I had had a heavier rig, it would have been easy — I could have let him tow me up in front of the camp and then yelled to Sam to come and brain him with the axe. But I couldn't do that, so I stood there in the boat and thanked the Lord that it was a steady old scow.

The skin wore off my thumb and my arms were aching and my heart was thumping at a merry pace — and then Mr. Fish began to vary his straight rushes with a little horseplay. He would come in quite close and then begin to run in circles. The rod bent double, and it was the devil's own job to keep the line taut. It had grown dark, and I was becoming exhausted.

My arms were trembling violently and I could hardly reel in properly, but luckily the big trout wasn't so frisky as he had been, either. About the time I was quivering with fatigue and my thumb was so painful that I was thinking of quitting in shameful despair (the trout meanwhile sulking fifty feet away in the darkness), a canoe came silently up beside me.

It was Sam and Vern, and they had a net in that canoe. My courage rose greatly — but, alas, prematurely. For though Sam got the trout in the net and even lifted him out of the water, he was too anxious, and consequently he slipped and nearly over-turned the canoe. There came a mighty splash in the darkness, accompanied by a mighty oath — and that was the end of my laker!

Sam sought to console me by reminding me of the tragic tale Hall had related to us concerning a twenty-five-pound laker of which we had seen a photograph in the Cold Spring Club office.

"That's the biggest trout ever caught in Little Averill," he told us. "A Doctor Friend from Middletown, New York, caught him — or rather, one of our guides did the catching for him. It's quite a story. Friend and Brousseau (the guide) were out in a boat, and Friend hooked this fellow. But when he got him up where he could see what a monster he was, he just let go of the rod and sat down in the boat like he'd been shot. Pretty near scared to death, Brousseau said.

"Brousseau grabbed the rod and managed to land the trout after an hour's fight. They brought him back to camp and took his picture and cleaned him and put him on ice. That night at dinner the doctor was so excited and nervous he couldn't talk, and his hands shook so he couldn't feed himself. He had to get up and leave the table — and he kept right on going, for he took the fish and he took Brousseau's raincoat and he left the same night. We've never seen him nor heard from him since."

"But had he been here before?"

"Yes. That's what makes it funnier. He'd been coming here for three years and he liked the place. I really believe it killed him. He had plenty of money, but when we wrote to him to return the guide's raincoat we never heard from him."

"So you see," said Sam consolingly, "if you had actually landed that fish just now, it might have given you heart failure, and pretty quick you'd be lying here all stiff and cold, just a pore lump of mortal clay."

"Poor lump of your grandmother!" snorted Vern. "If it wasn't for you we'd have caught the biggest trout ever seen in this lake."

"Oh no you wouldn't," Sam said. "There's trout in this lake bigger than you ever dreamed of."

"Hell!" said Vern. "You don't mean lakers, and the salmon don't run over eighteen pounds."

He stared at Uncle Sammy in perplexity.

"Where's your memory, boy!" Sam said, half affectionately, half irritably. "You was hopping like a flea all around this country forty years ago. Have you forgotten the golden trout?"

"By God! You're right. But it's been more than thirty years since they've caught one or I've even heard 'em mentioned."

Whereat they proceeded to tell to me as interesting a fish

story as I have ever heard. I took pains to verify it, both from local residents and by diligent research in libraries, so we have here the tale of the golden trout.

The *Salvelinus aureolus,* or golden trout, the loveliest and rarest game fish in North America, is found in only four places in all the world, and those are four widely separated lakes, all in northern New England: Lake Sunapee and Dan Hole Pond in New Hampshire, Flood's Pond in Maine, and Little Averill Lake in Vermont.

Few indeed are the men who have ever seen a golden trout, and even fewer are the fishermen who have caught one. But those who have unanimously agree that it is surpassed by no other freshwater fish in beauty and in fighting qualities.

I might say that while I was researching on the subject I found that Mr. DeRocher, superintendent of the Federal Fish Hatchery at Nashua, New Hampshire, has exhibited a tank of *aureolus* trout at the New England Sportsmen's Annual Show in Boston. He seines them from the spawning beds in Lake Sunapee.

Between 1880 and 1915 enough material on the golden trout appeared in sporting magazines and scientific journals to fill a large book, but the writers, one and all, confined their remarks to the Lake Sunapee trout. Flood's Pond, in Ellsworth, Maine, was ignored, the number of *aureolus* there always having been small. Dan Hole Pond and Little Averill were not known to contain golden trout until many years after they were discovered in Sunapee.

The *Salvelinus aureolus* was first noticed in Sunapee in 1878, in Dan Hole in 1889, and in Little Averill in 1898 — though reputable fishing-book writers did not learn this last fact until half a dozen years later, when government officials seined golden trout from Little Averill to exhibit at the World's Fair in St. Louis.

For many years attempts to transplant golden trout into other waters did not succeed, for besides needing deep water

trout were to be found in that vicinity. But that shortsighted person refused.

The seines came back and for years did deadly execution. *Aureolus* were taken out of the lake a boatload at a time. But after a few years the state went to work (acting on the supposition that the natural propagation of the golden trout was insufficient to keep pace with the demand) and stocked Little Averill with landlocked salmon (lakers were also introduced, by accident). The golden trout were killed off in no time.

"I was at Little Averill after that," Ed told me, "and the whole lake down near the outlet was covered with *aureolus* eight or nine inches long, floating belly up, bitten to death by the other fish."

The best and most reliable treatise on the golden trout is by W.C. Kendall in his monograph on the charrs, published in 1914. There he says that although there are stories of Sunapee *aureolus* weighing ten pounds, the largest authentic weight is less than nine, while the average is much smaller.

But in Little Averill the golden trout were not only immense in numbers. They were immense in size. Twelve and fifteen pounders were by no means uncommon, as a score of men will tell you, and there are stories of some that weighed as much as eighteen pounds. Ed swears he saw one that would have weighed over twenty-five.

"They won't take a fly like any other trout will," said Ed. "But I hadn't learned that yet, and one morning at sunrise I was out in my canoe casting away when I noticed something cutting through the water, leaving a wake behind it, and heading right for me. I thought at first it might be a muskrat, or maybe an otter, but then I saw it was the back fin of a fish.

"He came right up to me, slow, and I kept casting in front of him, but he never paid any attention. When he got up to the canoe he went right under it, and he must have touched the bottom, for I was looking over when he came up on the other side. There he was, not three feet from me, the biggest fresh-water fish I ever saw in my life. It almost scared me."

The golden trout has been the subject of more than one artist's brush. You will not be surprised, after reading this lyrical and exact description of the creature at the mating period, written by Doctor Quackenbos more than fifty years ago:

As the October pairing time approaches, the Sunapee fish becomes illuminated with the flushes of maturing passion. The steel-green mantle of the back and shoulders seems to dissolve in a veil of amethyst, through which the daffodil spots of midsummer gleam out in points of flame, while below the lateral line all is dazzling orange. The fins catch the hue of adjacent parts, and pectoral, ventral, anal, and lower lobe of caudal are marked with a lustrous white band.

It is a unique experience to watch this saibling spawn-ing on the Sunapee shallows. Here in all the magnificence of their nuptial decoration flash schools of painted beau-ties, circling in proud sweeps about the submerged boul-ders they would select as the scenes of their loves — the poetry of an epithalamium in every motion — in one direction uncovering to the sunbeams in amorous leaps their golden-tinctured sides, in another, darting in little companies, the pencilled margins of their fins seeming to trail behind them like white ribbons under the ripples. The wedding garment nature has given to this charr is unparagoned (sic). Those who have seen the bridal march of the glistening hordes in all the color and majesty of action, pronounced it a spectacle never to be forgotten.

Do you wonder that fishermen and artists alike become excited over them? But to get back to Little Averill — many of the young *aureolus* were killed or starved out by the salmon, and many of the old ones were caught, but they still survive in deep water.

People still catch them weighing five or six pounds, these remnants of a mighty race that have escaped the ugly jaws of the salmon. But a few times every season some lucky — or unlucky — fisherman comes back from Little Averill with his eyes sticking out of his head and minus much good tackle and nonchalance. He tells of hooking some monster of the depths that nearly pulled him overboard and finally departed with his minnow and a hundred feet of line.

"The fact is," said Sam, judiciously rubbing his chin as though to promote a clearer analysis of the phenomenon, "the fact is, they've hooked onto one of those old grandfather *aureolus* that are still alive way down there in the bowels of the earth."

And I think that Sam is right. One needs a special rig to fish for *aureolus,* and we didn't have it, so we caught none. I cannot tell a lie and say we hooked one that got away, but I am sure, from all the information I could gather, that somewhere down in the sparkling depths of Little Averill still live huge old *aureolus,* bigger than big lake trout — all that are left of the golden horde that sixty years ago the settlers were taking out of this beautiful lake by the barrelful.

It was a pleasure to drive about the country with a man like Sam. If he didn't know everything necessary about a given place or person, he had no qualms about drawing on his ample imagination and enriching the product with homely touches of verisimilitude. He claims to have discovered the "only genuine ice cave in New England" in Warner's Grant, and he makes such a good story out of it that I almost believe it is true.

On our way home from that fishing trip to Little Averill, we took an old back road down Canaan Hill rather than to return by way of Canaan, and every mile or so Sammy would point out a spot where a gruesome murder or lynching had occurred and tell us in great detail all about it. At least one of his stories was based on a fact that caused quite a stir in the North Country when it happened.

A cattle dealer named Job Cross was found in the woods on Canaan Hill shot through the head, and a native named Bunnell was arraigned for the murder. He was, however, acquitted.

"And we camped right there the night after they took Cross's body away," said Sam solemnly, "and his ghost came and scratched on the tent and wanted to come in, but one of the men was afraid of ghosts and he grabbed an axe and took a swing and knocked over a tent pole, and there we were, all five of us, under that tent and a wild man swinging an axe inside and a ghost scratching outside. I tell you it was awful."

"Why didn't you let him in and give him a biscuit?" Vern asked. "They say Job was awful fond of biscuits. That's probably all he wanted. And that ghost up on Indian, didn't he eat doughnuts?"

"If you go up on Indian Stream," said Sam to me, "you ask anybody about Greeley's camp and the haunt there. Vern doesn't believe it, but that's what turned Roaring Bert's hair white. He went in there and stayed, all alone, one night on a bet. I don't know what else it did to him, but I'll bet that ghost knew it had hold of something when it fastened onto Bert, for he's no puny lad."

"It's been years since I was on Indian Stream," said Vern. "Damned if I wouldn't like to go back there once before I die."

"I'll take you up," I said. And I did, but that is another story.

SIX

Old Ginseng Willard and the Forty-niners

VERN NEVER worked on Sundays. Not on account of religious scruples, but because he thought a man was entitled to one day's rest a week — "to catch up on his sinnin'," he used to say.

One Sunday we were reclining at our ease on the lawn and talking of this and of that when neighbor Hinman's boy walked into the yard, bearing a large platter covered with a napkin.

"Ma roasted a chicken," he said, "and she said she might as well roast two, and she sent this one over to you."

"That's mighty nice of your ma," said Vern. "You thank her for me. I don't suppose you like apples, do you?"

The boy — he was nine or ten years old — grinned. "I like 'em if they're good to eat."

Vern took the platter into the house and came out. Solemn as a walrus he led the boy to a Duchess apple tree. The ground beneath it was covered with big, ripe apples. First Vern had him fill his pockets — he was wearing knickers held up by suspenders. Then Vern pulled the pants away from his belly and stuffed apples down. Each leg filled up, the seat filled, so did the front. We could not help laughing.

"There, sonny," Vern said, "you run home and tell your ma to make you some apple sass."

The boy thanked him and waddled away, a ludicrous sight.

"He's a good boy," Vern said. "But ain't he funny as hell, his pants stuffed full that way?"

"His mother must like you," I said.

"I did her a good turn once. She ain't never forgot it."

He laughed. "By contraries, that puts me in mind of Leem Judd. He was a no-'count sort of a feller and he chummed around with Sile Brown, who was of about the same caliber. Brown and two other fellers committed a murder, and folks tried to make out that Leem was one of the two. I asked Leem's brother about it.

" 'Naw!' says he. 'Leem and Sile split up when Sile stole Leem's concubine two years ago and married her. Leem never forgave him for that — and Sile never forgave him for lettin' him steal her!' "

This led on to tales of other quaint characters, until finally I asked Vern who was the most unusual specimen of God's carelessness (a phrase of his own) that he knew of.

"The most unusual specimen of God's carelessness I know of up here?" he repeated thoughtfully. "That's quite a problem. Now there's Jack Haley, who lives all alone in a den on Sawyer Lake, and whose favorite pastime is shooting cigarettes from the mouths of passersby. He's what you might call quite a character.

"Then there's Philip Dumas, a Frenchman, who does a lot of beaver poachin' over on the Diamonds. They caught him once and took him down to Wilson's Mills, where a woodsmen's jury let him off on his own recognizance to go home to Canada and bring back a hundred dollars to pay the fine they assessed against him. He came back with the money, too.

"Then there's Ernest Nash, lives way up on top of Deer

Mountain. More'n seventy-five years old, and he went nudist a year ago, they tell me. He's quite a coon. But I guess when you come right down to it, it's a tie between Ervin Palmer, who lives down on Four-Mile Brook, and 'Ginseng' Willard, who lives over in Guildhall. Both of them fellers are different from the average citizen. Palmer ain't very talkative, but you'd like to meet old Ginseng. He must be most eighty years old. I worked with him in the woods years and years ago, and he was no spring chicken then."

"What is quaint about him?" I asked.

He chuckled. "Well, for one thing, he has some original ideas about the state of double-cussedness commonly known as matrimony. A lot of married men let their wives run all over them, but Ginseng always figured that if he was out earning a living for the family, his wife should tend to his well-bein'. One morning he got up at five o'clock as usual and did the chores and came in to breakfast, but Kate was still layin' in bed.

"Kate! he says, lookin' in the door of the bedroom, ain't you going to git up and git me my breakfast?'

" 'No!' she says, 'I ain't!'

" 'Why not?'

" 'Cause I don't want to!'

" 'Kate,' he remonstrates with her, 'you must git up and git my breakfast.'

" 'I ain't goin' to!' she repeats, and she turns over with her face to the wall, feelin' pretty bossy and independent.

"Ginseng don't say any more, but he goes across the road to the well, which has water cold as ice, and he draws a bucketful and takes it back to the house."

" 'Are you goin' to git up and git my breakfast, Kate?' he asks.

" 'Oh, go to hell!' she says.

"So he throws the whole bucket of ice water all over her, right there in the bed."

"What did she do?"

87

"She got up and got him his breakfast," Vern said dryly.

So we went calling on Mr. Willard. A strange-looking vehicle standing in the yard of his one-room home attracted all our attention as we drove in. A sign on the rear of the contraption announced: THE 49ERS GOING TO CALIFORNIA. It appeared to be an old-fashioned freight sleigh mounted on an automobile chassis. On top of the sleigh had been built an immense closed box surmounted by a roof on which was perched a row of singular-looking bird houses, deer antlers, hand-carved wooden animals, and other paraphernalia.

As we sat gazing in wonder at this odd sight, an ancient man emerged from the house and hailed us cheerily. At first glance, Mr. Willard appeared fully as strange as his caravan, if caravan it may be called. He was tall and spare. A black felt hat with a high crown ornamented with spangles crowned his snowy locks. A huge, ivory-handled Colt revolver sagged in the whetstone pocket of his overalls, and around his neck he wore a mighty necklace, composed, as I learned later, of a thousand porcupine claws, with a few bear's teeth sewn in for good measure. Such was Mr. George Willard, better known as "Old Ginseng," the first time that I ever saw him, and he was then in the seventy-seventh year of his age.

"Good morning, Mr. Willard!" Vern said in his loud voice and grinned.

The old man came closer and peered into his face. "You know me," he said, "but I don't seem to place you. Now don't tell me! Just let me think a little. I know I've seen that homely face of yours somewhere."

After a few seconds of searching back through the mists of memory, a grin cracked his leathery face. "By gum!" he exclaimed. "I know you now! You're Davison. Vern Davison. You was only a boy then. My, but that was a long time ago, wasn't it, when we were driving team for Van Dyke up on Indian Stream. Eighteen ninety-two, wasn't it?"

"Yup!" Vern boomed. "That was where you scared the

snubber to death after he sluiced you on Cowan Hill. Haw! Haw! Haw!"

The woods re-echoed his boisterous laughter. Old Ginseng chuckled.

"They brought me in to cure a pair of horses that had got sluiced," he grinned, "and then I got sluiced myself."

"But what in hell is this contraption in your front yard?" Vern demanded, after introducing me.

"That there is an old-fashioned Portland sleigh. Eighty years ago, everyone in this part of the country owned one. They got their name because they were used so much to freight up supplies from Portland. I doubt if you can find a single other one in all the North Country today.

"I fixed it up this way 'cause when I'm ready I'm going to buy a horse and go out to California just like the forty-niners did. You'll notice I've got everything they had —" and he unlocked the door of the sleigh and began to draw out hand-carved wooden animals, men, and other objects.

"Here's a six-ox team," he said, arranging them carefully on a board, "and here's the driver, with a gun in one hand and a knife in the other. And here" — producing more figurines — "are two armed guards on horseback.

"This here is a genuine old 'baker' such as they used to cook with, and I read once in a book called *Ned Bunting or Life on the Plains* how the forty-niners repelled an Indian attack with a swivel gun, so here's an old swivel gun that we'll put right out in front to protect the caravan . . ." and he proceeded to lay down a miniature brass cannon supported on two bicycle sprockets.

"There," he said admiringly, as he stepped back to survey his work, "isn't that pretty nice?"

We confessed that it was.

The inside of the sleigh was stuffed with unusual objects. Even the door, on its inner side, was covered with a curious collection and the old man gladly explained its meaning.

"There, first," he said, "are two thieves the forty-niners have

89

Ginseng Willard wearing a necklace he made from the claws of the "1,000 porcupines he had killed," and (right) *standing beside the coffin he made from two rosewood pianos. He slept in the coffin for two years "just to get used to it."*

hung by the neck. Then there's the forty-niners' pick and shovel, and a revolver and bowie knife. This is an old Indian tomahawk, over a hundred years old, and there in the right-hand corner is my gum-digger."

The old man rambled on, with an air half of sincerity, half of mockery, so that to save my life I could not tell whether he was serious or joking.

"Where's my old idol?" he demanded, feeling in his pockets. "Ah! here it is." And he produced an old cutty pipe. "Have to fumigate once in a while," he observed, as he loaded up. "That reminds me of an occasion some years ago I was out gumming and I came to a blowdown — a lot of spruce trees blown down in a heap, you know — and I'd clambered up on top of it, looking for gum, and I thought it would be a good place to fumigate, so I sat down and was just beginning to draw on the old idol when my little dog, Jack, came trotting up. He went in under me, and all at once there was a holler that made my hair stand right straight up, and a big black bear came bounding out from under me where he'd been asleep and I'd never seen him. He tipped me over on my back and away he flew through the brush with Jack yipping at his heels. Yes, I was scared that time," and the old man chuckled at the memory.

"Have I ever seen a panther? Well, no. Not exactly — yes. I did see one once. We knew there was an old he one hanging around, for we'd seen his tracks and heard him scream. One day I was out gumming and got into a thicket of spruce when all at once I heard something behind me, panting loud — 'Huh-uh, huh-uh, huh-uh,' like that — and I knew it was the panther, so I pulled out my revolver and turned around, resolved to shoot him in the eye the minute he showed his ugly face. He came pushing through the bushes on my trail, and finally he came into sight — and it was my neighbor's dog!

"Come on into the house and set a spell," he invited hospitably. "Yes," he told me, after we were comfortably settled and he and Vern had exchanged reminiscences, "I was born in

Guildhall and I've always lived here. That is, I've always had a home here, but I've been away a lot, all over this North Country. Now this place here I've lived in eleven years. Built it myself. It's warm as toast in winter. Double-sheathed with fir all the way 'round."

I looked around the one large bare room. An ancient, red-painted bed stood in one corner. Opposite it was a huge stuffed owl, perched on top of a large birdhouse. A small oil stove for cooking, a small iron stove for heating, a rough table, a dresser, a couple of mirrors, a posthole digger, a stack of dry wood, a small trunk, a sink, three comfortable but terribly worn chairs — such were the furnishings of that mountain hermitage. No, there was one more thing — a curiously chased pewter teapot enclosed in a stout cage of wood and wire.

"That," said Ginseng, noting my glance, "is probably the oldest pewter teapot in this country. I wouldn't take a thousand dollars for it. My ancestors brought it over from England in 1675. And the date 1503 is stamped right on the bottom. I built that cage for it 'cause it kind of sets it off," he added naively.

"Why do they call you 'Old Ginseng?' " I asked presently.

"Because for the last seventy years I've been gathering ginseng roots in these woods. I tried to cultivate the stuff once, and set out twenty-five hundred plants, but there was no market for cultivated ginseng so I gave that up. It's sold by the pound, you know. Takes three pounds of green root to make one pound of dry.

"A man was telling me last week it's worth twenty dollars a pound now. I can't see as good as I used to or I'd go out in the woods this very day and make a boodle of money. How much can a man average to find in a day? Oh, he could get a pound all right. I remember one day I'd been out in the woods since sunup, and it had been raining pretty near all day, too. By four o'clock I'd found just about one pound — and at five I was home with fifteen pounds in my bag. That's how it goes. So that's why they call me 'Old Ginseng.'

"Then I used to do a whale of a business digging spruce gum. I'd go out into the woods with a pan and a sack and my little hatchet I showed you, and I'd get it by the barrelful. I'd strip the gum right off the trees into the pan and then dump it into the bag. It used to be worth a dollar a pound. I've earned a lot of money in my day, mister. It's still worth a dollar a pound. Only there ain't any more trees. All the spruce has been cut off.

"After I got home, I'd steam it. That makes it pure. Takes away every bit of bark and dirt and impurities, and what's more, spruce gum that has been steamed won't ever get hard when you chew it. You didn't know that, hey? Well, it's a fact. After I'd steamed it, I'd strain it through spruce boughs, and it would come out clear as crystal. I used to make a lot of it up into sticks about the size of my little finger and sell 'em to a dealer for sixty cents a hundred. He got a penny apiece for 'em. Yes, there was good money in gum-digging.

"One time, it was while I was married, I went out on that hill you see over there, and in less than two hours I came back and I paid for a barrel of flour with the gum I'd dug in that time."

"So you've been married, Mr. Willard," I repeated. "Is your wife dead?"

"Gosh, I don't know. I got married when I was twenty-two years old. We lived together five years and then we decided to split muskrat skins. You see, I'd been working in the woods one winter, and I came home and found her living with another man. It annoyed me so I went down to Lancaster and bought a revolver, intending to shoot him, but I waited to get my hair cut, and when I'd got that out of my eyes, it seemed as if I could see clearer, and I said to myself 'George, it's more of a punishment for him to have to live with a woman like her than it would be if you killed him,' so I let him go. I guess he was sorry more than once I didn't shoot him," he concluded, grinning faintly.

"No," he went on, "it wasn't the only time I'd been suspicious of her. We had a neighbor named Charley Woods that used to hang around the house a lot, so one day I said to him: 'Charley, you've been coming over to my house too often. I don't want you to come any more. Stay away.' I went out to dig gum, and when I came home, as I came in the front door I heard him going out the back. I grabbed my rifle that stood in a corner and went to the back door and there he was, streaking across the field for home. I began to shoot at him. I'm a pretty fair shot, at least I was those days. I'd shoot at his right heel, and he'd jump sideways, and then I'd shoot at his left one and he'd jump back again. Believe me, he stepped some lively as long as the shells held out! No, he didn't ever bother me any more.

"Come on out and see my dance hall, The Bob-Cat," he said, and led the way across the yard to a long, low building that bore over its portal a painted likeness of a Canadian lynx. Inside, over the door leading from the vestibule to the hall, was a monster mounted lynx.

"That's a bay lynx," said Old Ginseng, "and not a real bobcat, but people down here ain't familiar with lynxes, so I call the hall 'The Bob-Cat,' and that's the reason. I caught this fellow right over there, in a swamp. He was a monster, too. He weighed most forty pounds."

The floor of The Bob-Cat was a very good one, but Old Ginseng told us he had lost money on the enterprise, and that no dances had been held there for several years.

"I built it ten years ago," he said, "for my son-in-law, who couldn't seem to find anything to do. I'm too old to run such a place myself, and besides I had to be away a lot. But the demon rum got too strong for the manager, and the second week, with over two hundred couples present, no orchestra appeared, none having been summoned. So finally it was closed up. I'm hoping to fix it up and put in a victrola and let people come in for a dime apiece and dance as long as they want to. It's the best floor in the North Country."

"What's that thing in the corner?" I asked, going over to look at a long rosewood box lying there. "It looks like a coffin."

"It is a coffin," Mr. Willard affirmed. "I built it myself out of a couple of grand pianos. I slept in it two years, just to get used to it. Yes, that's my last overcoat. I've made up my own epitaph, too," he went on. "Maybe you'd like to hear it:

OLD GINSENG WILLARD
Hermit, Hunter, Trapper, Gum and Ginseng Digger
Passed on to the beautiful
Spirit World
When
He stopped breathing:
He was a Funny Old Jigger but the Game
Always Dropped when he pulled the Trigger
Now his old Bones are smouldering in the Sand
While his Spirit roams the Happy Land
Where the Sun always Shines
With its golden, golden Glory.

"I often write poetry like that," he said. "It's no effort. It just comes to me, and I put it down on paper. I wrote down some thoughts once on that minister, Richeson, who killed a girl, you remember, and a man from New York saw it and told someone down there who came all the way up here to get it, and it was printed in the *New York Times.* I wrote another piece on Prohibition that a feller made a copy of and I think it was printed in the *Boston Post,* but I never saw it."

He showed us several notebooks full of "scratchings" as he called them, written in pencil, in a large, clear hand. All of them attested to the greatest originality and common sense, and dealt with subjects ranging from Prohibition to the Immaculate Conception.

"I don't believe," said Old Ginseng stoutly, "that the Manger Boy [for thus he always refers to the Saviour] was born any different from the rest of us, but his mother had beautiful

95

thoughts while she was carrying him. Beautiful thoughts — that's what makes beautiful children. I'll tell you something else. You'll probably think I'm crazy, but I *know* I've seen the Manger Boy face to face, and talked with him. It's happened to me twice."

The old man brought forth a Bible and expounded from the writings of the Apostles, but in no fanatical manner. Yet he told us one thing that was very curious.

"I stuck a rusty nail into my hand once," he said, "and it began to swell up and hurt like the Old Harry. That night, in the camp, I looked at it and began to think of what the New Testament tells us, and I said to myself, 'There ain't any pain!' and my hand stopped aching. I made a mitten for it that night, and worked all the next day, but it swelled up so it was clumsy and I decided to go to Lancaster to have it cut open. The doctor wanted me to take ether, but I wouldn't. I told them there wasn't any pain in it. So they operated on it and it healed up."

I asked him to tell us something about his boyhood.

"I don't know as there's much to tell," he answered, and took his old idol from his mouth to gaze at it reflectively, as if it were a fortune-teller's crystal.

"My father was the meanest man who ever lived," he said at last. "He was a big, strong man with an awful temper and no idea of how children should be treated. He was a carpenter by trade. One night, when I was seven years old, he came home and I was in bed and he yanked me out and took a sharp-edged ash stick half an inch thick and whaled me with it till it broke. I had scars on my back for two months from the licking. I tell you I was glad when that *** died.

"My mother's folks were among the first settlers in Guild-hall," he went on. "I've heard my grandmother tell how her grandfather, whose name was Schoff and who was part Indian, was one of the three men who buried the golden calf up in Pittsburg. You never heard about that? It was the time Benedict Arnold's men come home from Quebec. I wrote it all down here in my register, just as my grandmother told it, and you can read it if you want to.

"When I was thirteen years old I took an axe and went over to a logging camp on Nash Stream and the boss hired me. Pay was fifty cents a day and board. Those were the good old days. The camp had an open cupola in the roof and a fire was built on the ground, right beneath it. We all slept on the ground, under twenty-foot spreads made of cheap wool stuffed with cotton batten. When one of those things got wet, twenty men couldn't lift it. That was more than seventy years ago. Later, as they got more effeminate, they put a stove in the barroom (that's what we called the ram-pasture, you know) and built bunks, where only three men slept under one blanket."

"Remember that recipe of yours for curing pneumonia?" Vern asked. "You might like to know I tried it on a neighbor of mine some years ago, and it worked. Of course I told him it would, but I was really more surprised than he was when he got better!"

"Of course it worked," Ginseng said. "I've cured three different people with it myself."

"What is it?" I asked.

Vern laughed. "You know Hinman, that lives up there beside me? Well, he caught pneumonia, and the doctor from Colebrook gave him up to die. Said he had plural [I am sure Vern meant the opposite of singular] pneumonia and told his wife he had two days more to live. She told me, and I went in.

" 'Listen, Harry,' I said to him, 'the doctor says you're going to die.'

" 'That's what my wife tells me,' he says, looking pretty gray and feeble.

" 'Well,' I said, 'I don't believe in interfering with a man's business, whether he's living or whether he's dying, but if you *want* to live, I'll cure you.'

" 'I've known you to break every one of the Commandments

97

except the sixth,' he says. 'I've never known you to tell a lie, Vern. If you can cure me, go to it.'

"So I told his wife to put some lard to heating and to find some small sugar or salt sacks. Meanwhile I went out to the barn and got a panful of fresh cow manure and brought it into the kitchen. Ada didn't like that very well, but she knew better than to argue with me. I mixed the manure and the hot lard and put them in those little bags and put 'em on Harry's chest and kept changin' 'em when they were cold."

"And in less than an hour the congestion had gone out of him, and the next day he was all right," said Old Ginseng with conviction.

"It's God's truth," said Vern, "and you could have knocked me over with a feather when I saw it. It almost persuaded me to put out my shingle as a medicine man."

"I can tell you how to cure tonsilitis, too," said the old man. "Just take a live frog and bind him across the swelling, belly down. It'll kill the frog, but it'll cure the tonsilitis in less than fifteen minutes. An Indian told me that, many years ago, and one time I tried it on my grandson. It works."

"What do you do for a living, Mr. Willard?" Vern asked. "You say you can't go ginseng hunting any more. Have you got a gold mine somewhere?"

"I had quite a lot of money, once," said the ancient man slowly. "And I lost every cent of it. I invested it in human nature. In my relatives, if you know what I mean. Now I haven't got any more money, they don't come around to bother me — so that's one blessing. But I get along. I work in the woods in the winter and then I get jobs once in a while. I've just worked ten days for the town, cutting brush 'side the road."

"You're eligible for an old-age pension," I told him. "Why don't you apply for one?"

He looked at me in surprise.

"I've lived a long time," he said at last, with an unconscious little air of dignity. "Longer than most people, I reckon, and

I've earned my own living since I was thirteen years old. I've never asked any man to pay my bills and I'm not going to begin now."

We shook his hard old hand and left him standing before the door of his shack — no, of his *home,* his home, that he had built himself. To me that old man epitomizes the dauntless spirit of the pioneers, a spirit, alas, that is fast dying out of the land.

"What would you have done if Hinman had died under your ministrations?" I asked Vern curiously.

"Just like the other doctors," he answered. "Buried him!"

"I noticed you called him 'Mr. Willard' when you spoke to him. How come you were so polite all at once?"

"Young feller," he said, "I'm no model for a young man to pattern after, God knows, but I was brought up to speak respectfully to my elders, and it's a habit I never lost, especially when they are people I consider deserve my respect. And that old man there I figure is one of them."

SEVEN

Indian Stream

INDIAN STREAM REPUBLIC

THE NAME 'Indian Stream' fascinates me," I told Vern one day. "I've heard about murders and ghosts and gold mines and Indian burying grounds and a lot of other things there. Why don't you go up with me and point out the principal monuments?"

"I will! We can start tomorrow morning. Lafe Covell has a camp on Cowan Hill. We can stay there. Or I know the Millses at Depot Camp. We can stay there. Or I know Holden, who has a camp on East Branch. We can stay . . . "

"Hold on," I interrupted. "If we stay with everybody you know we won't be home till Christmas."

"Maybe you don't know," he said the next morning as we drove through a covered bridge across Indian Stream where it empties into the Connecticut and turned up the stream, "maybe you don't know that these meadows you're looking at are the best farmland in the state of New Hampshire, and that this was once part of the Indian Stream Republic that seceded from the United States and for four years maintained itself as a separate country. The smallest independent state in North America.

"It's a fact," he said. "I suppose it was the smallest, wildest and least-known of all the various republics that have flourished in this country. Al Stearns tells me there have been several others — one called Franklin, down in Tennessee, for example.

"Well, this one up here was only a tiny stronghold of rugged individualists, but it had its own constitution, it organized its own army (forty men) and it stood off Canada on the north and the United States on the south for four lively years — 1832 to 1836. It occupied the western part of what is now Pittsburg — which, by the way, is the largest township in the state.

"You know this country pretty well," he went on. "Well, you just try to visualize a map of it. You'll see that the boundary between Canada and the United States comes straight from the west until it hits New Hampshire at the Connecticut River, where it turns sharp north. The Republic really came into existence because of a long dispute concerning the line extending northward between New Hampshire and Quebec."

He continued as follows:

At the close of our Revolutionary War in 1783, the Treaty of Paris defined the boundary as the "northwesternmost head of the Connecticut River." That was all right in 1783, because the region wasn't surveyed, there weren't any maps, and nobody lived there anyway. However, six years later New Hampshire sent a Colonel Jeremiah Eames* to survey the boundary and

---

* This Eames was commandant at Fort Wentworth on the high bank of the Connecticut at Northumberland during the later years of the Revolution. Robert Rogers and John Stark had built the original fort in 1755. After the war, Eames built a splendid mansion near the fort that stayed in his family until about 1850. His grandson, John, who died in 1925 at the age of 101, cut a 14-foot-long timber out of the fort in 1841. As late as 1936 it was extant at the house of Eames's neighbor Aaron Potter. Maybe still is.

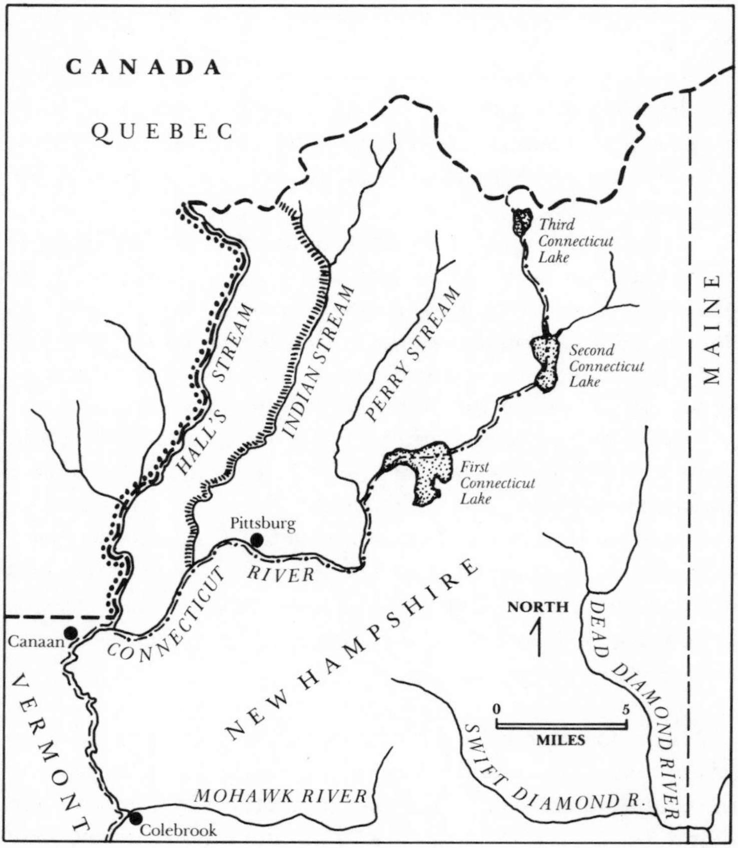

THE INDIAN STREAM REPUBLIC

·········· Line claimed by Col. Eames about 1800.

ıııııııııııı Line claimed by Canada about 1819.

·—·—· Line according to award of the King of Holland, 1831.

— — — Line of Webster-Ashburton Treaty, 1842.

– — – State lines.

establish markers. The colonel must have thought "head" meant "branch," or "tributary," for he made Hall's Stream the northwest bound of the state, which gave New Hampshire a good many extra square miles to the west of the true head of the Connecticut River, which is the Third Connecticut Lake.

New Hampshire accepted Eames's line, and Canada didn't make any objections at the time, so the colonel and three other promoters proceeded to buy the entire Indian Stream valley from Chief Philip, of the St. Francis tribe, in return for the promise that the chief and his two squaws should be given food and clothing as long as they lived and that all the Indians of the tribe should be allowed to hunt and fish there.

Of course the worthy colonel was merely wanting to make a fast dollar in land speculation, which you might say was kind of illegal the way he went at it, for buying land from Indians had been outlawed by the federal government some years before. His defense, of course, was that since the boundary hadn't been defined, the region wasn't part of the United States. This was also the defense of a rival land company run by an old Indian-fighter named Moody Bedel, who bought the whole north end of the state from the Indians at St. Francis for thirty-one hundred dollars. These enterprising gents would sell the same parcel of land to two different men, which caused a lot of confusion.

Well, during the next twenty-five years minor arguments between Canada and the United States kept cropping up about the land between Hall's Stream and the Connecticut River, with each claiming the entire territory, until about 1819, when the Canadians split the difference and named Indian Stream as the boundary. That decreased the area in dispute but it didn't eliminate it, and for some years thereafter the territory was a refuge for smugglers, what the historians call "border ruffi-ans," and other nefarious characters — to the annoyance of the honest citizens there.

Finally, in 1827, the two countries agreed to submit the boundary question to the King of Holland and to abide by his judgment. However, when the king decided that everything west of the Connecticut belonged to Canada, the United States thanked him for his services but refused to accept his ruling.

Then started the real confusion. Britain and this country had previously agreed that until the question was settled neither should extend any authority over the territory, but now the Canadians seemed to regard it as settled. In 1831 His Majesty's officers compelled some of the Indian Streamers to do military service. I don't think it was very serious — just summer camp training — but it was the principle of the thing that hurt. Those who believed they were citizens of the United States appealed to New Hampshire for protection, but they didn't get any. On the contrary, United States customs officers, apparently over-looking the official American attitude, began to levy duties on butter, cheese, and other produce brought into New Hamp-shire and Vermont.

Thus beset on one side by military conscription and on the other by customs duties, the harassed inhabitants decided to form a country of their own, owing allegiance to neither the United States nor Great Britain.

The first offical "declaration of independence" started over a woman. A young Indian Stream lothario, Moody Haynes — a relative of mine, incidentally — denied the validity of a breach of promise suit brought against him by one Melissa Thurston in a Coos County court.

"May it please Your Honor," said he on his appointed day of trial, "the alleged offense is said to have taken place in Indian Stream. I deny the jurisdiction of this court over Indian Stream."

He got away with it — and that started the ball rolling. For in challenging the court, Moody Haynes had challenged, by im-plication at least, the United States — and the territory was not long in following suit.

On June 11, 1832, the voters of the disputed tract came together and elected a committee of five, one of whom was named Luther Parker, to draw up a proper form of government. Within a month the committee reported in favor of a republic and submitted a constitution that was adopted by a vote of 56 to 3.

This constitution of the "United Inhabitants of Indian Stream Territory" provided for an assembly, a council, and a president. It contained a preamble and a bill of rights, the whole patterned somewhat after the present constitution of New Hampshire, but (said Vern) being a damned sight more amenable to change than the New Hampshire document, which is so bristling with legal and technical difficulties that the most determined efforts to bring it up to date have resulted in only three changes in a hundred and fifty years. The supreme legislative power of the Indian Streamers was vested in the assembly, which included everybody male and over twenty-one. Luther Parker was a member of the first council, and by the council he was later called "President of the Republic."

The "united inhabitants" also established a common school system, formed a forty-man army for protection against foreign invasion or domestic disorder, and levied taxes for local purposes. Likewise, the payment of debts, for the first time in the existence of the colony, was enforced by legal means. This caused some discontent, for a certain number of the citizens had come there to roost in order to escape paying their debts where they had been living.

The first criminal tried in the Republic was charged by a woman with felonious assault. The trial brought out a lot of ludicrous and contradictory testimony, but in the end the woman relented (her evidence wasn't of a very damaging nature anyway) and the jury handed down a verdict of "not guilty." The judge requested the defendant to stand up and listen to the verdict. Then he said to him:

"Prisoner at the bar. It gives me great pleasure to inform you that you have been honorably acquitted by your countrymen of the atrocious crime with which you are charged; but this court deems it its duty to admonish you that, if you are ever caught in another nasty scrape of this kind, you will be punished severely."

Vern laughed. "It makes me think of a letter the editor of the Colebrook paper showed me once, years ago," he said. "It was dated about 1883, if I remember correctly. A woman had sent it to him to publish, after her husband had posted her — you know, had put a notice in the paper he wouldn't pay her bills 'cause she'd left his bed and board. She allowed her husband wasn't any great shakes to begin with and had never paid her bills to end with, and in between she asked, 'What can you expect of a man who committed adultery with Beatrice Placey for seventeen sents?' She spelled it with an 's.' The price has gone up since those good old days," Vern added dryly.

He went on:

Well, for the first three years after the establishment of the Republic everything was fairly peaceful, despite the fact that they were recognized by neither the United States nor Canada. But on the fateful day of March 12, 1835, Deputy Sheriff Smith, of Colebrook, following the course of duty, tried to arrest a pair of Indian Stream boys. They gave him a licking and sent him back to New Hampshire. The next day two other deputies who had crossed the border to attach property were assaulted and driven out.

Wild reports of this resistance flew back down state. It was said that the people of the territory were raising an army and building a blockhouse — that they had made an alliance with the Indians to wage war on New Hampshire. The truth was that the Indian Streamers were building a jail for themselves so they could be a regular Republic — for how can you administer justice without a jail?

As a matter of fact, the lack of a penal institution was a prime cause of the Republic's downfall. The local sheriff, Reuben

Sawyer, used to keep his wards under a seven-hundred-pound iron kettle turned bottom-side up on a flat rock, but that would hold only one man at a time.

About this time the inhabitants of the Republic sent an ambassador to Colonel White, the sheriff of Coos County, to outline their position. The legate was instructed to say that the citizens were "unanimously resolved to abide by and support our own constitution and laws, agreeably to our oaths, until known to what government we properly belong, when our constitution is to end." Colonel White acknowledged their communication, but said he would have to consult with the governor.

You see, up to then it was pretty clear that the Republic aimed to prevent, and not foment, disorder. The affairs of the government were in the hands of peaceful, solid citizens who couldn't see any way out of the mess caused by the boundary dispute except to set up their own government until their official nationality was finally decided.

But the lawless element became more numerous, and in April, 1835, the Assembly of Indian Stream passed a law making it perjury to violate the oath of allegiance to their constitution, with a penalty of confinement in the stocks. They also forbade any "foreign" sheriff or sheriff's officers residing in Indian Stream or the United States to perform any duties within the territory, under the penalty of imprisonment.

That, of course, was a clear distinction against the United States. The inhabitants favoring the United States rather than Canada became alarmed, and on the same day they sent a petition to the governor of New Hampshire asking for protection against the action of those laws.

There followed a voluminous and confusing correspondence among the governments of New Hampshire, the United States, and Canada and the various factions within the Republic. Appeals were sent to both Washington and the governor of Lower Canada for protection from New Hampshire, which was determined to administer the law of Indian Stream until the whole affair could be settled.

Sheriff White visited the Republic and appointed a local citizen named Blanchard a deputy sheriff of Coos County. In October of '35, the said deputy sheriff tried to serve a writ on John Tyler, a citizen of the Republic. When Tyler refused to obey the writ, he was arrested, but his neighbors forcibly rescued him. At this point a Canadian judge named Alexander Rea who lived over in Hereford turned the tables and swore out a warrant for the arrest of Deputy Blanchard and his assistants for the crime of trying to serve papers not granted by Canadian courts. Blanchard was arrested by a posse of a dozen men and carried bodily off to Canada.

Then the fireworks started. A latter-day Paul Revere went galloping over the roads of Clarksville, Stewartstown, and Colebrook, spreading the alarm. His call to duty was answered by three hundred frontiersmen full of fury and old rum — one of 'em was Miner Hilliard — who gathered at Canaan all raring to go.

They rescued Blanchard and brought him back to Canaan, where, warmed with success and copious drafts of rum, they decided to invade Canada. In Hereford, Justice Rea and fourteen men met them on the King's highway — and ordered them to get off it. Eph Aldrich (Judge Edgar Aldrich's grandfather) — you remember I introduced you to the old judge once? — launched a mighty oath and a mighty swing with his old broadsword, felling a Canadian. There ensued a pitched battle in which three men and a horse were wounded. The invaders captured Rea himself and brought him back in triumph to Canaan, but after they'd held him prisoner a few hours they let him go.

Lord Gosford, who was governor of Lower Canada, wrote a strong letter of complaint to the New Hampshire legislature, and in Concord, Governor Badger appointed a commission to report on the matter. As a result of their investigation, a troop of militia was ordered to Indian Stream to help Sheriff White "uphold the integrity of New Hampshire laws."

About then, President Parker became discouraged (he'd already been arrested once by the Canadians and held in Sherbrooke jail for a spell) and emigrated to Wisconsin with his family in a two-horse wagon.

The "war" continued. Warrants were sworn out against several people said to be living at the house of a farmer named Applebee, on Perry Stream. Twoscore and ten brave militiamen surrounded the house on the night of November 13th and in the morning summoned the occupants to surrender. Applebee and his son came to the door, muskets in hand, and there would have been bloodshed and sudden death on the fair banks of Perry Stream if it hadn't been for a cooler head on the scene who persuaded them they had better come peaceably. As a matter of fact, poor Applebee was the only one who was ever punished during the whole war. He had to serve a year in the log jail at Lancaster.

About that time, Canadian authorities, aroused by the fireworks, came to see what was going on, but Captain Mooney's militiamen stopped them short and ordered them back to Canada, where they reported "an armed invasion of British territory." Lord Gosford wrote a sharp letter to the British Embassy in Washington, and trouble seemed to be in the air — but it was soon smoothed over.

The arrests of Applebee and a few others convinced the Republic that it would be to their best advantage to acknowledge the supremacy of New Hampshire and surrender their independent status. So the assembly adopted a series of resolutions which were published in the Concord newspapers, and the country was brought to an end. In 1840 the name of the territory was changed to Pittsburg, and in 1842 the Webster-Ashburton treaty at Washington established Hall's Stream as the international boundary. Thus the smallest republic ever established was legislated out of existence, and the state sold Pittsburg to speculators for about twenty cents an acre.*

The last survivor of the Indian Stream Republic was Charles D. Parker, who as son of its president had participated in the war at the age of nine as a musket-loader. Later he became lieutenant governor of Wisconsin and died in 1925 at the good ripe age of ninety-seven.

As for Captain Mooney's company of the 24th Regiment of the New Hampshire militia, comprising one captain, one lieutenant, one ensign, four sergeants, two musicians, and forty-two privates — what of them? When they were disbanded after the Indian Stream War in 1836, they were considered veteran soldiers, and each was granted 160 acres of government land.

"And," Vern concluded, "I know a lawyer up in Colebrook named Johnson who is a Son of the American Revolution and is so proud of it that he always signs his letters: 'Tom Johnson, S.A.R.' I thought once I might sign: 'Vern Davison, S.I.S.R.' But then I got to thinking maybe my grandsir fought on the wrong side. What do you think?"

KIM DAY

After cutting through broad and fertile meadows, the road we were driving on wound uphill through woods for a mile or two. Here we found quite a sizable clearing, with an occupied set of farm buildings.

"Frank Holden lives here," Vern said. "He's one of those fellers who like to get away off from the settlements, and clear land and farm and hunt and fish. Lucky for him he's got a wife who doesn't mind it. We'll leave the car here."

* An ancient and substantial citizen of Lancaster named Fred Amey, whose grandfather was, like Vern's, an original Indian Streamer, told me that the speculators got those lands for *two* cents an acre . . .

Mrs. Holden, a woman by no means small, was frying doughnuts. She gave us a couple, and permission to leave the car in the barn.

"Hard times haven't made you fade away any, Cora, have they?" asked Vern, regarding the buxom woman admiringly.

Mrs. Holden laughed. "Hard times?" she repeated. "Shucks. Frank says it's always been hard times on Indian Stream. But it never helps to go around complaining about them. We manage to get along. Seems to me that the people that crowd into cities and go on the dole could come out onto these abandoned farms and make a living, even if they didn't become millionaires."

"But, Cora," protested Vern, reaching for another doughnut, "then they wouldn't be able to have oranges and grapefruit for breakfast, and two kinds of cereal. And if they earned their own living, they couldn't afford to buy rubbers and parasols and have beauty treatments. Haven't you any humanitarian feeling for the forgotten man, Cora?"

"Shucks!" said Cora, so contemptuously that I burst out laughing. "I'll bet you never owned a pair of rubbers in your life, Vern, and your poor little frame ain't been stunted any, that I can see. I don't hold with letting anybody starve to death, and never have. We help our neighbors when they need help, and they help us. I'm not forgetting the time you pitched in and did all our work for two weeks when Frank broke his leg. But I don't see any use in taking money away from hardworking people and giving it to a lot of loafers to buy stuff I can't afford to. Our kids go barefoot most of the year and it doesn't hurt them any. So could other people's."

"The trouble with you," Vern said as he went over to the sink and drew a dipper of water to wash down the doughnuts, "the trouble with you, Cora, is you're one of these rugged individualists that are still living in the horse and buggy age."

"Maybe so," she admitted. "But the horse and buggy are paid for, and the way I was brought up that gives me a mighty comforting feeling."

"Is she a fair sample of North Country womanhood?" I asked, after we had bid her farewell and had gone on our way.

Vern rubbed his ear reflectively. "Yes, I guess she's a good sample. There's some that are more shapely, and there's some that are more shrewish. But she's the kind you can depend on. And there's a surprising lot of them like her, I can tell you.

"The people up here," he went on, "are a good deal like their environment. Narrow and contracted in some things, but hard and rugged and kinda elemental in their ways of thinking and doing. They ain't bothered much by false values. They expect life to be hard — but they take a sort of pride in being hard enough to stand it and enjoy it.

"I've heard my old grandfather tell that in the early days, when crops were uncertain, the men all wore belts with holes punched in 'em halfway around. If they had to go without food one day, they took the belt up one hole. They got so they knew just how far they could take it up. But they never went around howling that the government owed them a living. The thought never occurred to them. In fact, the more the government let them alone, the better they liked it. And that spirit of self-sufficiency ain't half so dead as you might think.

"Of course humans are humans anywhere, and a lot of people up here do get what they call 'relief.' Just because they know they can get away with it. But bless you, if the relief was taken away from them, you'd see them go to work.

"I know a Frenchman down in Milan and he was being supported by the town. He has thirteen kids and he lives on an old back road up on a mountain and one winter there came a hell of a fall of snow and this bird waited for 'em to come and plow him out, but they didn't come. So he sent a boy down to the nearest neighbor to phone to the poormaster that he couldn't get out to get provisions for his starving family and furthermore his kids couldn't get to school.

"I happened to be visiting with the poormaster when the boy

phoned. 'What would you do in a case like this?' Winslow says to me.

" 'Christ Almighty!' I told him, 'he can walk down to the main road, and pick up a ride from there to the store. I'd tell him if he was too damn lazy to do that, he could starve to death!'

"And Winslow told him just that. That feller travelled out all right. When Winslow heard about it, it encouraged him a little so that spring he took all their relief away. Told them there'd be no more. What happened? Hell! The feller went to work and put in five acres of potatoes and made enough off 'em to keep him in luxury all the next winter. Don't worry, all the people up in this neck of the woods will find some way of managing. If they can't, they wouldn't be worth saving, would they?"

The road meandered on, due north, far up above the stream which was on our left. Vern stopped and pointed.

"That was what we called the High Landing," he said. "I saw a man killed there one spring. His name was Johnny O'Hara. He slipped, and the rolling logs caught him. We didn't find enough of him to bury."

The road was full of little bubbling springs. We tramped for more than an hour, and then, without warning, came out into an immense clearing. The road ran along the edge of the trees and swung to the right, up a hill, only a tote road from now on. To our left, the cleared land extended down to the stream, a furlong away, and even across it. Directly ahead of us stood a log cabin.

"That must have been a mighty farm once," I said.

"It was a mighty man who cleared it," Vern replied. "It's the old Kim Day place. When Kim was on earth there was a big, three-story house, painted white, where that shack stands.

"The drive was going down Indian and the rivermen had filled the oven of the stove in the house with dynamite to thaw. I read in some scientific magazine not long ago — I picked it up in a barbershop in Colebrook — that it is a popular fallacy that heat will cause dynamite to explode. It must be *jarred!* Hell! If the goddamned fool who wrote that had been in Kim Day's house that morning, *he'd* have been jarred. For that ovenful of dynamite exploded and blew the house all over the farm. Ed Hilliard was just driving into the clearing when she lifted, and he said the air was just chuck-full of flying timbers.

"Old Kim," Vern went on, "was a very religious man. He was a Seventh Daysy, as the wits around here call the Seventh Day Adventists. And he had a familiar spirit that accompanied him through the woods disguised as a wildcat.

"It's a fact," he persisted, noting my look of disbelief. "Ask any of the old-timers in Pittsburg about Kim Day's 'Indian Devil.' I've seen its tracks myself. What it really was, it was a panther that made its home near Kim's place. Like all panthers, it was chuck-full of curiosity, and it used to walk along beside him when he went back and forth between his farm and the settlement.

"Kim never feared it, because as I said, he was a religious man, and those chaps, when they are sincere, *know* the Lord is behind them, so they don't fear anything. Any ordinary man would have been scared to death to walk through these woods at night, alone and unarmed, knowing that critter was loping along in the brush beside him. But not old Kim. They do say that the night the old man died, the animal was heard outside, screeching something terrible. No one ever heard of nor saw it after that night.

"There's a song about the Day family. It's called the "Old Dan Day" song, after Kim's father, Dan, who fell out of a sleigh one night when he was drunk, and froze to death. Let's see if I can't remember it."

We tramped along in silence for a few rods, until Vern cleared his throat loudly and burst into the following ditty:

114

OLD DAN DAY

There lives an old man in Pittsburg here
Who sometimes drinks rum and sometimes beer
Or a little cold water when rum ain't near.

Every night when he goes to bed,
He places a bottle under his head;
And in the morning when he awakes,
A jolly good dram this old man takes.

(Chorus — to be repeated after each stanza)

I wish to God the time would come
When Old Dan Day won't drink no rum;
But you might as well wish for the day of his death,
For he'll drink rum as long as he draws breath.

He had a son, his name was Zeke,
I've heard them say that the truth he couldn't speak;
But I know better, for I've heard him say
He believed the very devil was in Old Dan Day.

He had another and his name was Sam,
He drinks so much rum he ain't worth a damn;
He drinked and has squandered all his property away,
He's following the example of Old Dan Day.

He had another and his name was Dan,
If 'twa'nt for his failings he'd be quite a man;
But you that know them know what they be,
And if I don't tell you, why you can't blame me.

He had another and his name was Kim,
All the men in God's world couldn't beat him;
He likes to be with the women alone,
Other men's wives as well as his own.

He had a daughter and her name was Sue,
I don't know but what I'd kiss her if I wanted to spew;

115

It's enough to gag the devil when she puckers up her
    mouth,
I'd rather kiss a nigger from away down South.

He had another and her name was Jane,
I think that her character is deeply stained;
With old Doctor Robbins she used to lay
When her husband was far away.

He had another and her name was Ab,
Selden thought he'd got the first grab;
But over to 'Lonzie's they say she went,
To ride old Rob was her intent.

There's one thing more that I do crave,
That this old man shan't have no grave;
Throw him into a watery hole.
The sharks take his body and the devil take his soul.

Now my song is at a close
And those that don't like it can turn up their nose;
But those that do, in a smiling way,
Give three rousing cheers for Old Dan Day!

(Chorus)

"I ain't much of a songster," Vern said, laughing. "I've got
enthusiasm, but that's all. The tune to that song is really something like 'Little Brown Jug.' In the old days, people sung a lot,
not only in the camps, but in the evenings at social gatherings.
It helped to pass away the time and kept 'em from thinking.
Nowadays they play bridge or listen to a radio. Someday I'll
take you over to see Stonewall Jackson on Sims Stream. He
knows dozens of those old songs. Feller could make quite a
collection of those that originated and grew right here in the
North Country.

"I told you Kim was a Seventh Daysy? Well, one day he and
some others of his faith was having a banquet at a house over

on Hall's Stream. The table was set on the piazza, and a place at the head was left for the Saviour, in case he should come. Everyone was seated and they was just about to say grace when in strides Kim's brother Sam, whose failings I just sung to you. Seeing a vacant place at the head of the table, he sits himself down in it.

" 'Just in time,' he remarks cheerfully, and was going to ask 'em to pass the potatoes when someone remonstrates:

" 'But Mr. Day, you can't sit there. That place is for Jesus.'

" 'Huh?' says Samuel. 'Well, I don't see him yet, but if he comes, I'll get up and give him the seat.'

"Kim's boys (Vern continued, as we strode on through the forest) "weren't as religious as their sire, and they played a mean trick on him one night. The old man believed that the 'last trump' was to sound on a given date, and that night he wrapped himself in a sheet and climbed into an apple tree, ready to be carried aloft.

"But he went to sleep, sitting in a fork of the tree, and when the boys saw it they got a big pile of straw that they placed beneath him and set on fire. Then they shouted. Kim woke up and saw the flames shooting up around him.

" 'Oh my God,' he hollers, 'here I am in hell, just as I always knew I would be.'

"Old Dan Day had other children, who don't appear in the song," said Vern. "There was the triplets, for example, Lum, Peen, and Lay. Over on Perry Stream is the 'Day Settlement' where they were born. The natives up here have a kind of joke about it. They say it's where occurred the only thing of its kind on record, namely 'where they made three Days in one night.' "

He laughed. "When the triplets were born, old 'Lonzie Perry, a neighbor, was congratulatin' Dan on his prowess as a begetter.

" 'Yas!' Dan says, 'and if my foot hadn't slipped, I'd have had a whole basketful!' "

"He shouldn't have taken off his spiked boots," I said.

My aphorism must have conjured up a picture in Vern's mind, for he burst out laughing.

"I hadn't thought of that," he said. "Damned if you ain't showing signs of almost human intelligence this morning!"

SLUICED

As we tramped on up the stream, Vern continued to regale me with talk of murders, suicides, and sudden and violent deaths. Every bend in the trail called up some stirring memory to him. At Graham's Dam he pointed to the ruins of an old, old logging camp. Only a few timbers left in the grass of the clearing remained.

"That was where Old Ginseng and me drove team for Van Dyke so many years ago," he said. "This here is Cowan Hill, and over there is where Ginseng got sluiced.

"What does 'sluiced' mean?"

"It means any accident in which a team of horses is involved. Specifically, it means when they get away from you going downhill and the load tips over. Or even if it doesn't tip over," he added grimly.

"Did you see Old Ginseng?"

"I did so. I was right behind him, waiting for the snub warp. You see, we had a snub-hill over there nearly eight hundred feet long. Ginseng came down there one forenoon with five thousand feet of twenty-foot logs on a bobsled. We used three binding-chains for that kind of work — two bunk-chains, one on each side, on top of the sled-bunk, and then a thirty-foot topchain full of logs on top of the first two.

"That was a hell of a big load he had on that trip, but he was a hell of a good teamster. He stopped at the top of the hill, threw the snub-warp, which was a two-inch manila rope, around the bunk and the load, tied a bowline knot in it, and started down. The snubber, the man who pays out the warp

118

off a stump at the top of the hill, was a little French-Canadian.

"He had three coils of rope wound around the stump, separated by big wooden pegs driven horizontally into auger holes bored in the stump. Those kept the warp straight. I've seen snubs where they just threw one coil of warp around the stump, and paid it out by hand, but that can be mighty dangerous if it's slippery. On this one, the snubber had a wooden lever set in a mortise, and all he had to do to slow up the load was to bear down just a little on his lever, which tightened the warp.

"Ginseng had gone down about two hundred and fifty feet when the snubber got careless and bore down too hard on the lever. Consequently, with all that length of rope out, one of two things had to happen — either when the slack was taken up the load would be jerked back up the hill, or else the warp would break. Well, the warp didn't break — that time — but the load, horses and all, leaped backwards up that icy hill a dozen feet, as if they'd been shot out of a cannon.

"Only Ginseng, standing on the front end of the logs, kept right on going down the hill. He shot out on the pole between the two horses, right over the neck-yoke, and landed on his face and hands in the middle of the road. It jarred the soup right out of him. I thought he was killed, and so did he. He slid more than three rods down that road on his face and stomach. But he wasn't killed. He had sense enough to realize what had happened, and that if that snubber eased off on the warp again, the horses and logs would come smashing right down on top of him. He rolled off into the snow beside the road as fast as he could.

"But the snubber had heard him yell when he went diving over the neck-yoke, and he saw what had happened. So he held the warp tight until Ginseng got back onto the load and started again. But that last yank on the rope had been too much for it. It was getting old and weak, and he was just easing down onto the next hogback when it broke.

"He didn't look back, but he knew the instant it parted that

119

ABOVE: *Biggest load of pulpwood ever hauled out of the woods by two horses (a little more than twelve cords).* BELOW: *Sluiced! A pair of horses running away with a load of four-foot pulpwood.*

he was sluiced. I tell you, young feller, I've been in some pretty tight places in my life, and I've never been scared, really scared, but just that once — watching another man riding to hell. God! Even today I can remember just how prickles of fear went all over me, from my scalp to my toes!

"There were ledges and trees on both sides, so it was impossible to turn the horses out of the road. Ginseng should have jumped right there, but he wouldn't leave his horses. And a second later it was too late, even if he'd wanted to.

"The road down that snub-hill wasn't straight, nor was it level. There was a curve near the foot, and there were hog-backs, or benches, maybe ten feet long, before each steep pitch all the way down. When the sled struck the first bench, I thought the binding chains would break. They groaned like a wounded bear.

"Ginseng told me afterwards that right then he felt something clutching at his foot. He tried to move it, but it wouldn't come. He looked down. The logs had begun to roll and they'd caught the rubber heel of his boot and held it like a vise. Lucky for him he was wearing felt boots like everybody did those days. He pulled his stockinged foot out of it in a hurry. The logs rolled up that bootleg halfway to the knee! Of course they rolled back again after a while, but that wouldn't have done him any good.

"He went shooting down those pitches hog-wild. The horses couldn't hold back. They weren't even really running. They'd jump and strike, jump and strike, and every time they hit the edge of those little flats, the logs would come sliding down the pitch behind and jam them forward something desperate.

"Ginseng stood on the top of the load as firm as the rock of Gibraltar, helping 'em all he could, and a teamster who knows his business can do a lot with horses, even in a place like that, so he managed to keep them on their feet and in the road till they got to the last curve. It was just at the foot of the last pitch, and he couldn't swing the horses around!

121

"By God, he *couldn't* swing 'em around! That five thousand feet of green timber gave one last hellish lunge just as he tried to swing 'em, and it pushed 'em ahead so fast they shot right straight across the road. There was a big spruce tree, three feet through, blown down, or uprooted, rather, right in front of them, leaning at an angle of maybe twenty-five degrees, its top lodged in the crotch of a big yellow birch.

"The heavy load fairly hurled the horses right up that tree trunk, one on either side, and they hung there by the neck-yoke, kicking into space. The pole lay along the trunk, and when the bunk of the sled hit the tree, of course the whole thing stopped. It's a wonder it didn't break that big spruce right in two.

"Ginseng didn't feel like taking another header off that load, and just before the bunk hit, he jumped. He landed in a couple of little balsams and bounced off them into a snowdrift. He wasn't hurt. He picked himself up and ran back to his team. Their hind feet was on the ground, but they'd have choked to death pretty soon, lying on the neck-yoke that way. They were too tight to unhitch.

"He had an axe sticking in one of the logs on top of the load. He grabbed that and crawled out on the pole. Those horses knew he'd come to help 'em. They stood as quiet as kittens while he chopped the neck-yoke in two and let 'em down. So all the damage was a broken warp and a chopped neck-yoke. Oh yes, and one missing French-Canadian snubber.

"After Ginseng got the horses free, he came back up the hill to talk to that snubber. He had the axe in his hand. I'd run down the hill to meet him, but he never noticed me at all. I don't know whether he intended to kill the snubber or not. But *he* thought so. When *he* saw Ginseng coming with blood in his eye, swearing at the top of his voice, and swinging that four-pound tomahawk, he turned and ran like a fox. He must have run clear to Canada. Anyway, they never saw him on Indian again."

ORA MILLS

That night and the two succeeding ones we stayed with Milt Mills at his camp far up on Indian. His brother, Ora, he told us, had got a job guiding a city man and his two half-grown daughters over to Parmachenee Lake via Moose Bog, and would not be back for a week.

But that same night, Ora, a small, bushy-haired man with a harelip, came in from Burnt Dam, a pack basket of provisions on his back.

"What in hell are you doing *here?*" Milt asked in polite surprise.

Ora slipped the straps from his shoulders and sat down with a sigh of relief.

"Damn 'ports!" he grunted disgustedly. " 'Ey tried to make a fool out of me. I yef 'em over 'ere in Moose Bog."

"Great blushing geranium!" cried Vern. "They'll get lost and die in there!"

" 'On't care if 'ey do," said Ora indifferently. "But 'on't worry. Joe Parrault was over here and I yef him to 'ake care of 'em."

"Had your supper?" Milt asked. "No? Well, I'll get something for you to eat. What was the trouble, anyway?"

Mollified at this kind reception, Ora unburdened himself. The " 'port" and his daughters, aged sixteen and fifteen, had wanted to walk across country to Parmachenee, where the papa was a member of the Parmachenee Club. Ora was sitting on the Camp Idlewild piazza at Second Lake when papa drove up, chauffeur and all, and as he was the only guide available, he was hired.

"We went over to Bog," Ora said, "and make camp. 'Ey want 'rout for supper. I say ' 'Aw right, I get you some 'rout.' I go down to 'ream to fish. I see hell of a big 'rout in 'ere. 'E girls follow me. I say, 'Be careful, 'on't show yourselves in 'e water, you 'car 'e 'rout.' 'Ey just yaugh. 'En 'ey pick up hones and frow

123

'em in pool. 'At big 'rout run off. I get mad 'en. I 'rab 'e biggest girl and give her damn good 'pankin.'

" 'E old man come runnin' down. ' 'On't you 'are yay your filfy hands on my daughter,' 'e say. I say — 'I'm in charge of 'is party. If 'ey 'on't have any manner, I 'each 'em some.' 'E say — 'you're fired!' I say — 'Go to hell! I've quit aweady.' So I come on home.

"But I met Joe Parrault. 'E over 'ere pickin' spruce gum. I told him to go yook after 'ose 'ports, and 'e do it all right."

"You should have spanked the old he-one," commented Milt.

"If I was big as Vern here, you bet I 'pank him too," said Ora darkly. "Damn 'ports! 'Ink a guide is a yackey 'ey can order around!"

"They can certainly be aggravating," Vern agreed. "And women are always a damn nuisance in the woods anyhow."

"Do you think," I asked him the next day, "that Ora did right to leave his party in the woods like that?"

"No," he answered, "I don't. If you take on a contract to do a thing, you should finish it, come hell or high water. You understand, I don't blame his feeling that way a bit, and it's the way all these fellers up here would feel. They ain't any of 'em rich, but they can all read and write, and they figger they're just as good as the next man. Being independent is their particular pride, and they won't let any employer step on their tails, not when they think they're in the right. They don't have to, for they ain't afraid of getting fired, you see. On the other hand, they'll work themselves to death for a man who gives them a fair shake.

"But still and all, Ora shouldn't have quit like that. It reflects on all guides. And there's other ways of handling such situations.

"I remember once two city fellers came up to Windigo to go fishing. They were friends of O.B. Brown, and Ralph Sawyer, who had charge there, took 'em on what we called the 'grand circle,' a week's trip through a chain of lakes. Those fellers were an awful trial, Ralph said. But when he worked for me, I'd brought him up to hold his temper, and he held it, though sometimes he had to dash off into the woods and claw the bark off trees.

"But on the fourth night out, when one of those sports woke him up and told him to pull the mosquito netting over him, Ralph lost patience. He woke up the other man and then proceeded in a few well-chosen words to tell 'em what he thought of 'em. At least that's what he said. Knowing Ralph pretty well, I can imagine that the words really weren't so few, but they probably were well chosen.

"When he run out of breath, he counted ten, and he counted it slow, like I had taught him. Then he said: 'I was sent to guide you around the Circle, and I'm going to do it. I'm responsible for you, and I'll get you back safe to Windigo. But when we get there, I'm going to take both of you to once and give you the goddamnedest licking you ever heard tell of!'

"Well, sir, those sports were sweet as little lambs after that. Ralph said he'd never seen a nicer, more considerate pair of fellers, and when they got back to Windigo they gave him a ten-dollar bonus."

Each day there at the Mills's camp we went fishing, but that took only a small amount of our time, for in half an hour we caught all the four of us could eat — and the four of us could eat an astonishing quantity.

One afternoon a large deer came out to graze on the hillside in front of the camp and, as the larder was short of venison, Ora lazily got his rifle and prepared to kill the creature.

"I'll shoot him right through the heart," he said. He rested the gun on the windowsill and took a long, still aim. He fired, and the buck leaped straight up into the air and fell backwards. And never moved again. We strolled over to get it. It was shot through both eyes!

"I forgot to tell you," yawned Milt, "that I was monkeying with the sights on that gun yesterday."

"That Milt is quite a quaint character," Vern observed one morning as we sat on the porch and watched our hosts depart to wash gold in the stream. "One time he had a little difficulty with a trapper from Pittsburg named Jack Chapple who owns a camp way down below Cowan Hill. Milt had a line of traps set for sable along the height of land. As everybody knows, sable will follow a spotted line, and since the height was already spotted, it saved Milt that work. Somebody — Milt thought it was Jack — came along and urinated beside each trap, which of course would scare away all the sable.

"So Milt girds up his loins, like Samson of old, and goes forth to shoot his enemy. Jack was away from home, so Milt wrote a note stating he would slay him the first time he saw him, and nailed it on the door. Jack got home pretty soon after Milt left, and when he read that note his whiskers curled with rage.

"He took the paper in one hand and his rifle in the other and set out for Depot Camp as fast as he could caper. He overtook Milt at Graham's Dam, and there the two warriors stood — or, to be accurate, I presume they skulked — and did their best to put each other out of business. But one was scared and the other dassen't, so neither succeeded. But they're good friends now."

LOST GOLD MINE

"Is there really any gold in here?" I asked Vern.

"Oh yes. The Mills boys make day's wages washing it out of the main stream. You know that Annance [he accented the name on the last syllable] Gulch I showed you yesterday when we were fishing? That's where the original gold mine in the valley was probably located, though nobody is quite sure. Anyhow it was named after Archie Annance, and Archie *did* have a mine in here somewhere.

"Archie was a red Indian. His family lived over on Moosehead Lake. Some of 'em still do. Quite a respectable outfit, too.

Old Louis Annance especially. Some of 'em even went to Dartmouth College. Archie himself went to college, and he specialized in mineralogy."

"Did you know him?"

"Yes, I knew him when I was a youngster. I was working on the drive in 1885, and Archie had charge of the wanigan. I remember what elegant handwriting he had. You remember that Lewis Leavitt I told you about? Well, he helped Archie trace a mineral vein from Ditton, in Quebec, more than eight miles down to Lake Parmachenee. Archie used to drink like a fish. I don't know when he died, but I'll bet I know what he died of!

"Back in 1865 he was prospecting in what is now Ditton, just over the height of land from here. It was all woods then, belonging to the government. Archie found a mine and he took out a little free gold by panning, but it wasn't a placer deposit, and he needed money to take out a mining permit and locate his claim. But that would have cost him two hundred dollars, which was a lot of money those days.

"He tried to borrow it from a politician named Pope who lived in Cookshire, some miles to the north, and was fool enough to tell him what he wanted it for. Pope offered to lend the money in exchange for an interest in the claim, but Archie wouldn't do that. Then Pope sent men to trail him, in order to find out where the mine was, but Archie knew they were after him and he always lost 'em.

"Finally, Pope, who was afraid Archie might raise the money some other way, got a man to give Archie a job of some kind so's the Indian could earn the two hundred dollars. Then Mr. Pope, who was a member of Parliament, went to the Ministry of Mines or wherever it was Archie would have to go to file his claims, and said:

" 'One of these days an Indian named Archie Annance will come in here to take out a mining permit. When he has described the location, you keep a copy of his description, but tell him that the claim has already been filed on.' "

"And that's just what they did. They whipsawed the Indian out of his mine as pretty as you please, and of course he couldn't do a thing about it, being a poor savage."

"What would you have done, in Archie's place?" I asked.

"I'd have scalped him, sure as hell," Vern said indifferently.

"Well, they worked that mine for years and years and took a lot of gold out of it. A Mrs. Ives up in Cookshire owns it now. I've heard tell there's a barbed wire fence and an armed guard around it all the time.

"But Archie had learned something from dealing with his Christian paleface brothers, and pretty soon, when he'd discovered a placer over here on Indian, he had sense enough never to tell anyone where it was. But when he needed any money he'd come in here and get as much as he wanted.

"For years people hunted for his mine. Some of the first ones found a wheelbarrow, taken apart, and a spade, hidden in a spruce thicket, and they found some diggings had been done on the main stream, but that was all. They found more signs on Annance Gulch, but that doesn't prove anything. But at least it gave the brook a name."

When the Mills "boys" came back (they had spent more time fishing than gold washing) I asked them about mining on Indian, and they confirmed Vern's story. Also they showed me a couple of bottles of gold dust they had accumulated in their spare moments.

"There's gold all through this valley," said Milt, "but it's in such small quantities that it doesn't pay to dig for it. That was proven some years ago. To be exact, in 1901, when Judge Aldrich, a native of Pittsburg, organized a company, or association, to prospect here. He and Tom Van Dyke and Jones of Portland (the 'Jones's Pale Ale' man) and seven others put up a thousand dollars apiece and started in.

"Of course they'd always known about Archie Annance, but they were sort of warmed up because an old prospector from Rumford Falls named 'T-Bone' Jackson had been up the East

Branch prospecting and in his first pan he washed out a twelve-dollar nugget. Jackson had some sort of an obligation to Judge Aldrich, so he let him in on it. I suppose they promised Jackson some reward for his information and services.

"The first thing they did was to hire a quartz mining expert from New Mexico, a man named Newell, to examine the country. He did most of his testing on the East Branch, and blasted and dug for many feet on different quartz veins. But he didn't accomplish much except to undermine the Klondike Falls dam, which made George Van Dyke swear at his brother Thomas.

"They got rid of Newell and sent for a placer expert from Colorado, a man named Bachelder. He knew Newell, and after he'd taken a look at the land he said: 'Newell should have known right away that this is no quartz country.' He went to work and jabbed test holes all over the valley from Moose Pond (which is on the height of land above the Kim Day farm) to Greeley's camp, and from Teapot Brook to the West Branch — and he found color everywhere. Sometimes more.

"But fortified by T-Bone's big nugget, he concentrated his efforts on the East Branch. He drove his test holes up and down and back and forth and at last he limited the deposit to a plot three rods wide and less than half a mile long, beginning about a quarter of a mile above the junction of the East Branch and the Main Stream.

"The company hired twenty or thirty men from Pittsburg and put them to work there. They built sluice boxes and riffles and they shovelled and sweat and they got gold. At the end of each three days of sluicing they'd take out the riffles and clean up. The most they ever got at one cleanup was fifty-five dollars.

"Judge Aldrich himself came up one afternoon (on a cleanup day) and when he saw the yellow gold glittering on the riffles he got so excited that he insisted on staying all night, so he built a fire on the bank of the brook and slept there beside the riffles with a rifle in his hand.

"The next day was when the cleanup showed fifty-five dollars. Some evil-minded people say that the men from Pittsburg working there swiped part of the gold on other occasions. It's probably true. Anyhow, when Bachelder was all through, he informed the company that there was seventy-five thousand dollars worth of gold in the gulch, but it would cost a hundred thousand to get it out.

"So the company disbanded, and nothing else has ever been done on Indian in the way of big scale mining. Ora and I pan a little every summer. So do other fellows who come in from Pittsburg. But it's more of a recreation than a paying proposition. I know two men who spent all one summer panning gold here, and in the fall they had a gross profit of one hundred and ninety-two dollars, which isn't good wages. But then, they really didn't know much about panning, and like most of the rest, they spent more time fishing than gold hunting."

THE HAUNTED CAMP

It was while we were staying at the hospitable log castle of the Mills boys that Vern and I became involved with the famous Greeley's ghost, or "haunt" as the natives call it.

Newhall (the CVL engineer), Tom Cozzie, and our old friend Sam Martin and a young fellow named Clyde had been running a height-of-land line, and they came down to stay at Mills's camp one night before finishing their work in that region — the final piece of work being to run out the main stream and tie into the international boundary several miles to the north.

"It's a long day's work," said Newhall, who was a small, quiet man, with clear-cut features and steady brown eyes. "We'll have to leave the stream at the upper dam and strike for the line. And we won't have time to get back here at night. According to my map, Greeley's camp is only three miles below the boundary. I think we'll stay there. We can get back that far before dark."

Then it started. The Mills boys, along with Sam, warned him of the "haunt," and told of the mysterious deaths associated with the place. Some of the stories I had heard before, and some of them I hadn't.

It seems that Greeley had built the shack some six years earlier. He lived in Massachusetts and intended to come up deer hunting every fall with a party of friends. The first fall he came in with a party. One of their number was a young man named Foster. He was no woodsman, and the third day he went out and did not come back. It was late fall and there was no snow for tracking.

A searching party of over fifty men, gathered from Pittsburg and adjoining towns in Quebec, hunted three days for him in vain. Not a sign — except that one man came in at the end of the third day and said that late in the afternoon he had seen a crazy man carrying a gun who had turned and run like a deer.

The searchers shook their heads, told a few tales of men gone mad when lost in the woods, and returned to their homes. For three years Indian Stream valley was the home of a wild man who was seldom seen, apparently being afraid of his own kind, but who left unmistakable signs of his presence.

He broke into sporting camps in the winter and lived in them. He stole grub and ammunition from the Mill's camp, and one summer he started a fire that would have swept the whole valley if the fire warden on Deer Mountain had not seen it in time. But three years before (that is, before we heard these gruesome tales at Mills's camp) a skeleton had been found in the woods by a pair of timber-cruisers, and it was identified by means of a ring on one finger. So ended "Crazy" Foster, the first victim of Greeley's camp.

But once, shortly after Foster had gotten lost, he came back to Greeley's camp and wrote on a piece of notepaper a curse, if it may be called such, in which he stated that every party staying overnight in that camp would lose one member. He signed his name and tacked the paper on the door. Milt Mills came by there hunting one day and found the paper. He kept it.

The year after Foster's disappearance, Greeley came up again — and died. He had gone out and killed a deer (the biggest deer, incidentally, ever killed in the North Country), hung it up, and was returning to camp. For more than a mile his snowshoe tracks pointed straight for home. So he was not lost. The searching party found him standing bolt upright between two little spruces, dead and frozen. He was a healthy man, and no one knows the cause of his death.

The next year a party of three men came in to Greeley's camp by way of the boundary trail, from St. Malo. Halfway in, one of them became very sick, and the other two made a stretcher. But instead of taking him back to the railroad, they lugged him five miles farther into the woods before one of them went out for a doctor.

Meanwhile, the sick man died. The other two stayed a week until they had four deer; then they sent out to Pittsburg for a man to come in with a pair of horses and a sled. They piled the deer onto the sled and the corpse on top, and started out. Five or six miles from the road a terrific snowstorm struck them, forcing the teamster to unhitch his horses and go home. For a week the body lay there, alternately thawing and freezing.

By that time, the natives had become chary of Greeley's camp. Foster's curse was a thing to be reckoned with. The trappers and woodsmen shunned the place — all but big Roaring Bert, who feared neither God nor man nor ghost. But what Bert saw the night he stayed there, no man knows; only all men know that his hair turned white before the morning.

"It's Foster's curse," the natives say. "That crazy sport hoodooed the place. I wouldn't stay there overnight if you gave me a hundred dollars."

132

"Perhaps it isn't the curse," said Ora Mills in his own peculiar speech, "but it *is* mighty queer that every party that ever stayed there has lost at least one man."

"How about the last three years?" I asked. "Has anyone died since then?"

"There has," said Ora. "Three years ago and two years ago the camp wasn't used, but last fall a man was shot for a deer by another member of the same party. He was shot through the eyes, just like I shot that buck the other day. The man who did it committed suicide the next afternoon. They found him lying in his bunk with the top of his head blown off. He'd taken off his boot and pulled the trigger of his rifle with his toe.*

"And there's things prowl around there nights, too. I don't mean animals, either. I've lived in this valley thirty years and I know the animals and the noises they make. I came in from St. Malo one night this spring and I was half drunk when I started. I must have been, or I'd never have started at seven o'clock at night — on that trail.

"By the time I got to Greeley's I'd walked most of the liquor out of me, and I was pining for another drink. There was a light in that camp, and voices of three different men talking and laughing. I could hear them, but I couldn't make out what they were saying. I said to myself: 'It must be a party of fishermen from Beecher Falls,' and I went over to ask them for a drink. When I knocked on the door that light disappeared and I couldn't hear a sound. I opened the door and turned on my flashlight.

"There wasn't a soul in there, but I heard the damnedest weirdest noise — right on the back of my neck, it seemed. 'M-m-m-woo-oo-oo-oo,' like that. I didn't stop running until I slipped on a rock in the stream two miles below and fell in all over."

* Several years after this, Ora, who was living alone in a shack at Second Lake dam, killed himself the same way. His head was splattered all over the shack.

"Do you expect us to believe that story?" Vern asked.

"I don't care whether you do or not," answered Mr. Mills indifferently. "I've met quite a few odd things in my life, and I was in France fighting a year, but I never ran from anything yet except that camp."

"It's too bad you're afraid of it," said Newhall slyly. "I was intending to ask you to go up with us to find it. This map isn't too accurate, and it would save time."

"Oh, I'll go with you," Mills replied promptly. "There's nothing there daytimes to scare anyone."

Vern and I went along with them the next morning, curious to see the famous camp. It was in the gloomiest location — right in the center of a clump of second-growth spruce where hardly any light could get at it. And to give us a final warning, a skeleton lay before the door.

"Died this spring," Ora announced after a cursory investigation. "Not a sign of who he was, either. Well, here's your Greeley's camp. I wish you luck — and if you all come out alive you'll be the first party that ever did!" With these cheerful words he turned and disappeared among the trees.

Newhall regarded the skeleton thoughtfully.

"Two or three are found up here in the woods every year," he said, "and most of them can't be identified. Though this is the first one I ever knew to be right beside a camp."

Then, in a more matter-of-fact tone, he added: "You, Sam, bury this thing and clean out the mice and snakes and fix up the bunks. It ought not to take long, and when you get through you might go catch some trout for supper. The rest of us will try to finish that line by night."

Off they went. Vern and I offered to help Uncle Sammy by catching the trout, so we went back to Schoppe's upper dam and fished down the main stream. When we came to Annance Gulch I proposed that we explore it. Vern was willing.

All the way up its steep and rocky bed we found signs of pick and shovel work. We heard a partridge drumming, and Vern proposed that we go watch him, so we climbed out of the gulch and crept as stealthily as a pair of Indians toward the sound. It was exactly like a roll of distant thunder, and we had no trouble locating the drum-log, but the grouse had departed.

"If you can sit still and keep absolutely quiet," said Vern, "he'll probably come back pretty soon, and we'll see him drum. It's a sight worth seeing."

So we sat down with our backs against a rock and waited, motionless as graven images. We waited for half an hour and then we heard a dainty, cautious footfall behind us. If I had not been perfectly still I would not have heard it at all. I looked sideways at Vern without moving my head. He winked portentously.

I craved mightily to turn around and see if it was a bobcat or a wolf, but if Vern wasn't disturbed, I figured I needn't be. Those slow, long-spaced footfalls came closer and closer — and presently there stepped past our rock a large and handsome doe.

I think something had frightened her and she had been running away from it, for she kept looking back over her shoulder. She stopped not six feet from us and did that. Then she moved on through the trees, slowly and daintily, looking back from time to time.

I was watching the bushes close behind her when a rustling in the leaves announced the return of our drummer boy. He leaped onto the log and walked slowly back and forth, becoming more important and more ruffled every minute. His beautiful fan-shaped tail spread out and up, and his ruff stuck out all around his neck until he looked more than twice as large as he really was.

After a few turns to get his courage up — for all the world like a violinist tuning his instrument — the bird halted near the end of the log and began to drum. His wings beat his sides faster and faster — it is the wings striking against the air that produces the drumming sound — and the faster he drummed the farther he leaned back on his tail, and at last the beats of the drum merged in one long roll. He stood there for half a minute, fan spread, neck stretched, wings going like mad. Then he subsided. Vern clapped his hands in spontaneous applause, whereat the noble bird lifted up over our heads in a startled whirr. We got up and stretched.

"Feller can have a lot of fun, sitting still in the woods waiting to see what'll turn up," Vern said. "I've done it lots of times. Takes some patience, though."

"And you aren't exactly a patient man," I told him.

"I am and I'm not. I guess I'm what you call a paragon. Now these partridges," he went on, "they're really ruffed grouse. Birdologists claim that the drumming of the cock partridge is a part of their lovemaking, of their mating dance. That's true, too, but it's also a fact that they drum sometimes just for the sake of the noise — just like so-called civilized human beings turn on a radio — or git drunk.

"There's another kind of partridge — the spruce partridge — you'll see in these parts occasionally. When he drums, he flies through the air, rolling like thunder. But spruce partridge are so stupid you can kill them with a stick. I caught a grouse once in an unusual way. You know they don't fly far at a time, but they travel like a bullet while they do. I was helping a man sugar one spring and I'd just jumped off the draw-tub sled. I had a twenty-quart pail in my hand and it was held up in the air, straight out. The feller I was working for was off to one side and he scared up a grouse that came, like I say, just like a bullet, and flew smack into that pail the instant I was holding it straight as I jumped off the sled. Broke her neck."

"How about that Indian burying ground?" I asked him. "Isn't that near here?"

"Yes," and he rubbed his right ear thoughtfully. "It's between the Main Stream and East Branch, so it's got to be somewhere around here. Lafe Covell showed it to me once when I was hunting with him. There was snow on the ground then, but I guess I can find it again."

136

"I've heard there are five thousand Indians buried in it?"

"Yes, that's what Lafe claimed, too. But I think it's a damned lie. There was never five thousand Indians in the whole state of New Hampshire. But we'll look for it, if you want to."

We tramped through the woods for hours, until I was completely lost. We ate lunch, but still we had not found the burying ground. But at last we remembered we had promised those surveyors trout for supper, so we pointed our noses westward and followed after.

And we ran right into the Indian graveyard. An acre and a half — my informant had been right about that — and laid out in orderly rows, evenly spaced, mound after mound. Why, there might have been five thousand of them! I said so to Vern.

"Ayuh," he assented doubtfully. "But you'll observe that this burying ground, if it is one, faces west, and if I'm not mistaken, Injun burying grounds always face east. I'd say that a hurricane had swept through here, and those little mounds were where the trees were uprooted. Only we don't see any signs of stumps or anything. I guess you'll have to bring some anthropophagist up here to investigate."

There was nobody at Greeley's camp when we arrived, carrying a creelful of trout apiece. Before the door was a pile of fresh turned earth where lazy Sam had buried the skeleton, but of Sam himself there was no sign. We shouted for him in vain. We were about to hit the trail to Mills's camp when the surveyors came into sight. Sam brought up the rear.

"He came tagging along in the afternoon," explained Newhall. "Said he wouldn't stay around this camp alone for all the money in the world."

Newhall did not believe in ghosts.

They had packed in some provisions and Tom made a fire in the stove and got supper. Then it was dark. We had no means of illumination except matches, so we crawled into our bunks. Vern and I in one, Newhall and Tom in another, Clyde and Sam in a third.

A fearful yell awoke us.

"What is it?" "What's the matter?" came the voices of Vern and Newhall simultaneously.

Sam answered. "It's the phantom," he said, so solemnly that we had to burst out laughing. Clyde was the one who had cried out. Newhall struck a match and held it up to him. The boy was white and trembling.

"It went up the wall," he chattered. "It was on my throat and face and I hit at it and there wasn't anything there and it went up the wall!"

We looked skeptical.

"It's so," he repeated. "Listen!"

A light rain had begun to drizzle down onto the tar paper roof, and the wind was moaning through those spruces, making a dismal, lonesome noise that somehow made me feel that I was shrinking together. I felt glad that Old Vern was there beside me.

We stood there in the blackness, not seeing one another, although we were so close we touched. Then something crawled up the side of the shack, crossed the roof, and went down the other side. Then it climbed up the end of the camp to the ridgepole. From there it began to race: up, across, down, and then back. Then came the sound Ora had told us about. It seemed to be all around us and not to come from any one place — "M-m-m-woo-oo-oo!"

Clyde cried out hysterically and I felt my hair stand up. Vern growled a tremendous oath, while Newhall hissed something under his breath and strode to the door. He pulled it open and looked out. It was as black as ink. Our visitor ran once more across the roof and was silent. The room was full of that strange moaning. It wasn't the wind and it wasn't a bear. God alone knows what it was. It stopped soon.

We went back to our bunks and after a while to sleep. Once Tom woke us up by crying out, and once more Clyde did the same. Both times the men leaped up and seized their axes, but when we had lighted matches, nothing was to be seen. Yet both men admitted the same sensation — some tangible something crawling over their faces and throats. Newhall said nothing, but he told me afterward that he had felt the thing when Tom woke up and yelled. But he could offer no explanation.

At half past two in the morning Clyde cried out again and again. We jumped. It was still pitch dark. The rain had grown into a steady downpour and the wind was swishing through the spruces. Again came that strange moaning. This time it sounded right outside the door, and Newhall opened it again. As he did so, Clyde stepped past him and out into the blackness.

Newhall had just struck a match. When it flared up, it was on a level with Clyde's face as he passed. His eyes were wide and staring and he was as white as a sheet. Newhall swore and seized him around the waist. The match went out.

A terrific struggle began there in the inky darkness. I crouched in my bunk and moaned with terror. Sam was so frightened he lost control of his bowels. Luckily — or unluckily — he had not removed his pants. Newhall called hoarsely for help, and with a roar Vern leaped for the center of the noise.

Of course he couldn't see, but he was as strong as three men, and half-crazed with fright as I was, I remember thinking it would go hard with that ghost when Vern laid hold of him. Afterwards I thought of big Roaring Bert alone with that damned "thing" all night long, and I could understand why no man in the North Country ever called Bert a bluffer.

The noise died away at last. Tom struck a match. Vern held Clyde under one arm like a sack of meal and Newhall was just scrambling to his feet. He looked as if he had gone through a threshing machine.

There was plenty of wood. We started a fire in the stove and left the rimmers off. It gave a ghastly light, but it was very welcome. In a couple more hours it was daylight. We ate breakfast before we left. Clyde had become quiet after the fire was started, and he was in as good condition as the rest of us.

"Let's stop a minute after they go," Vern said to me. "I want to do a little investigating. Now you," he said, after the surveyors had departed down the trail, "you're educated. You know the difference between Fanny Burney and Fannie Hill and everything like that. Now me, I'm ignorant, but I'm not so goddamned superstitious as to believe that there's any ghost in this camp."

"Neither do I."

"I know you don't. I know you well enough to believe that. But you was scared last night. You was damn near as scared as Sam was, I'll bet a cookie! But what was you afraid of? That thing that run over the roof? That couldn't hurt you either. That thing the men felt clambering over their faces? That didn't hurt them either, did it? But what were those things? That's the question. I tell you that was a squirrel running over the roof!"

"I'm not an authority on squirrels," I objected, "but are they in the habit of running over houses in the middle of a rainstorm, at night?"

"No, they ain't, and that's a fact. But it's the exception that proves the rule. You know that. And I've personally known squirrels to run back and forth over a camp roof several times in succession — though I'll admit it was in the daytime. So we'll say that thing was a squirrel. It *could* have been."

"Okay. It could have been."

"Now for the noise. You follow me, and I'll show you what made that noise!"

Full of curiosity — and, I must confess, disbelief — I followed him around the camp to the back. An empty whiskey bottled protruded by the neck from a knothole not far below the ridgepole.

"See that?" and he pointed triumphantly. "That board had a big knothole in it, and some smart sport who was up here thought it was cute to stick that dead soldier in it. Now there's two panes broken out of that window beside the door, isn't there? Notice where they are? The upper ones — and right in line with this bottle. Well there was a wind last night, and when the wind comes through those open window panes, it hits that empty bottle just right to make that 'woo-oo-oo' sound! If there was too much wind, or too little, we didn't hear it. It had to be just so!"

"Check again. It could have been."

"Could have been! Hell! It *was!*"

"All right. I believe you. But how about the thing the men felt?"

"I don't know what that was," he confessed. "But you notice it didn't try crawlin' over me!"

A WILDERNESS ODYSSEY

The day after the mix-up with Greeley's ghost, Newhall and his crew were moving down the stream to the Kim Day place, and as our eventful visit to the valley was over, we decided to go with them. We went more for the sake of Sam's company than for our own convenience, as I shall soon make plain.

There was only one man in the North Country who would undertake the onerous task of moving the surveyors down the roadless river. This was Bill Bacon, from Happy Corner. He had come bumping up the stream the day before, to take them out. So the outfit was loaded, a tarpaulin spread over it, and down the stream we went.

It was the strangest cavalcade I ever saw. First came Tom and Newhall, "feeling the way" so to speak. When the water was up to their waists, the two would push into the thick brush lining the bank, but two or three feet of water daunted them not at all. Next came a pair of mules, drawing a lumber-wagon. The mules were thin, hard-looking animals, but they had plenty of spirit. In the wagon was packed the entire wanigan, ours included.

The doughty William was perched on the load, where he looked for all the world like a Chinese idol — except for a two-inch red bristle which obscured nearly all his face.

"Remember the walking boss at Camp Seven?" Vern asked. "He didn't indulge in hyperbowl when he said Bill was a tough nut to crack. He's a little older than I am. I seen him ride a log through the Horse-Race at the head of the Fifteen-Mile Falls for a bet. I'd do it, too, if my life depended on it, but not for any damned ten dollars.

"He ain't a big man, but he's cordy as hell. I'll bet he could pick up as much as I can, and walk off with it. One night a feller that thought he looked easy picked a fight with him in the barroom of a camp on Cedar Stream. Bill's a peaceful gent. He doesn't drink, and he hardly ever swears, even at those ornery mules of his, but he doesn't like to be picked on. He and this feller were slamming and biting each other something terrible, when the feller drew a knife and stabbed Bill in the chest. That made Bill lose his temper. He drove into him head first, like a bull. The feller upset and dropped the knife. Bill jumped on him like a wildcat and began to whang his face into the floor. He'd have killed him sure as hell if we hadn't dragged him off.

" 'Let me at him!' he squalls. 'Let me at him! He had his chance at me. Now let me have mine!' "

Behind the wanigan splashed the rest of us. It had rained hard the night before and the water had risen considerably. Bill, from observations taken the previous day, usually managed to keep going, but sometimes he miscalculated. We four behind him were marching along with our heads down when there came a yell from the teamster.

With his charming disregard for consequences, and the pointed directions of the men ahead, Bill had driven into a hole so deep that the mules were forced to swim, and the water had lifted the wagon body off the front wheels. Scarcely had we taken in these details when Bill went over the edge and sprawled like a great and awkward fish at the end of the reins, on which he never relinquished his grip.

We rushed forward, and with the water up to our shoulders managed to catch the front end of the body before its precious contents got wet. The hole was not very long, and we swung the vehicle sideways so that when Bill, thoroughly soaked, backed up, he was able to hitch on and continue. It was all in the day's work. Nobody minded it.

A few miles farther on we came to a beaver dam — or rather, to the upper end of the flowage.

"By God," grunted Bill in disgust. "I made a great big hole in that dam yesterday, to let the water down, and now those beavers have gone and fixed it all up!"

We were delayed half an hour at that dam. Then it began to rain, and it rained and it was cold and we were cold. We shivered and cursed, and the drops fell thick into the stream with a cold, spatting noise and the water in our boots sloshed and sucked at every step. Also it was hard work wading in water above our knees.

Twice we saw bedraggled deer standing among the sopping balsams at the edge of the water. They eyed us disconsolately and never moved. And once we met a wild duck with nineteen ducklings and were momentarily cheered by chasing them. They were not old enough to fly, but they stood up in the water and beat their little wings and proceeded with a fine splashing and spattering. Several times we cornered them in sharp bends, whereupon they would dive and escape in the muddy water.

We did not stop for dinner. We got some cold food from the grub-box and ate it as we splashed along. After a while it stopped raining, although the sky was still a leaden gray, and a warm breeze sprang up that chilled us through. The stream wound through some magnificent forest, but we were not in a mood to appreciate scenery. We busied ourselves counting off the miles.

"It's only two more to Kim Day Pitch," said Sam at last, "and that means five to go."

"Why do they call it that?" Clyde asked.

"After old Kim Day," Sam answered. "You know the place we're heading for now is the Kim Day shack. Kim lived there thirty years ago. He was one of these Seventh Day Advents and had lots of religion. One day his son Howard, who was twenty-eight years old and couldn't swim, fell into the stream. Kim couldn't swim either, so he flops down on his knees and prays: 'O Lord give me strength to walk upon the water and save my drowning boy,' and then he walked off into the river. Only he fell through, and if some rivermen hadn't been building a sheer boom just below, and pulled them out, they'd have both drowned."

Bill rested his mules on a sandbar and waited for us to catch up.

"See that hole?" and he pointed to a deep hole beside the bar. "Well, forty-five years ago I was coming up the tote road on horseback when a big buck crossed the road like a bat out of hell and jumped into that hole and stayed under, all but the tip of his nose. I'd never seen a deer do that before, so I tied my horse to a tree and went over to look.

"The horse snorted and I looked back and there, not ten feet from me, stood a big gray wolf — what they call a Canada wolf — his front paws up on a mossy log and his red tongue hanging out about a foot, and he was looking right at me. Now I tell you I was scared. I let out a yell and he ran off a little ways and I climbed onto my horse and we lit out for camp. They killed a Canada wolf that winter on Perry Stream and I guess it was the same one. Anyway, they've never seen one in New Hampshire since."

"Another mile," grunted Sam, "and we'll strike a tote road ourselves and leave this damned water."

His teeth chattered like castanets as he spoke.

Tough old Bill looked down at him with pitying concern.

144

"Here, Sam," he said, "take my raincoat. It'll keep the wind off you," and he passed it to the other.

"But what'll you do?" chattered Sam.

"Oh, I'll be all right," Bill answered, and with a yell he swung the mules into the stream. Sam gratefully put on the proffered garment, the skirt of which floated lightly behind him like a huge green lily pad. I looked at Bill occasionally and noticed him shiver, but he made no complaint.

The streambed became very rough, full of boulders and ledges. It was terribly hard going — hard on the mules, hard on the teamster, and hard on the wagon. It was slippery and rough, and we cursed heavily as we plunged along. For half a mile this kept up. Then Bill saw clear sailing ahead. "The worst is over," he yelled and started to sing.

As he did so, the wagon hit the last of the rocks, and four spokes went out of a rear wheel. We groaned, but the amazed and pained expression on Bill's homely, hairy face as he turned and saw the damage, caused us to roar with laughter. And laughter was what we needed. We cut a birch pole and bound up the injured wheel and kept on. Soon we came to the Kim Day Pitch, a very short and very savage rapid.

The men ahead stood on the left bank. "I guess you can get out here, all right," called one, and without hesitation Bill headed his mules for the bank. But as it happened, they couldn't get out. After several futile attempts, during which both beasts fell flat and had to be unharnessed before they could get up, we cut a passage around the Pitch, on the other bank, and passed along.

Then we struck the old tote road, with three miles to go. That rear wheel had lost three more spokes and was swaying wildly. After a couple of miles it collapsed completely.

"Talk about Ulysses and his twenty years!" ejaculated Vern. "He didn't have anything on us and our twenty miles!"

It was a tough job, repairing that latest break, but finally it was done, and as the clouds parted to show a splendid red sunset we dashed down a hill to the Kim Day shack.

Rest and warmth were what we craved — especially warmth. We knew there was a stove in that shack — but I'll be darned if someone hadn't stolen the stovepipe! I would have sat down and quit, but Tom, the ever resourceful cook, went out to the dump and brought back a dozen peach cans. We soon had a short and many-jointed stovepipe that didn't smoke half bad.

After supper Vern and I plodded down through the woods, the ancient habitat of Kim Day's "Indian devil," to Holden's farm. We got into the car and drove away in the starlight. When we got back to Lyman Brook we slept for a night and a day recovering from the effects of our wilderness odyssey.

EIGHT

Lost in the Woods

ONE MORNING in early April, when all the land was soggy with melted snow, when the North Country streams were white and roaring, and flocks of cawing crows squatted lazily around the constantly contracting snow-patches still remaining on the upland pastures, and when the Lyman Brook road was a slippery ribbon of mellow mud studded with sinkholes into which various travelers had thrown rocks and old fence posts, I arrived at Vern's mountain farm just as a woman was walking out of the yard. I recognized her as the wife of a man named Harry Boucher, who lived down the road a piece.

"You came just in time," Vern told me after we had exchanged greetings. "They've got Harry in jail up to Stewartstown, and I've got to go and see him. Maybe you'll drive me up? If you've never been in a jail it will be a new experience for you."

"I suppose you are well acquainted with jails," I said jokingly, as we jolted down the mountain.

"I've been in more than several," he answered. "Either as a

visitor or as a guest. When I was a young man I was quite a hand to drink rum. Like most of the old rivermen, I could drink raw alky without even taking the chaw of tobacco out of my mouth. I'd come out of the woods in the spring and draw my winter's pay and it seemed I couldn't get drunk fast enough. But after a while I acquired a few more brains and I sort of tapered off.

"But it was the thing to do in those days, when a lumberjack got drunk, to throw him into jail until he was sober, and then let him go. Sometimes it took the whole village police force and a couple of hastily sworn-in deputies to subdue him, but numbers always prevailed. They often didn't even fine him. There was no stigma attached. Lots of woodsmen never got farther south in the spring than Beecher Falls," he added, laughing. "Or maybe North Stratford.*

"You see, when the railroad ended there (before Van Dyke persuaded the Maine Central to build a branch line up to Hereford) every bit of traffic or freight coming into the North Country had to pass through Stratford. All the camp supplies went north from there by tote-team. There was always a hundred horses in the livery stables, and when the CVL had its offices in Bloomfield the teamsters came out of the woods in the spring and left their teams there. And then they'd git drunk and they'd begin to fight. You know that crooked road coming north out of the village? One night I counted nine separate fistfights going on at once on that hill. That ought to constitute some kind of a record.

"Speaking of jails," he went on, "you'll meet the Stewartstown jailer. His name is Ford Moore and he's quite a quaint character in his way. He and his brother used to run a little weekly paper in Stewartstown called *The Frontier Gazette,* and

* There was no jail in North Stratford. Malefactors were taken to the county jail in Lancaster before the West Stewartstown calaboose was built.

one fall, in deer season, he and some other fellers were staying at a hunting camp on Cedar Stream. You know Cedar Stream? It's an immense, shallow valley, easy as pie to get lost in.

"Well, Ford went out hunting on a Thursday and didn't come back that night. He didn't show up Friday, either, nor Friday night. So the word went out that a man was lost in the woods, and Saturday forenoon every man who could come was present at the camp. There were one hundred and thirty-seven of us who lined up and received instructions. We were told to advance from the stream in a long, unbroken line, sixteen feet apart, to the top of the Swift Diamond height. I qualified as an expert woodsman and they put me on one end of the line. Win Schoppe was at the other end.

" 'He's probably dead,' Doc Allen told us, 'so don't be looking for a man running through the trees. Look on the ground for a corpus. At that distance — sixteen feet apart — there won't be any chance of missing him. Don't leave the line. When we get on the height we'll form again.'

"And I was to hang a spot on a tree at my end of the line so we could tell where to start back on the next lap. So there we went, up through the heavy timber, pushing our way through the brush and over the rocks. A rabbit's corpse couldn't have escaped us, to say nothing of a full-grown man. But when we got to the height we hadn't found anything, and what was worse, when we counted noses, two men were missing!

" 'Two more crazy coots to hunt for,' Bill Fuller says to me, but we checked into it and found the two missing fellers were Win Schoppe and Lafe Covell.

" 'Of course *they* can't be lost,' says Doc Allen fretfully, 'but why in the devil did they go off and leave us?'

"I cut a club and began to beat on a beech tree. The noise carried far. We waited. A good thing we did, for pretty soon we heard a faint shout down on the Diamond side of the height. I kept on beating the tree and after a while Win and Lafe came in, supporting Ford between them. He was wild-eyed and haggard and about all in. His rifle, which he had been using as a cane, was plugged from muzzle to breech with dirt.

"We gave a mighty cheer and began to crowd around.

" 'Stand back!' orders Doc. 'This man needs a drink! Hasn't someone got a flask?'

"It's a picture I'll never forget, for in the wink of an eye one hundred and thirty-seven hands shot to one hundred and thirty-seven hip pockets, and one hundred and thirty-seven flasks glittered in the cold sunlight!

"But the strangest part of it is that Ford wouldn't admit, then or ever, that he had been lost. The boys expected to read at least a note of appreciative thanks in the *Gazette* — but behold, the next issue contained two columns relating how Ford Moore had found over one hundred men lost in the woods and guided them back to camp!

"Of course everyone thought his dreadful experience had left him a little cracked," Vern went on, "but it's a curious fact that men lost in the woods, whether they eventually find their own way out or are found by searching parties, never will admit they were lost. I've seen it happen many times. They always say they were right on the road home all the time and knew where they were . . . "

"How about yourself?" I asked. "Do you talk the same way? Or weren't you ever lost?"

He chuckled. "I'm like old Daniel Boone. Someone asked him that question once and he said, 'Well, I don't know as I was ever lost, but once I was *bewildered* for about three days.'

"It reminds me of one winter I was working in a camp near Mooselookmaguntic Lake and there was a sixteen-year-old boy cookeeing there . . ."

"What's a cookee?" I interrupted.

"Why, he's a cook's assistant. He splits wood, carries water, builds fires, washes the floor — and learns to be a cook. You know Orrie Crawford up in Colebrook? He runs a restaurant there, on a side street, a damn good restaurant, too. He got his start cookeeing for Joe Bully more than forty years ago. Joe was the most famous cook that ever worked for the CVL. He was a French-Canadian and some people thought he was a little dirty, but he was the best damn cook I ever knew anywhere. His thick pea soup was famous. Canucks are famous for their pea soup anyway — there's a little rhyme everyone knows:

> Pea soup and johnnycake
> Makes a Frenchman's belly ache.

"I know a wealthy businessman down in Lancaster who years ago worked for Van Dyke. I saw him last summer and we were talking of the old days and I happened to mention Joe Bully.

" 'Vern,' he says to me, 'I'd give five dollars right now for a plate of Joe's pea soup!' and tears came into his eyes when he said it.

"You know a cook runs his department in a logging camp. He knows what to do and he does it. Even a walking boss doesn't dare to give him orders. One night, when supper was half through, Charley Layton (who was camp boss at Teapot Brook) comes up to Joe, very apologetic, and says, 'Joe, I've just got word twenty men are coming in from Paquetteville tonight. They'll be here in about twenty minutes. What shall we do?'

"Joe just turned around to Orrie and said, 'Orrie, t'row anodder pail of water on de soup!' "

Vern laughed again. "Years after that, Joe came down out of the woods one spring and put up at the Stewartstown House. Pat Hinchey was running it then — by the way, years ago a feller named George Pike run that hotel. He also managed Camp Idlewild, up at Second Lake. He was a tall, slim man, hell of a good feller, and he had a wife named Mary and a brother-in-law named Ed Callahan, a big strong Irishman who tended bar for George. The ceiling was kinda low in the barroom and one day a riverman named Ed Roby was in there feeling soulful and he challenged Callahan to fight with him. Ed vaulted right over the bar and took him by both shoulders and snapped him like you'd snap an empty meal sack. Roby's spiked shoes flew up and hit the ceiling and the print of those calks stayed in that ceiling till the old hotel burnt down. I've heard that Callahan went out to Montana after that where someone shot him between the eyes for cheating in a poker game.

"But as I was saying, Hinchey says to Joe after he'd given him the key to his room, 'Oh, by the way, Joe, you aren't lousy, are you?'

" 'If I ain't now, I will be by the time I come down from dat room of yours,' Joe told him.

"I guess that's what Shakespeare would call the retort courteous, wouldn't you say?"

"Did the men always get lousy in the camps?" I asked.

"Of course! In some of those louse-bound logging camps that had been running for years those great gray old cooties had CVL stamped right on their backs! There's a famous lumberjack song you may have heard. A couple of lines of it go:

'And there on a Sunday about all you could see
Was a dirty old cook and a lousy cookee . . .'

"What does it mean? It means we never saw the camp by daylight. Not even on Sunday. They used to put Sunday away in the wanigan when the camps opened in the fall, and never took it out again till come spring. The first time I left home to work in the woods I was sixteen years old. I went in to a camp on Paul's Stream and I stayed there 125 days and I never saw that camp! About five o'clock in the morning a cookee would yell 'Turn Out!' and we'd set down to baked beans and hot biscuits and gingerbread and black molasses and black tea strong enough to float a half-inch nut, and then we'd take our axes and go out to work and get to the place where we were going to fell trees, just at daylight. At dark we'd shoulder our axes and start back to camp."

"It doesn't sound precisely sybaritic," I said.

"No, I guess it would seem kinda rugged to a young feller today, but it didn't bother me any then. I remember the night I got there there were two empty bunks in the barroom — one on the second tier and one on the bottom layer. I tried the upper story the first night. You remember Ginseng Willard mentioning those twenty-foot spreads? That's what we had there. The worst thing about 'em was if some feller would fart. That was a mighty bad thing, I can tell you, to fart under those spreads.

"I stood it one night up there in the warm and fetid air, but the next day I shifted down to the last bunk on the ground floor. It was right up against the end logs of the barroom and a hell of a great icicle about four feet long and thick as my arm was wedged between two logs within an inch of my nose, if I turned that way. I guess that icicle was the reason nobody wanted that bunk. Well, I slept cheek by jowl with that icicle the whole winter, and never had a trace of a cold. And I remember it snowed every one of those 125 days. I never saw another winter like it.

"But as I was sayin', we had this young cookee and at noon he was sent out to a distant job where eleven men were working, carrying eleven dinner buckets slung on a pole. The men would build a fire in the snow and warm the food over the fire. The boy got lost. We searched for him and found him late the next day. He was still carrying the eleven buckets on the pole. When he got back to camp he was hungry as a bear and ate enough for three men. He'd never thought to take food from those pails he was carrying.

"It ain't only young, inexperienced fellers that can git lost in the woods," Vern went on, as the active fingers of his memory clutched into another episode. "The Brown Company has a woods boss named Henry Mullen, a big, black-moustached Irishman, and one fall he was inspecting a camp on the South Branch of the Little Dead Diamond — Ed Groleau's Number

Two camp it was — and Ed wasn't there, but a phone call came in saying there was a forest fire spotted behind a hill over east of the camp, and to take what men he could scrape up and hustle over there.

"So Hank gathered up the clerk and a few other loafers and stormed out into the pathless forest. After about an hour and a half he broke out of the trees into a clearing and in the clearing was a logging camp, and settin' in front of the cookshack was a bald-headed cookee peelin' potatoes.

"Mullen knew there wasn't another camp within five miles of Number Two, and he couldn't figure out where he was. He strides up to the cookee and bawls, 'What camp is this?' The cookee looks at him with his mouth agape, as the storybooks say. 'I asked you whose camp this is!' Mullen roars.

"Says the cookee, settin' back on his bench and holding a potato in one hand and his paring knife in the other: 'If you're such a damn fool you don't known your own camp, Mr. Mullen, I ain't going to tell you!' "

Vern rolled down the window and spat tobacco juice onto the highway. "Speaking of Mooselookmaguntic," he went on, rolling the window up again, "you know I still sometimes take a little red-eye though, bless you, I know it does me no good. And more than once my abstinence has probably saved my life. Have you ever met Jack Haley? Jack used to be a great booze-fighter. He kept it up until one time he got the horrors. He saw pink snakes and green elephants, and right then and there he decided he'd had enough. He never took another drink. One of the few men I've known who decided to lay off the stuff and then stuck to it.

"It never hurt his shooting eye any, though. I've known some first-rate rifle-shots up here in these woods, but I never knew one who could beat Jack. And he's just as good with a revolver. The drive came into Holyoke one summer and they put us up in a hotel there and Jack and I and a few boys came

154

out of it one afternoon just as a peaceful citizen passed by smoking a big cigar.

"'Want to see me ash his cigar?' Jack asks, and he yanked a revolver out of his pants and shoots the cigar right out of the feller's mouth. Right on Holyoke's main street.

"But what I was going to say is that at that same camp on Mooselookmaguntic, the next fall, before the men came in to the woods, I passed one of the wildest nights of my not exactly cloistered life. Me and Jack and Johnny Arsenault and Mike McCabe and one or two other men were all that were there. We were staying in the cookshack, which had a separate bunk-room behind it, connected by a door.

"Bob Campbell came in driving a tote team and bringing the mail, and the four mail pouches full of pint bottles of whiskey. And he had two cute little whores with him — they came from Rangeley, so they said. So there we were, half a dozen men and two women and rum enough to float a bateau. Well, I stayed on the wagon. I didn't want to see the camp burn down. It damn near did. They got to fighting over the women, and three times that red-hot stove tipped over and three times I got it righted before anything caught on fire.

"McCabe would have killed Johnny Arsenault that night. He had him by the throat with one hand and struck at him with an axe, but I had a little bull-bitch that Johnny had been kind to, and it saved his life, for when Mike swung up the axe the dog jumped on his back and grabbed him by the collar — he had on a roll-neck sweater — and he was drunk enough and off balance enough so that sent him to the floor and then the stove went over again and one of those crazy fools — it was Jack — drew a revolver and began to shoot out the lights.

"Bullets were flying wild and Johnny and Mike were tearing into each other like a pair of wild bulls, and the stove was on its side and the women were yelling in the bunk-room, and there was I, cold sober, the only one in the lot who wasn't happy."

"What did you do?"

155

"I finally yelled to Jack to open the door and I picked up the two warriors, one under each arm, and threw them outside. 'Fight there all you please,' I told em, 'but I'm tired of picking up that hot stove for you!' At long last everyone calmed down, but it was really quite a night."

Vern was still entertaining me with his reminiscences when we came to the Coos County poor farm and brick county house, which, together with the jail, are the first buildings one comes to in West Stewartstown when approaching from the south. The villagers are justly proud of the layout. The county house possesses the best-equipped hospital north of Hanover. Even Lancaster, the county seat, has not so fine a one.

The inmates are mostly aged men. The able-bodied ones among them, and also the less violent prisoners in the jail, are put out to work in the fields belonging to the institution. In the summer, the prisoners wear overalls which have one leg brown and one blue, in order to lessen chances of escape and as a means of identification. In the winter they wear pants of which one leg is black and the other brown. But do not be alarmed if you happen to meet on the street men thus attired, for the county house inmates also sometimes wear the same rig, although they are not required to.

Sometimes the prisoners escape across the Connecticut into Vermont, but this does not happen often, for it means they will miss free board and lodging, and besides, it's too much work to swim across the river.

The jailer, Mr. Moore, a thin citizen no longer young, was glad to see Vern. Neighbor Boucher was produced, and Ford, who was proud of his calaboose, offered to show it to me. It contained a few prisoners who scowled or grimaced at me from behind their bars. In one cell three disreputable malefactors were playing cards, and when the jailer left for a few moments, one of the three, a hard-boiled young hooligan, called to me out of the corner of his mouth — "Hey, buddy, give us a cigarette!" No answer. "Hey, buddy, will you give us a cigarette? Say! If you don't give me a cigarette, I'll throw a louse on you!"

Before he had time to carry out his horrid threat, Mr. Moore returned. "Shut up, George," he said pleasantly. "You know better than to talk to visitors."

To my surprise, the prisoner did shut up. I voiced my surprise to Ford, who laughed unmusically and answered that insubordination was not condoned in that institution. I believed him after he had showed me the "solitary" cell for "insubordination."

"Bread and water for three days in that hole usually tones 'em down," he remarked grimly.

The jail had a well-stocked library for such prisoners as could and would read. Several hundred volumes lined the shelves. But when I looked at them more closely I found them in singularly fresh condition. In fact there wasn't one that was thumbmarked or dog-eared. I saw three copies of *Pilgrim's Progress,* a remarkably well-preserved copy of Kant's *Critique of Pure Reason,* and another entitled *The Moral Maxims of Mr. La Rochefoucauld.*

I mentioned the elevating spirit of the books to Vern, as we drove home.

"What the hell," he answered, in pious perplexity, "they can't give those birds wild West novels and gangster stories, can they?"

To which I had no answer.

NINE

The Art of Running Rum

BOUCHER will git out of jail pretty soon," Vern told me as we drove back home. "You ought to go call on him. He's our principal local bootlegger up this way and he might have some interesting stories for you. Of course he ain't in the class of the Parker brothers, but then, they aren't local."

"What do the people up here think of rum-running?" I asked him.

"Oh, up here along the border I suppose everybody is mixed up in it a little, more or less, according to his mother's teaching. Some fellers just go up to the Line House and buy a quart and bring it back. Others take a truck. Of course there's always been smuggling along the border. The Indian Stream Republic was formed largely because of that. But nowadays of course it's booze that forms the 'piece of resistance' as the French say. Only last week I met a two-horse load of the stuff coming down that back road on Canaan Hill."

"How did you know what it was?"

"It was my horses hauling it. Harry had hired 'em."

"I take it you're not an ardent Prohibitionist?"

"No, I'm not, and that's a fact."

"Yet I've heard its proponents say that it's been a good thing, at least for the workingman. How do *you* think?"

Vern rubbed his right ear reflectively. "To be fair about it," he said at last, "I guess maybe it has. When I think of it, I can remember how in Berlin when the millmen got their pay they'd stop in the nearest saloon to cash their checks and then they'd have to drink, and lots of times their wives and kids at home didn't have enough to eat. When the saloons closed their doors that sort of thing stopped. So I guess maybe on the whole Prohibition has benefited factory workers. At the same time it benefits scofflaws like me and Boucher."

"According to the papers," I said, "the country is full of bootleg booze and everyone is making his own besides."

"Yes, I read that, too. All the papers are howling for repeal. But I don't believe it. It certainly isn't the Prohibitionists who want repeal. And if everyone can git all the rum he wants, why isn't everyone else satisfied, too?"

He thought it over for a few moments. "It's probably this way, sonny," he went on. "You see, there's money in those pants pockets, and there's people who know if they can begin making rum legally again, they can git it, instead of it all going to people like Harry Boucher and Al Capone. Furthermore they can advertise, and bootleggers can't. I've seen indications of what's coming. You'll see more and more stuff in print about how bootleggers cause 'crime,' and how much nicer 'legal' whiskey is than illegal, and how the government will get big juicy taxes from it, and of course we'll never git back the awful old saloons, and of course the liquor industry will be 'regulated,' and not allowed to advertise its pernicious wares . . .

"Well, young feller, I've had quite a lot to do with the rum business in my life, and if you want to listen to a minor prophet, you mark my words — they'll repeal Prohibition, but it won't stop moonshining, they'll still have saloons, only they'll call 'em by some sweeter-sounding name, and the liquor industry *will* advertise, and all the seventeen army alcoholic hospitals that have been closed down since 1919 for lack of customers will be opened up again!

"And I'm not in favor of Prohibition, either," he repeated. "Still, there's two sides to every story. A few years ago I had charge of a string of camps for the Brown Company over on Clear Stream. A bootlegger named St. Pierre kept bringing booze into the camps and selling it to the men. Even the camp bosses bought it.

"Well, a boss doesn't git his trees cut down and cut up by a crew of drunken woodsmen. I finally called on the bootlegger.

" 'Listen, St. Pierre,' I said to him, 'I don't like to interfere with another man's business, but you're interfering with mine. Now you just take and move the seat of your activities to some other place than Errol and Clear Stream, at least until I get through logging there.'

" 'Maybe,' says he, real contemptuous, 'you don't know who I am, me?'

" 'Listen carefully,' I said to him, 'for I sha'n't tell you twice. I don't give a good goddamn who you are, but I know who *I* am, and if you bring any more booze into this valley I'll put you out of business, sure as hell! I know you killed three men in that joint you run over on the Magalloway, and they've never done anything to you for it, but you ever try to tangle with me, I'll make you one sorry Frenchman!'

"I did, too."

"What did you do? Shoot him?"

"No, I did worse than that. I hurt his pocketbook. I learned he was coming down with a two-horse sled loaded with rum one night in January. Christ! It was a cold night, twenty-four below zero, and I froze one ear and part of my face, but it was worth it. You know that little hill and a curve in the road, between Errol and Aker's Pond? I knew he'd have to be walking up that hill, and just as he came to the top I rose up out of the snow and stopped him.

"He had a feller with him and they both had rifles, but I had a feller with me, a man named Albert Kier, from down in Berlin, and we had rifles, too. It was about two o'clock in the morning. We took their guns and team and drove down to Errol full gallop and hid the booze under the hay in the barn back of the Umbagog House and turned the horses loose. They found the horses eventually, but they never did find the liquor. By that time I found out my face was frozen and it made me so mad that I took Kier and went up to an old camp where I knew they had some more liquor cached and we abstracted that, too.

"No, he didn't bother me any more. I guess he figured I was bad medicine. And not long afterwards he murdered a man up in Hereford and the Canadian authorities caught him and hanged him higher than Haman. They don't fool around with murderers up there, like we do."

A few days later, as I was walking past Boucher's house, I saw him out on the lawn tinkering with a child's cart. I stopped to pass the time of day. He knew who I was and did not mind telling me about his hazardous profession. He informed that he had been shot at several times, had paid many fines, even had been jailed once and again. He had been one of the first to go into the rum-running business, back in 1920, and he was still carrying bravely on.

His purpose, when he started, so he told his wife, was to make a thousand dollars. But before he had quite earned that sum he was arrested, his car confiscated, and his savings were sadly depleted by a fine. So, of course (said he), he had to keep on until he had recouped his losses. By then he was in the game for keeps.

He made a lot of money — some eighty thousand dollars — which (on the advice of interested friends who wanted to sell it to him) he invested in worthless stocks. At present he had only one old automobile — "but it'll hold thirty-five cases," he said bravely.

A "case," I learned, contains twenty-four pint bottles or twelve one-quart bottles. When Harry first started, in 1920, he and his men used to drive up to the government liquor store in Sherbrooke (Quebec) and load up quite openly. A man was only allowed to take two bottles at a time out of a Quebec government liquor store, but you could go in and out as often as you like.

"We used to hire a bunch of bums to go in and get it," he reminisced. "We paid them twenty-five cents a bottle. And you'd be surprised how quick they could bring out a carload — two bottles at a time!"

"How much profit do you make on the stuff?" I asked.

"It differs according to the price of the goods. We pay all the way from $1.40 a pint to $16.00 a quart — that's for fancy brandies — only we don't handle much of that expensive stuff. On an average I figure to make a profit of forty percent."

"How do you bring it across the Line?" I asked. "A car heaped full of booze in plain sight is bound to be examined, isn't it?"

He grinned sourly, either at my ignorance or at some memory my question roused in his mind.

"You see," he explained, "the car isn't heaping full. You take out the rear cushion, you know, and there's room for a good many cases. The Parker boys used to run it through loaded clear to the top, but believe me, they got caught, too!"

I pricked up my ears when he mentioned the Parker brothers. They were, at that time, almost as famous in the North Country as the Smith Brothers, which is saying a good deal, considering they never had to pay for publicity. They were the most desperate rum runners in northern New England. Chased, arrested, let free by judges who didn't believe in enforcing the Prohibition law, arrested again, sometimes fined, their car operator licenses were revoked. They had bought an airplane and used it for some time, but this machine, too, was finally confiscated and their pilots' licenses revoked. Their life was a veritable comedy of errors, and a notable example of the old adage that "honesty is the best policy." Harry admitted he wasn't in their class.

"But," he went on, "you were asking me how we get by the customs. Why, there's nothing to it. The thing is to get someone to drive your car the officers won't suspect. Take your own self, for instance. You could bring down a whole load of booze and they'd never bother to look at you until you got to coming too frequent. The best driver to get, though, is a cleric."

"I suppose you have no difficulty in finding gentlemen of the cloth for the job?" I ventured.

"No," he answered. "They aren't hard to get. I had a minister's son drive for me all one summer. Paid him $50 a day, and he was worth it. But he used to drink, and one night — he wasn't driving for me then — he got into a row with a customs officer and after that they laid for him. He was coming across the Canaan bridge and they chased him and he left the car and ran. They shot his heel off but he got away. That was on a Saturday. The very next Saturday they caught him again and that time he didn't get away. Of course I paid his fine, but he wasn't any use to me after that."

"Did you lose the booze?"

"Not on that trip. I was right behind him — stopped at the customs when he did — and when I saw what was going to happen I declared the stuff before they had a chance to say anything. When the case came up, Dick was charged with violating the tariff act — but he hadn't done so, for everything was declared — so the case was dismissed. In fact, I didn't even have to pay a fine that time, now I think about it. You see in those early days they weren't clear about the Volstead Act. He would have been sunk if they had charged him with violating that."

"Have you ever been caught yourself?"

"Oh yes, several times. They caught me in West Stewartstown once. I tipped over turning the corner. I spent some time in jail. But we had a good time there — all the rum we could drink, good food. Just like a vacation."

"But didn't your business suffer?"

"No. I directed it from behind the bars — just like our colonel during the war. He sent us out to do the fighting and the government pinned medals on him when we won.

"There was a bootlegger in North Stratford," he went on, "who had a system you might like to know about. He bought twenty horses and led them up and down through the woods between Stratford and Norton Mills, which is on the Line. When they'd got used to it, he'd let them go two or three days without eating and then take them up to Norton Mills and load them with gunnysacks full of bottled rum — the sacks hung down on each side and were tied, of course — and then start them toward home. Of course they come right down through the woods to Stratford. He has a scout trail along beside 'em to see that nothing happens to the loads. Of course if they're caught nobody can identify the owner, so he only loses his horses and that one cargo. I know he got caught once. The horses were sold at auction. I saw some of them. It was a shame how they'd been treated — all galled and sore and bruised from lugging the stuff."

"You are still in the business, aren't you?" I asked politely.

"Yes, and I'll be in it as long as I live, I guess."

"Then you'd advise a young man looking for a profession to pick this one?"

"No, I wouldn't," he said decidedly and to my surprise. "It's a dog's life. You're bound to have more or less rows with this damned rum and it's a mighty poor way to live, I can tell you. I wish I could get out of it for the sake of my wife and kids, but I can't. I've been in it too long. Easy come, easy go!"

He spat bitterly on the ground.

TEN

North Country Folk Songs

I T WAS A Sunday afternoon in mid-October. I was on my way
south from Montreal, and had stopped at Vern's the night
before. The mountains were ablaze with color; the maples
flaming like huge bonfires, spotted here and there with the
dark green of the spruce, while the white birches stood out like
slender virgins, their russet leaves heaped like skirts around
their feet.

We strolled down the road, admiring the flaming hillsides
that rose up in jumbled masses as far as we could see to the
west, and presently we began to talk of folk ways and of folk
songs.

"Yes," said Vern, "I've known fellers who could sing for eight
hours at a stretch and never git hoarse and never repeat a song,
either. Willis Danforth, up in Pittsburg, is one. Lafe Covell
knows a lot, too, and Abe Washburn and Elwin Trask and
Stonewall Jackson. Stonewall lives the handiest to here. Up on
Sims Stream. If you'd like, we'll go and call on him and you can
git some real old songs."

At the fork of the river road and Sims Stream, an unusually attractive group of tourist cabins caught my eye.

"Those belong to Charlie Pinckney," said Vern. "It shows you what a man can do in this day and age when it's all the fashion to yowl that a man hasn't the opportunities to make a living he had thirty years ago. Charlie started out there with one cabin, a few years back, and now he's got ten. They're all furnished in tip-top style and I expect he's got ten thousand dollars invested there. But he's full up every night all summer long. I imagine he's got all his stuff paid for by now, and what he takes in is mostly pure profit. Of course it took him some years — but now he's sitting pretty.

"There's a woman named Julie, over to Bayview, just before you get to the Thirteen-Mile Woods," he went on, "who runs a set of overnight cabins, and she had a tame bear tied to a post out in the yard to attract tourists. She'd sell bottles of colored water to 'em for a dime apiece, and they'd give it to the bear to see him set up on his hind feet and drink out of the bottle. She did a right good business. That bear had a funny habit, too — he'd trot around the post at the full length of his chain, but every time around, at a certain place, he'd turn a somersault. Nobody could ever figure out what made him do it. Finally a Harvard professor of biology happened along and explained that it was physiological, not psychological — seems that at a certain point in his circle the collar pressed down on the vertebrae in his neck in such a way that he couldn't help goin' head over heels. Just like you strike yourself under your kneecap and your leg'll fly up.

"Well, one day the bear got loose and took for the woods. Julie was pretty vexed. 'Damn it!' she said to me. 'Why couldn't it have been my husband? He'd ha' come back when he got hungry, but that bear will never come back!' "

"I know you can find a lot of cheap people up in this country, and even a lot of poor damned degenerates," the old man went on, "though I don't know as they're any thicker, proportionately, than they are in Boston or New York. But you'll also find a pleasing lot of people who are up and doing something for themselves, like Pinckney here, or Hortense Quimby, or even Tom Cozzie, to take a less spectacular example.

"Hell! There's all kinds of ways a smart man can make a living in this North Country if he only tends to business and don't spend all his time and money chasing over the roads in an automobile. There's just as many opportunities as there ever was, only they're different kinds. Take it thirty years ago, and Pinckney couldn't have made ten cents with his tourist cabins."

As Vern finished this exposition of dynamic economics, we drove into Mr. Jackson's yard. Stonewall was a typical high-country farmer — insofar as those individualistic mountaineers may be said to form a type. He was lean and sinewy, with hard hands and a twinkle of laughter at himself and the hardships of this world lurking far back in his steady eyes.

This Sunday afternoon we found him sitting on his porch, a Bible in his hand and a pitcher of hard cider beside him. A homely brindle cat lay supinely across his knees. The family, he gravely explained as he went into the house to requisition two more glasses, had gone over to the neighbor's to help piece a quilt.

"I see you're gittin' religion, Stonewall," said Vern interestedly. "Have you come to Deuteronomy 25:11 yet?"

"I'm surprised you even know there is a Book of Deuteronomy in the Bible," Stonewall replied. "But as a matter of fact, I always read the Scriptures for an hour or so every Sunday. I do it instead of going to church and listening to a sermon on the Russian situation, or on the sins of my neighbors."

"Do tell! Have your neighbors been sinning some?"

"Well," said Stonewall, "I was just reading a passage here that tells us to let him who is without sin cast the first stone, and when I consider my own youthful days, and moreover think of yours even now in your old age, I don't know as I have the right to call it sinning. However, it's a fact that Baldy Kegman's

167

daughter had a baby and the state came and took her away."

"Wasn't Kegman's widow living in a state of carnal concupiscence with some feller?"

"Not only concupiscence," corrected Stonewall with a trace of humor, "but also concubinage. But he up and married her when he got scared the state was going to investigate Matildy's case. Then he went crazy, and they took him off down to Concord."

"What a hell of a mess!" said Vern. "But that Matildy can't be more than thirteen or fourteen years old. That man didn't sire her young one, did he?"

"No. It was a boy in high school. Too young for them to do anything with."

"The whole family hasn't brains enough to pound sand into a rathole. They should have taken and cut Kegman the night he got married."

"Well," said Stonewall thoughtfully, "if they applied that rule everywhere, I'm afraid there'd be a frightful increase in neurotic females — and that would probably be even worse."

"Damned if you ain't right! I hadn't thought of that before."

"Live and let live is my motto," said Mr. Jackson. "I don't aim to let any man run over me, but I don't condemn my neighbors' pleasures, and I'd hate to have it said I'd ever kicked a man when he was down. I speak figuratively, of course," he added hastily as a gleam came into Vern's eye.

"Would you kick a man literally, if he were down?" I asked.

Mr. Jackson pondered, his half-empty cider glass in his hand, his heels hooked over the rungs of the straight chair tipped back against the wall.

"My father brought me up," he said at length, "to never get into a row if I could help it. But if I was ever compelled to defend myself, he told me that the first thing I should do was to kick my opponent in his private parts. Then strike him as hard as God would let me under the ear. Then to jump on him with both feet.

168

"Since I was sixteen years old I have had just three occasions to put the old gentleman's precepts into practice. Once was at a dance, when a fellow insulted a girl I was with. Once was when I was a deputy sheriff and I had to arrest a cantankerous citizen. And once was when a fellow tried to hold me up in Montreal."

"I expect," said Vern dryly, "that you found the old gent's advice tolerably sound?"

"Both sensible and salubrious," agreed Stonewall, a twinkle of humor in his blue eyes.

"To take up another phase of your sinful youth," said Vern, "Bob here wants to hear you sing some of the old songs. By the looks of that pitcher, I should judge your voice ought to be pretty well oiled by now?"

"Of course my voice isn't so good as it used to be," Stonewall apologized, "but I'll try to oblige. I haven't done any singing for ten years. I'm seventy-two years old next week," he added. "Still, I guess I can remember a few of the old songs. It's mostly at the sporting camps in the fall when the boys are sitting around the stove full of red-eye that the old tunes come back to us."

He smiled. "I suppose you know the 'Old Dan Day' song?"

"I sung him that," Vern said.

"It's a good song," said Stonewall. "It's kinda rough in spots, but everybody in Pittsburg knows it. I've even heard women sing it, though they omitted the stanza about Abigail. But it has a nice tune. How about 'It's Hard Times in Lancaster Jail?'

"That's a hell of a good one!" Vern affirmed. "You sing it and I'll come in on the chorus."

"This song," Stonewall explained, "was composed by a man in Colebrook named Ed Shallow. He was drunk and disorderly in Lancaster one day, and an influential citizen named Colby had him arrested. Judge Ray sentenced him to jail."

Whereupon Mr. Jackson cleared his throat two or three times and began to sing:

169

IT'S HARD TIMES IN LANCASTER JAIL

A prisoner's fate let me tell you is hard,
The doors they are locked and the sills they are barred;
With bolts and with bars they will make you secure,
God damn 'em to hell and they can't do no more.

(Chorus — to be repeated after each stanza)

And it's hard times in Lancaster jail
And it's hard times I say.

The food that you have is a loaf of brown bread
As hard as a rock and as heavy as lead;
Or a pint of bean soup, and your meat it is stale,
You're bound to go hungry in Lancaster jail.

Oh the bed that you have is the dirty old rugs,
And when you lie down you're all et up with bugs,
For the bugs they swear they'll never give bail;
You're bound to get lousy in Lancaster jail.

There is old Colby, a very rich man,
He spends all his time in loafing around.
Your boots he will raffle, your clothes he will sell,
Get drunk on the money, God damn him to hell.

Now there is young Ray, he's a dirty mean crew,
He'll look at his men as if looking them through,
To Lancaster jail he will send you to dwell;
For one pint of whiskey he'd send you to hell.

Now to conclude and finish my song,
I hope that I have sung nothing that's wrong.
May the Stars and the Stripes together prevail
In hell with old Colby and Lancaster Jail.

"It isn't a song for the Epworth League," said Stonewall,
"but it's very popular in the camps. At least it used to be. It has

170

a sort of a lilting tune that is quite catchy. You have probably heard variants of the chorus if you've been around the North Country much."

"Sing us 'Bright-Eyed Etta Lee,' " urged Vern, and Stonewall obliged:

BRIGHT-EYED ETTA LEE

In the golden vale of Pittsburg
Down by the Connecticut Stream,
There dwells a maid that holds my heart
And haunts me like a dream.

At night my rest she do disturb
My mind is never free,
All wishing her to be my bride,
My bright-eyed Etta Lee.

O Pittsburg you are beautiful
As everybody knows;
The Connecticut River full of fish
Down by our dwelling flows.
It's not the river nor yet the fish
That dwells so on my mind,
Nor with the town of Pittsburg
I've any fault to find.

The one I love is fairer than
All other female kind,
Her skin is whiter than the foam
That floats on the silvery tide,
Her eyes they sparkle like the sun
That glitters on the sea,
And cheeks that make the red rose pale
Has bright-eyed Etta Lee.

Was I governor of this state
Pittsburg at my command,

Or was I William McKinley,
The man who rules this land,
I'd give up my robes of office
To the people under me,
I'd give her all my fighting ships
That's on the briny sea;
A beggar I would go to bed
Wake up content and free,
If by my side, all for my bride,
I'd find fair Etta Lee.

So fare you well, my Etta dear,
No more for you I'll moan
While there is breath in this fond heart,
'Twill beat for you alone.
Both night and day, for you I'll pray,
No matter where I'll be,
That the hour of death
My dying breath
Will murmur "Etta Lee."

"Jack Murphy, a teamster, made up that song," Vern said. "I was there the winter he did it, too. It was in 1900, at a logging camp on Perry Stream. This Etta Lee was a good-looking girl, who wasn't any better than she should have been. A lot of the men were chasing her, but finally the competition narrowed down to Jack and another teamster named George Hathorne. You knew him, didn't you, Stonewall?"

"I knew Murphy," said Mr. Jackson. "I've heard of Hathorne, but I never saw him that I know of."

"Well, Jack lost out finally. George got the inside track, and Etta told Jack to stay away. Of course that made George feel good, but Jack got kinda gloomy. He was normally a gay cuss, and he had a good voice and knew all sorts of songs and he used to entertain the men nights by singing, but after Etta gave him the mitten he got glum and despondent and we didn't hear his silvery tones any more.

"George took delight in devilin' him. He'd call on him at night when the men were sittin' around the barroom to give 'em a song, and inquire what ailed him, and everything like that. Two months or so went by, and one night when George begged him to sing he promised to sing a song if George would promise not to leave the room until it was finished. Of course George agreed, and then Jack sung this song, which he'd been busy composing all the interim.

"George wanted to get out, but he didn't dare to, not after saying before all the men that he'd stay. Of course they all knew about him and Etta, and what kind of a girl she was. He had to suffer the rest of the winter from *sotto voce* remarks about his Bright-eyed Etta Lee."

"What does *sotto voce* mean?" Stonewall asked.

"Why," Vern explained blandly, "it means the same as *sub rosa*. Ain't that right, Bob?"

"It probably is in this case," I agreed.

"I'll sing you a song that must be very old," said Stonewall. "Some people call it 'Young Albion,' and some call it 'Amanda, the Captive.' The Pemigewasset river, mentioned in it, is what they call the upper end of the Merrimac. It rises in Franconia Notch. I worked for Ave Henry down in Johnson one winter, but I never heard this song there. But it's known all over Pittsburg."

AMANDA, THE CAPTIVE

The sun had gone down o'er the hills in the west,
The last beams had faded on Moosehillock's crest
When at midnight of hour the red lightning flashed
And far down the mountain the cataract dashed.

At intervals came the hollowing sigh,
The hoot of the owl and the catamount's cry,

173

The howl of the wolf in his low cavern cell
And the crash of the dead forest tree as it fell.

At the foot of a hemlock the wild game was flung,
Above on its branches their rude armor hung
While from battle and plunder each warrior reposed
From the toils of the day which evening had closed.

They led in a captive, unfriended, forlorn,
Her feet bathed in blood, and her clothing all torn.
She scorned the vengeance and wrath of her foes
And sighed for the hour when her sufferings would
    close.

Ere the blushes of morning again should return
Amanda was destined in torture to burn.
Amanda, the pride of her village and home
Afar up the Merrimac waters had come.

The pile was constructed, in the red torches' glare,
Amanda was bound, her white bosom bare
While around her stood gazing the merciless throng
Impatient to join in the war dance and song.

Young Albion, the chief of those warriors, stood near
With eye like an eagle, and foot like a deer,
A heart that would scorn a moment to crave
A tear for her suffering, a sigh o'er her grave.

One moment he gazed on the charms of the fair,
Her dark hazel eyes uplifted in prayer.
Half hidden from view was her bosom of snow
By her dark auburn hair that in ringlets did flow.

"Forbear!" cried Young Albion, "your torches forbear,
Amanda shall live, by my weapons I swear
This night if a victim must burn at the tree
Young Albion, your chieftain, that victim shall be."

To rescue Amanda then forward he rushed.
The tumult was ceased and the revelry hushed.
Oh! how mute stood that group of warriors around
While Young Albion the cords of Amanda unbound.

Down the Pemigewasset at the dawn of the day
A white birch canoe was seen gliding away
As swift as the wild duck that swam by their side
Young Albion and Amanda together did ride.

At dusk of the evening her white cote was seen,
The smoke curling blue o'er the willows so green.
Oh! What was her joy when she landed on shore
Where she met with her father and mother once more.

Young Albion stood gazing to see them embrace,
His kind heart affected, tears ran down his face.
All the favor he asked them was shelter and food
With joy it was granted to the chief of the wood.

So Amanda returned to her village and home,
Lamenting that Albion a savage was born.
O long may the praises of Albion be sung
Till civilization unites them in one.

"That song is another thing I've done some researchin' on,"
Vern said. "It's never been printed anywhere.* And the inci-
dent isn't recorded in history. And nobody ever heard of an
Injun chief named Young Albion. I've often thought it might
refer to old Metallak, the last of the Coo-ash-aukes. He was
once chief of the St. Francis Indians, but he told Grandma
Fickett, over on the Magalloway, that he'd been deposed for
saving a white captive from torture."

* Vern was mistaken. Mrs. Fannie Eckstorm, Maine's eminent folklor-
ist, told me that "Amanda" is without any historical basis, having
been composed "out of whole cloth" by one Timothy Alden and
published by him in 1816.

175

"You're wrong there, Vern," said Stonewall. "For the captive he saved was Major Whitcomb, the famous old hunter and trapper of Guildhall. My folks came from Guildhall. The story was well-known to the old-timers there."

"Was Whitcomb the one who shot a British general and was captured by the Injuns and one of 'em saved his life because Whitcomb had saved his years before? Yes? I thought the name was familiar. I heard Ginseng Willard tell that story forty years ago. Quite a quaint character, the old major was."

Stonewall laughed. "He was quaint all right. Did Ginseng tell you of the time he crawled into a hollow log when the Indians were hot after him and he'd no more got in when a spider began to weave a web across the hollow end? The Indians came up and leaned on the log, and one of 'em suggested crawling in to investigate, but the other one looked and saw the web and decided no man had gone in there in the last half hour."

"No. I never heard that. But I begin to recall the other story now. Whitcomb ran across all of Lower Canada without stopping, with the redskins right tight to his heels."

"Tell us the story, Mr. Jackson?" I asked.

"After I get some more of these songs off my chest, I will," he promised. "Now here's one that was composed by a man up in Columbia. It's about a family named Stanton that lived on Clarksville Hill, just across the river from Pittsburg village."

THE BULLDOG SONG

There was an old farmer who lived on Bulldog Hill.
He raised a pack of bulldogs, his neighbors' blood to
   spill.
He raised a great big Charley, the fiercest of them all.
He'd get a chance to steal a sheep, he'd eat it wool and
   all.

(Chorus — to be repeated after each stanza)
Laddely doo a dang, laddely fol de doo a da dee
Laddely doo a dang, laddely fol de doo a day.

He has another son and George it is his name.
He's got lots of money but git it if you can.
He walks about the street, he thinks he's mighty smart;
If he cannot bite you, he'll snap his teeth and bark.

He has another son, his name it is John.
He thinks that he can do nothing that is wrong.
He'll run all over the country for a job sawing wood.
He'll beat Bill at sawing by lying if he could.

He has an only daughter, Palmyry is her name.
I think that her character is just about the same.
She married George Chappel down by the riverside;
'Twould have been a blessing to him if he'd in his
    cradle died.

It's lying and dishonest this old man always was.
His Maker's Name profaned, he regarded not His
    laws.
No more from the peddler's cart the barley he'll pro-
    long [purloin].
Old Lull has done his peddling, because he is dead and
    gone.

Now to conclude and finish, I'm going to end my song.
I hope that I have said, sung, or done nothing that is
    wrong.
If that they should hear of this, they'd make a terrible
    brawl
And to make my escape I should have to climb the
    wall.

"Didn't Abe Washburn make up that song?" Vern asked.
"Maybe, maybe," Stonewall answered. "Now here," he

177

went on, "is a song that's a favorite of mine. The men in the camps used to like it, too. They was always asking me to sing it."

JACK HAGGERTY

My occupation is a woodsman, where the wild winds
    do blow,
My name is engraved on the rocks of saint shore;
From Hashop to Bashop I'm very well known,
And they call me Jack Haggerty, the pride of the town.

I'm the boy who stands happy in the white foaming
    stream,
My thoughts are on Annie, she faltered *(sic)* my dream.
She's a blacksmith's daughter of the Flat River side
And I always intended to make her my bride.

I dress'd her in jewels and the costliest of lace;
The finest of linen to her I did embrace.
I gave her my wages all for to keep safe;
I begrudged her of nothing I had on this earth.

One day on Flat River a letter I received.
She said from her promise herself she'd relieve
To marry a lover who had long been delayed,
And the next time I saw her she'd ne'er be a maid.

On her mother, Jane Tucker, I laid all the blame.
She caused her to forsake me, go back on my name;
She cast off that rigging that God would soon tied,
And left me to wander on the Flat River side.

I'll bid adieu to Flat River; for me there's no rest.
I'll shoulder my peavey and go to the west.
I'll go up to Higgins, some pleasure to find,
And leave my true love and Flat River behind.

Now come all you bold woodsmen, with a heart brave
    and true,

Ne'er depend on a woman; you're beat if you do.
And if ever you meet with a dark chestnut curl,
Just think of Jack Haggerty and his Flat River girl.

"I like that about as well as any lumberjack ballad I ever heard," Vern said. "Although it ain't a native to this neck of the woods. I think Flat River is up in Canada somewhere. You remember McKelvie? He was out in Muskegon in 1888 and he said they were singing it out there then. How about the one on the man who was killed in the woods, Stonewall?"

"You mean 'Peter Anderbell'? Wait til I get a drink. My throat is getting hoarsed up."

Mr. Jackson went into the house (we had been sitting on the piazza) and got a drink. Then he returned and obliged:

PETER ANDERBELL

My name is Peter Anderbell
As you shall understand.
I was born in Prince Edward Island
Near to the ocean strand.
In 1881, the flowers were in bloom,
I left my own dear native home
My fortune to presume.

I landed in New Brunswick,
In that lumbering countree.
I hired to work in the lumbering woods
Which proved my destinee.
I hired to work in the lumbering woods
Where we cut those spruce logs down,
It was loading sleds while from the yard
Where I received my deadly wound.

There's danger on the ocean wild
Where the sea rolls mountain high,
There's danger on the battlefield

179

Where the ragged bullets fly.
There's danger in those lumbering woods
Where we cut those spruce logs down.
It's there I fell a victim unto that monster snare.

There's adieu unto my father;
It was him that drove me here.
I thought him very cruel,
His treatment being severe.
It is not right to press a boy,
Or try to put him down.
It will repulse him from his home
When he is far too young.

There's adieu unto my dearer friends,
That is my mother dear.
She reared a boy that gave her shame
As soon as he left her tender care.
Little did my mother think
When she sang sweet lullaby
What countries I might travel in
Or the death that I might die.

Adieu unto my dearer friends.
The island girl so true.
Long may she live to bless the day
When first my breath I drew.
The world will roll on just the same
As before I pass away.
For what is less than mortal man
When anchored in the clay?

I know my luck seems very hard
Since death has proved severe,
But victim *(sic)* death is the worst can come;
I'll be no longer here.
I'll allow these deadly pains

180

Will elaborate me soon.
I shall sleep that lone and lonesome sleep
Called slumbering in the tomb.

There is a world beyond the tomb
Lo that I'm nearing on,
Where death is more than mortal,
And death shall never come.
The thought of death, it blacks my eyes,
I can no longer hear,
My spirit takes a heavenly flight
Unto some heavenly sphere.

There's one thing more that I do crave
When I am dead and gone;
That some heavenly father will bless my grave
For I've done nothing wrong.
Here in Prince Edward Island
My mouldering bones do lay
To wait my Savior's calling
Unto the Judgement Day.

"That song ain't right!" objected Vern, when Stonewall had finished. "What in hell do you mean by 'those deadly pains will *elaborate* me soon?' "

"It doesn't make much sense," Stonewall agreed, "but you know how we get those songs. They travel from mouth to mouth, from one camp to another, and it's a wonder they don't get corrupted more than they do. Now I'll sing you one about Roaring Bert Ingersoll."

THE BALLAD OF ROARING BERT

Come all you honest lumberjacks,
A song to you I'll sing
Of how the famous Roaring Bert
Was licked by ancient Win.

Now Roaring Bert was walking boss
That winter on Cedar Stream.
A bigger, better walking boss
I'll say I've never seen:
Full four axe-handles wide was he
And very strong and tall,
And he roared before the camp one night
That he could take and fall
A spruce tree quicker than any man
In all the North Countree.
And slammed upon the deacon seat
Ten bucks in good monee,
And dared the men to call his bluff,
If bluff they thought it was.
But all the men knew Roaring Bert
And you didn't hear a buzz
Out of all that crew of hardy lads —
Full thirty-five were there —
Until a chap in a corner dark,
Where he sat in a barrel-chair,
Spoke up in a voice so soft and low
But full of amusement too:
"Now Mister Bert, I'll take that bet
And I'll win ten bucks from you.
I'll get a man from this North Countree.
He'll be here tomorrow night,
And he will fall a big spruce tree
As quick as his axe can bite,
And he will beat you all to hell,
Or my name ain't William Blight!"

When Bert heard this, he roared aloud,
Like a he-wildcat in pain,
And he swore such a man could never be found
Though they went to the state of Maine

Where men are born with an axe in their hand
And a peavey 'twixt their teeth.
But William Blight did only smile
Until the roaring ceased.
And then in accents mild and calm
He spoke when Bert ceased to rave:
"The man who'll win your ten bucks for me
Is the ancient, decrepit Win Schoppe
Who has one foot in the grave."

Now six years had passed since men had seen
Old Win in the woods, you bet.
But the fame of his name was very green
Wherever woodsmen met.
And the thirty-five in the barroom there
Sent up a silent cheer
And waited with breathless eagerness
To see what they would hear.
They gazed at their boss, big Roaring Bert,
The best man in the land,
A man who'd never been licked in his life,
And a man chuck-full of sand.

But this time Bert knew he was done,
And though it grieved him sore,
He stood up straight, full six foot two,
And cried in his famous roar:
"In forty years in lumber camps
I've held my own and more,
And by the Roaring Jesus, I've never backed down
    before;
But here, Bill Blight, is your ten bucks,
You've earned 'em fair and free,
For even with one foot in the grave,
Win's a better man than me!"

"By God!" said Vern when Stonewall had concluded this song, "I never heard that before! You must have made it up yourself, Stonewall!"

"No, I didn't. I heard it somewhere and I took it down and memorized it. They say it actually happened, though."

"It happened all right. I was there that night. Bert was blowing off steam like he always is. But it was five dollars he bet, not ten. Of course Bert is a hell of a good axeman. Probably the best in the North Country. But he'd forgotten all about old Win. Win was 'most eighty years old, then, too. When that feller said it was Win Schoppe he'd put up against Bert, Bert nearly fell over. But he knew when he was licked. He handed him the five dollars right then and there.

" 'By the Roaring Jesus!' he says. 'Take your money! Win's a better man than I am, I don't care how damned old he may be!' "

"From all I've heard of Roaring Bert," I said, "he isn't the kind of a man to back down for anyone."

"It's the only time he ever did it," said Vern. "But nobody thought any the less of him for it. It was old Win who taught Bert all he knows."

"Why didn't you take him up yourself, on that bet?" I asked curiously.

Stonewall coughed discreetly and grinned. I thought Vern flushed beneath his indelible tan, but he laughed when he answered:

"I did once, some years previously. I didn't care to lose another five dollars!"

Stonewall sang us many more songs: "The Maid of the Mountain Brow," "The Girl I Left Behind," "The Lass of Mohee," "Flying Cloud," "The Lousy Cook," "Jordan Hill," "The Van Dyke Familee," and others. Together he and Vern roared out "Maggie Gray," a lovely song of over two hundred verses that recounts the adventures of a pioneer woman who got lost in Charlestown, New Hampshire, and wandered clear around the Connecticut River to appear opposite her old home six months later. Her baby, who had been with her, died meantime.

"My repertory isn't exhausted," Stonewall said at last, "but my throat is. I'll give you one more and then I'll have to quit. This is called the 'Moose Pond Song,' or sometimes the 'Song of the Four Cousins.' Moose Pond lies on the height of land between Indian Stream and Back Lake. In the winter of 1853, four young men, Ransom and George Sawyer and Smith and Ben Currier, went there to haul logs with oxen. From the tracks in the snow it was deduced that one boy had fallen through the ice with the oxen, and the others were drowned while trying to rescue him."

SONG OF THE FOUR COUSINS

All young people far and near,
Attend my words and you shall hear.
'Twas of four cousins and their fate,
The circumstances I will relate:
In eighteen hundred fifty-three,
They left their homes no more to see.
To get some timber, so we find,
Return that night was their design.
Their payrents, so I understand,
Gave them strict charge to keep on dry land,
But for some reason no one knows,
They lies (sic) in water they did go.
They rallied all the neighbors round
To see if those children could be found.
They came unto the pond that night
And there they waited until daylight.
Early next morning they did start,
With tearful eyes and aching hearts,
They searched until the spot they found
Where those four cousins were all drowned.
They took them up and carried them home

185

And then conveyed them to the tomb;
Their bodies lay all in one grave,
Their spirits gone to God who gave.
Oh Mr. Sawyer's loss is great,
He must submit unto his fate,
Neither murmur nor complain,
For what's his loss is their gain.

Mr. Currier he must be
Contented with his destinee,
Remembering also that he must die,
Pass from time to eternity.

Now those four boys are dead and gone
Their friends for them do deeply mourn;
May they be found in worlds on high,
Reigning with Christ above the sky.
And now may this a warning be
To all mankind as well as me,
To raise to God a prayer each breath
That we may be prepared for death.
For when our Savior was on earth,
He spoke concerning a new birth,
He says there's one thing does remain —
The sinner must be born again.

"And that," said Mr. Jackson, "is what the shoemaker threw
at his wife. I've got to go milk now, anyway. Come up again
when you feel you can stand a little more, and we'll have
another session. I'll tell you that story about Major Whitcomb
then."

We thanked him and drove away up the road heading toward Gadwah.

"How come you ever took time to memorize that Maggie
Gray song?" I asked Vern. "It's inordinately long."

"I liked it," he said simply.

Presently we came abreast of a squalid farmhouse, its un-painted clapboards flapping in the wind. In the doorway, smok-ing a cigarette, sat a blowzy, untidy female, her bare and hairy legs spread wide to catch the breeze. Several dirty, half-clad children were running around the yard.

"All tits and tuppence," Vern remarked with his usual can-dor and pungency. "That's the Kegman female Stonewall was telling about."

"Is the community proud of her?"

"No, they ain't, and that's a fact. She's what you'd call 'poor white,' I guess. You'll find 'em scattered here and there all through these hills. People whose brain stopped growing when they were ten years old, and who'd rather starve than work enough to earn a decent living. Of course I mean the men especially, not the females."

"Are they the good old Yankee stock?" I asked, a bit mali-ciously.

"They are so," he answered decisively and without hesita-tion. "Almost all of 'em. They're the examples that have gone to seed. But I reckon every stock can show similar specimens."

"Some high-minded communities I've been in," I told him, "they'd run women like her out of town on a rail."

"Yes. But I guess up here we're a leetle more tolerant of our neighbors' failings. We ain't so damned self-righteous that we go in for community lynchings and tar and feather parties. If one of us don't like a man, we may knock him down and step on him, but we don't have to get twenty or thirty fellers behind us to bolster up our courage."

"What did Stonewall mean by saying that song was what the shoemaker threw at his wife?"

"The last and the awl, of course. Hah! Makes you blush, doesn't it, you missed that one! Haw! Haw!"

"Didn't I see you blush, when I asked you about Roaring Bert?" I retorted.

He rubbed his ear. "It seems to be a human idiosyncrasy to

187

blush at one's mistakes," he said. "There's no harm in that. Of course a man don't want to make too many mistakes. But let me tell you, young feller, don't you ever try to deny 'em in public. As soon as you admit 'em, people forget about 'em, but if you try to cover 'em up, they'll be uncovered every time, and people *never* forget that."

"You're a philosopher," I told him.

"I'm a tough old coot that lives way back in the woods," he said, "but it's been some time since the lanugo wore off me."

ELEVEN

The Old Pepper

SEVERAL years after I had first met "Uncle" Sammy Martin, I came up one July to spend a couple of weeks with Vern.

"You got here just in time," he said with a chuckle, after we had shaken hands. "I've got some news for you. I was walking along the street in Stewartstown the other day, and there was Uncle Sammy sittin' on a piazza, the most mournful-lookin' object of pity you ever laid eyes on.

" 'What's the matter, Sam?' I asked him. So he tells me the whole story. It seems that Sam was working last winter for a doctor, and the doctor had a big old Brahma rooster that weighed ten pounds and was ugly as sin. Years and years ago, there was an epidemic of cockfighting in these parts, and Sam thought of it, and figured out he could make an honest dollar with this old Brammy, as he calls him.

"So, with cunnin' words and clever propaganda, he managed to stage quite a few fights between his fowl and the champions of other barnyards. There's always a lot of these sports, you know, who think whatever they have is superior to anyone else's, even if it's just an ugly barnyard rooster. Of course there weren't any great sums wagered, but Brammy always won, and so Uncle Sammy got all swollen up with pride and profits.

"And that was what got his neck in a noose, and what was making him feel so dolorous when I saw him. There's a man lives up at Bear Rock named Deacon Wallace who had a Rhode Island Red rooster he thought was pretty mean, and he got the unhappy idea of pitting it against old Brammy. Brammy killed him.

"Now Sam has worked up quite a reputation as a cockfighting man, and a sport in general, and you know what he's like anyway. Well, just a couple of days ago, while Sam was sunnin' himself with half a dozen of Stewartstown's young bloods around him on Hinchey's piazza, up came the deacon and proposed a new duel.

" 'I've got another rooster over home,' he said, 'and I'll bet you, Sam, exactly one hundred dollars that he can lick your Brammy all to he — heck!'

"He slapped his hand on his hip pocket and regarded Sam with a stern and challengin' eye. Of course Sam couldn't disappoint all the hero-worshipers loafin' around.

" 'We'll let Hinchey hold the stakes,' he said, real nonchalant. He didn't even bother to ask the deacon what kind of a bird he had got, he was so confident of Brammy. So they put up the money and the fight is going to take place tomorrow in the old livery stable. Fight till one bird quits. That's all."

"Well," I asked Vern, "what's so sad about that? I don't see how that put Sam's tail in a crack."

He chuckled hugely. "The deacon," he explained, "has sent off somewhere and got a genuine fighting cock. He paid sixty-five dollars for him. It has got a pedigree a mile long, and has had experience and everything. He'll make short work of Brammy. You can't pit bulk and bad temper against skill and speed. And that was why Sam was sitting there lookin' like a

190

bass drum broken in two in the middle! Well, I guess we'll go, what?"

"We'll go," I said.

The great rooster fight was to begin at three o'clock. At two-thirty the livery stable was swarming with men impatiently awaiting the arrival of the principals. No bets were being placed. The story of the deacon's guile had gone abroad, and not a man would take a chance on Sammy's bulky Brahma.

"Well," boomed Vern cheerfully. "I've fought for many a lost cause before, and seen it come through. I'll put down ten on Brammy. Who'll give me odds?"

A dozen men were prompt to take him up at odds of ten to one.

"You and Van Drew must be lousy with money," said one of them. "He's the only man besides you that has wanted to bet on Sam's rooster. But he don't like the deacon is why he bet that way, I guess."

A few minutes later, Vern beckoned to me. He was talking with a man who might have been thirty-six or thirty-eight years old, but who looked to be fifty. He had been a big man once. Now he was thin and rather cadaverous looking, though his warm gray eyes were full of fire, and the thick iron-gray hair covered a high, thinker's forehead.

"This is Van Drew," said Vern, and presented me. "Us two," he grinned, "are Brammy's only backers, so we kinda have to stick together."

"Are you betting?" asked Van. "No? You'd do well to put a few dollars on Sam's fowl. I think he has a very good chance of winning."

"What makes you think so?" Vern demanded. "Personally, I don't think he has the chance of a snowball in hell. Though I'm betting on that chance."

Van smiled. "I saw considerable cockfighting when I was in France," he said. "From my experience and observation there, I prognosticate in favor of Brammy."

"I'll shoot ten more," Vern proclaimed. "You'd better do the same, Bob."

"Put me down for five," I told him, more to be a sport than because I thought Brammy might win.

Then Deacon Wallace arrived. He pushed his way to the center of the crowd, ordered the men to step back and form a hollow square, and put his foreign fighting cock on the floor. It was a regulation fighter all right. Not much body, a great deal of neck and legs, a fierce glare in its yellow eyes, and an ugly way of drawing its long, vicious spurs across the floor that made the gooseflesh come out on those present.

Then Uncle Sammy came through the crowd, Brammy under his arm. "All ready," he announced briefly. He set the big bird on the floor in front of the deacon's champion and the two men moved the birds up close to each other ("breasting" them, Van called it) to make them more angry. Then they moved back to crouch on one knee and watch.

Before Brammy could move, the other dashed in and struck like lightning with both feet — long, ripping slashes that brought blood to the breast of his huge opponent.

"Ten to one on the 'Deacon,' " called someone, but he got no taker.

Again the "Deacon" struck, leaping over the astonished Brammy's back and raking him along the spine. Now the big rooster was thoroughly aroused. His eyes flared wickedly and he advanced, earnestly desiring to slay his puny-looking foe. But alas! He was far too slow. Again he was raked and slashed. Sammy shook his head and muttered dolefully under his breath. The deacon grinned in triumph.

Then it happened. The long-legged fighting cock, wishing to give the spectators a little variety, darted in, intending to bury his beak in Brammy's breast. But the old veteran managed to interpose a solid wing to this laudable attempt, and so far as the spectators could tell, the shock stunned the "Deacon."

He began to run in circles, shaking his head from side to side as if clearing his brain of cobwebs. That was all Brammy needed. He leaped upon the small bird and sank his big beak into the back of its neck, just behind the head. That was the end of the "Deacon."

In the midst of a solemn and open-mouthed silence, Sammy collected the stakes and the side bets. So did Vern and Van Drew. Then, bidding a condescending farewell to those present, Sam gathered his rooster under his arm and started for home. We, his faithful backers, accompanied him.

Vern was rubbing his right ear as we walked along. Finally he reached out a big hand toward Brammy. Sam slapped it indignantly away. Van winked at us, and Vern burst out laughing.

"What did you put on him, Sam?" he asked. "It must have been powerful, for it certainly made the deacon's bird dizzy."

"It's an old Spanish custom," Van explained. "We took and powdered him thick with cayenne pepper, all except his head. It got into the other bird's eyes and he couldn't see. The deacon played me a dirty trick once, and so I showed Sam how to do it, just to get back at him. It's a trick I learned in the army."

"The old pepper," chuckled Vern. "And it earned me just two hundred dollars in about two minutes."

TWELVE

How Van Drew Came Home

T HAT FELLAR Van Drew," said Vern as we drove home
from the cockfight, "has had quite a history. I've known
him ever since he was born, and I know all his family.
When he was a young man, he was rugged as a bear. Got a
good education, good looking, full of hell. Everybody liked him.
Now he don't amount to a damn. Just tears around gittin'
drunk and chasin' women. He's a veterinary by trade. A good
one, too, when he's sober. He should have been a physician.
He's only got one lung, and there's enough shrapnel in him to
sink a ship. Also he's got a croix de guerre with palm. But he
just can't stay still. Acts as if each day is the last he has to live,
and he intends to make the most of it."

"There must be a reason," I said.

"There is," he answered. "I just said I was an old friend of
the family's, so to speak. Well, I'd been cruising for timber up
on the Saint Maurice from the summer of 1919 to the summer
of 1920. Of course I knew Van was fighting in France, but the
last I'd heard, he was dead. So you can imagine how I felt one

night soon after I got back when I walked into a speakeasy in Colebrook and there he sat — or what was left of him — drunk as a dog. He didn't even recognize me, but I knew him all right.

"So I ambled right up to his house. There wasn't anyone at home except his sister Helen. She was sitting on the piazza. I went up and sat down beside her.

" 'I just saw Van downtown,' I said. 'Then he wasn't dead after all?'

" 'No,' she said. 'It was a false report. Or rather, we were mistaken.'

" 'He seemed to be celebratin' winnin' the war,' I said.

" 'Yes. He's been that way ever since Mother died. That threw him all off. He wanted to go on studying medicine, but he lost his grip. Well, you can hardly blame him.'

" 'I didn't know your mother was dead,' I said.

" 'Yes, she died just after Van came home.'

" 'Do you want to tell me about it?'

"She didn't say anything for a while. Then she frowned a little and then she said:

"Yes, Vern, I'll tell you. You know," she says, "I've always liked Van best of any of the boys. He was always so — so efficient. He could do anything and do it well, and he was generous, and always smiling, and ready to help with anything.

"You know he left college in 1915 and went across and enlisted in the French army. He used to write fairly regularly at first. We knew that he had been wounded and decorated, and after the A.E.F. went over, he wrote that he had transferred to the American Army.

"Then for a long time there was no word. Finally, in July of 1918 we had a letter from him. He was in a hospital in France, badly gassed and shot to pieces with shrapnel. The letter was brief and stern, and it ended: 'Good-bye for the last time. Van.' We knew that he must have been pretty far gone or he would never have written to Mother that way.

"She aged quickly after that. I guess you saw her a month later, didn't you? Well, we never heard from Van again, so we knew he was dead. Our attempts to trace him were of no use.

"One afternoon in August last year I was sitting here on the piazza, reading, with my back to the road. The sun had just set, and the sky was red as blood with the afterglow. Mother and Dad and Babe had gone over to the woods to pick berries. I sat there reading when I heard someone come up the walk. He came slowly, dragging his feet, and when he got to the steps he halted on each one as though he were lame. He could not see me, because I was hidden by the back of the chair.

"All at once the thought flashed through my mind: 'It's Van come back!' and I jumped up and faced around. And it was Van. But dear God, what a different Van! He had on a uniform that hung loose all over him. He was frightfully thin and white, and he tottered rather than walked. How he had ever walked up from the station is a mystery. He could not speak three words without stopping to get his breath. He was dying on his feet. He just held out his arms to me — me, whom he had held up above his head with one hand the day he went away — and said: 'Well, Sis, I've come home to die.'

"And then he began to cry. I put him in the big chair and tried to soothe him. I thought he'd never stop. He cried in a way that racked him all to pieces — terrible, moaning sobs that made him cough until it seemed that he might strangle. But after a while he became quiet, though tears ran down his poor wasted face like water. I was crying too. I was so glad to see him that I was fairly foolish.

"When he had cried himself out, he leaned back in the chair and asked where Mother was. Then he told me he had been transferred to another hospital in England, that he had written several times, but evidently the letters had never arrived. He had intended to send a telegram from New York, but decided not to, as he was not sure he would live to follow it. He was so miserable he didn't care a darn anyway.

"But pretty soon I heard the folks coming back. It was quite dark then.

" 'Here they come,' I said.

" 'Is it mother?' Van asked eagerly.

"He got up and stood straight, with his shoulders back, though it nearly killed him — I could tell by the way his face twisted — and he marched into the house, straight as a ramrod, the finest exhibition of grit I've ever seen, even if he is my brother.

"He went into the house and got to the piano and he started to play 'Marching Through Georgia.' It was the only tune he knew, and we used to make fun of him for playing it all the time.

"The folks were just at the gate when Van started to play. They couldn't have possibly been thinking of him but the moment he began to play, Mother cried out: 'It's Van come back!' and she dropped her pail of berries and ran up the steps and into the house. And she had thought Van had been dead a year.

"He got up and stood there with his arms around her, trying to comfort her, and all the time his breath was coming in those horrible choking gasps. I'd got over my first surprise and joy, and I began to notice that breathing. It made me afraid.

"Mother," she says, "Mother died there in Van's arms. Died of happiness. Now do you wonder he doesn't take more interest in himself?"

"I reckon," I told her, "that he's been through enough to excuse anything he does."

She got up and went into the house. I watched her go, but young feller, what I saw walking through that doorway was a white-faced, crippled lad with a uniform hangin' loose all over him, and his shoulders held straight; and an old woman droppin' a pail of berries to run up the steps to find a son she thought was dead.

THIRTEEN

The White Death

I T WAS DEER season, that is to say, the end of November, and Vern and I, after a long and fruitless day's hunt, were sitting before the fireplace in the barroom at Camp Idlewild on Second Lake. A dozen other men, hunters and guides, were grouped around us.

Even if a man is not a hunter, and is constitutionally opposed to the slaughter of game, he has missed a pleasant and unforgettable experience if he has never been at a sporting camp in deer season and sat before the fire at night listening to the wondrous tales that the spirit of the occasion evokes from the Nimrods gathered there.

"More deer have been shot around this fireplace than ever were in the woods," Vern chuckled, and I believe it.

It is impossible to reproduce on the printed page the rare flavor of these marvelous stories. To be fully appreciated, they must be heard when rendered orally, with much gesturing and slapping of knees and rolling of eyes and blasphemous invoking of the name of the Lord; with rank tobacco smoke filling the room, and accurate, long-range expectorating to punctuate the high spots — and to give the narrator more time to think up a more impressive lie.

Yet, most of them are *not* lies. But they are so wonderful, so breathtaking, so out of the normal, that you just can't believe them. And yet you will hasten to cap the last one with an even more remarkable relation of your own.

It is the custom of the guides to shoot deer and sell them to unlucky hunters for ten dollars apiece.

"Once I made seventy dollars that way in one day," rumbled Roaring Bert, a strong-thewed, handsome, ruddy-faced man. "Got seven deer, and it was snowing to beat hell all day, too. Got three in the forenoon and four in the afternoon. Two of them were bucks fighting each other. They never saw me. I walked right up beside 'em and let 'em have it."

"Jodrie over at Hellgate," spoke up someone else, "killed seventy-five deer last winter for the camps. One day he saw a deer's head looking past a little tree right at him. He up and shot, quick as a wink, but the deer never moved. He shot again, and missed again, but the deer kept standing there looking at him. He shot seven times, and then, when his rifle was empty, he walked up to the deer — and there it was dead as a doornail with seven bullets in its head. It had been standing behind a tree with its head sticking through a crotch, and the fork had held it up after it was dead."

"I shot a big doe late one afternoon over near Long Pond," contributed Vern, "and shot the insides out of her so they hung down on the ground. She broke through the skin ice on the shore and swam across the lake and I had to go around after her. There was a frightful lot of dry kye and driftwood on the shore. I couldn't see any tracks where she had come out, so I figured the doe must be hiding somewhere near. It was gittin' dark and I was cold, but I didn't want to leave her there wounded like that. I kept pokin' around, and all at once she came up from almost under me, with a big *whoosh!* and lit out for the water. I dropped her just before she got there. But just think, there she'd swum half a mile in ice water with her guts dragging, and she was still able to run."

This tale of course evoked the old classic: "I shot a deer once, it was on a sidehill, shot her so all her innards fell out. She ran down the hill, and her heart fell out and rolled down the hill too, and you could see it beating as it rolled along."

"That's right," affirmed half a dozen solemn voices. "I've seen the same thing."

An ancient man, his white whiskers and blue eyes gleaming in the firelight, piped up to tell how the caribou came drifting through there in the "seventies."

"I've counted twenty-three of them at one time out on the ice of Second Lake," he asserted. A solemn grunt from another oldster backed him up. But such mighty tales of the old-timers made the younger men move impatiently, and they interrupted loudly, to declaim once more on their own prowess.

We heard a car drive up outside, and presently a man and a woman came through the barroom on their way to the rear of the building where the manager's wife stayed.

"Hello Ed, hello Ina," Dick, the manager, greeted them. The couple paused and chatted a moment before going on. Vern knew them, and as we were sitting in the corner next to the door, he introduced me to the man. After they had gone along, Vern said:

"I didn't introduce you to the lady because I wasn't quite sure what name to use."

"You seemed to know her well enough. You called her Ina."

"Of course I know her. Known her ever since she was born, but you see her husband swapped her off the other day to Brown here, and it's a sort of ticklish business introducin' her. You see, I really didn't know what name to use."

"Listen, Vern," I answered. "I may be a stranger up here, but I know better than to believe any such story as that. Now just what do you mean, 'Her husband swapped her off?'"

"Why," replied Vern in a hurt tone, "I mean just what I said. Lots of men up here sell their wives just like they would a horse. This fellow bought Ina, I understand, for fifteen dollars, good will thrown in. Isn't that right, Dick?"

"That's what Brown told me himself," said Dick.

"But surely this must be an exceptional case," I protested. "You can't mean 'lots' of men do it."

"Well," Dick said, "there's old Harv what's-his-name, down on the back road. He sold his wife for ten dollars and a driving harness."

"And," chimed in Roaring Bert, "there's that restaurant feller and his wife down in Pittsburg village. You must know them both. He bought her for five dollars and a pint of whiskey."

"But do the women always go along peacefully?"

"Sure! Why shouldn't they? They haven't anything to lose, and they kinda like a change, I suppose."

While I was meditating on this pleasant North Country custom, a stranger, his mackinaw collar around his ears, and carrying a pair of snowshoes in his hand, blew into the barroom. He uttered a vast grunt of relief, nodded dourly to several of the men, put his snowshoes in a corner, and took off his mackinaw.

"What's the matter with you, Mr. Nash?" Vern inquired, and I knew it was the old fire warden from Deer Mountain, far up above Third Lake. "You don't seem to be your usual cheerful self tonight!"

"By God," growled the tall, wiry old man, "you wouldn't be your usual cheerful self either if you'd seen what I just saw!"

"What was it?" asked half a dozen voices.

Nash spat viciously into the fire. "When I left my cabin up at the tower," he said, "I nailed up everything so tight that a grizzly bear couldn't have broken in and went down to Maine for the winter. But I found there was something I just had to

201

have, so I came back here to Idlewild this morning and put on a pair of snowshoes and climbed up there.

"And I'll be goddamned if four skunks from Pittsburg who have camps over on Indian Stream hadn't come and broken down my door with an axe — and there they were, packing all my stuff onto a toboggan, ready to lug it away! Say! Did I ever read those gents the riot act! If I'd had a gun I'd have shot every last damned one of them!

" 'Why Nash,' they said, 'we just needed some supplies, so we came to borrow some from you. It's nothing to get mad about. You know you're always welcome to come and borrow from our camps.'

"They had guns, and I didn't, and there were four of them anyway. But I knew them all, and I told them to git, and git fast, and if I ever saw them up there I'd shoot 'em on general suspicions, just like I would a skunk. They won't come back!"

"Go on out back, Nash," said Dick, "and Mother will fix you something to eat. Then you'll be your old cheerful self again, and you can tell us a story."

Nash snorted and went away toward the kitchen. The men laughed, and a number of tales of other depredations were evoked.

"Nash," Vern told me, "loves to talk, and he's a born story-teller. We'll git him to tell about the lost trapper he found one winter across Second Lake here. The feller died, and they never did find out who he was, but he told Nash some of his story, and the old boy reconstructed the rest."

The other men were interested, and we agreed to let Nash have the floor. He returned in a few minutes, his "cheerful self" once more, and this is the story he told us in a slow, convincing tone, his eyes closed, and apparently seeing in his own mind each thing he described so vividly:

It was a freezing day in mid-February. The cold sun was a sulky red disk balancing on the crest of the steep, spruce-crowned hills to the west, as a lone man on snowshoes came swinging down a tortuous, frozen watercourse, its icebound heart covered with three feet of powdery snow, its banks lined with balsam and spruce interspersed with many bare old hardwoods that flung out their gaunt gray arms in a mute gesture of desolation. It was a silent, hostile-seeming land, and one not good for a man to travel in alone.

The man evidently realized this, for a worried frown appeared between his frost-rimmed eyebrows as he cast a calculating glance at the sinking sun. But though he increased his long stride to its utmost, he failed to reach his trap line camp-shelter before dark.

It is not wise to cut wood with a sharp axe in the dark, and the man knew it, but without a fire he would freeze, so he started to chop a fallen log before the camp. He worked cautiously, but in spite of his care the steel blade came down on a frozen knot and glanced. The man felt it bite through his moccasin into his right foot, and he knew it had bitten deep, but with remarkable willpower he restrained a mad desire to throw down his axe and examine the wound. Instead, he continued methodically to chop wood in the cold darkness.

Then he built a rousing fire on the ground toward the front of the rude pole-and-brush shelter of which the back was a great boulder that reflected the heat. He boiled tea and ate his supper; then he heated water in his teakettle. All this he did calmly, efficiently, without undue haste. At last he was ready to look at his injured foot. But by then it was so swollen that he could not take off his boot. The man took his hunting knife and slit the moccasin until, half filled with blood, it fell from his foot.

After he had removed the stockings, he found a deep gash across the instep that cut the foot half in two. The man turned pale beneath his short, blond beard when he saw the gaping wound. Around his ankle he twisted a rude but effective tourniquet made of a strip cut from his shirt, and he washed and bound the foot the best he could.

Curiously, it did not hurt him much. Barring the danger of infection, he would probably get over it in a few weeks. And in that cold clean air you would not expect it to become infected. But the trapper was deathly afraid of it just the same. Tough as rawhide and inured to deprivation and physical hardship, his healthy constitution was not adapted to fighting germs and he knew it. The summer before he had lost a finger from blood poisoning, caused by the prick of a fishhook.

Grimly he weighed his chances, and grimly he made up his mind. He was ten miles from his main camp, where he could get no help. Thirty miles to the southwest lay First Lake, where men lived and where he could be taken to a doctor. But it was thirty miles of tangled, steep, heavily forested hills where better woodsmen than he got lost every winter and left their bones to be gnawed by the wildcats and foxes. Yet it was the trapper's best bet. Having made up his mind, he threw the rest of the wood onto the fire and went to sleep.

In the raw, gray cold that precedes the dawn he awoke, boiled his kettle, and prepared to hit the trail. He wrapped his foot in furs and rigged up a harness that enabled him to lift the snowshoe with his hand, thus avoiding any strain on the wounded foot. Thus equipped, his short rifle in his left hand, his right grasping the rawhide thongs, he hobbled away from the line camp and the thick spruces closed behind him.

At nightfall the man calculated he had covered ten miles, but he knew he would never do as much again, for his foot and lower leg had become black and badly swollen, while constantly recurring pains shot through his groin until he had to grit his teeth to keep from crying out.

That night was very cold and clear, and as the man was cutting his firewood he noticed an emerald glow in the northern sky, and later, as he lay in his blankets, racked with pain, his fevered eyes beheld the northern lights creep up across the heavens.

The spectral, coruscating flames shot up and up from the

204

edge of the world, heatless, mirthless streaks and bands of colored, frozen fire thousands of miles long that leaped and flamed like live things. Slowly they faded and died, and only the bright, pulsating stars were left, and big and clear though they were, the earth and sky seemed plunged into darkness after the disappearance of the lights.

Then the silent loneliness of the frozen land pressed down on the man like a tangible weight, and for a moment he was afraid, with the disintegrating, belly-weakening fear that can drive a man stark mad.

But the man was born a fighter, and presently the courage that had oozed out of him came rushing back. He lifted his fist and shook it across the fire at the cold silence surrounding him, and spoke aloud, gritting his teeth as the agonizing pains shot through his groin:

"I'll beat you! Damn you, I'll beat you yet!"

And as if in answer to his puny words, a little breeze came from nowhere and stirred the branches of the snow-laden spruces in a whisper of derision and of mockery. To the man it seemed that the white silence was taking up his defiance, and the idea was born and continued to grow in his pain-racked mind that all this nightmare was a fight between him and it. Then the man swore a mighty oath that he would never give up until he dropped dead, and that thought stayed with him and drove him on in the days that followed.

The middle of the third day found him facing into a howling blizzard. He had not noticed the approaching storm until it was too late to seek shelter, so he kept doggedly on, knowing that if he stopped he would freeze to death where he lay. The fine, hard crystals of snow shot and whirled and bit into his face like bits of steel. The storm-wind shrieked and howled, and in the middle of the white, swirling hell everything was as black as death.

The man dropped his rifle. He hobbled slowly, and ever more slowly, but he moved. It never occurred to him to give up.

He did not know whether he was limping straight ahead or in a circle, and he did not greatly care. His short, thick beard was stiff with frost and icicles, and the whirling, stinging fury of the storm blinded him, but he hobbled painfully on, bumping into trees and stumbling over fallen logs. Once he fell over a ledge and tumbled sprawling into the soft snow six feet below, but he was not hurt. He untangled his feet, groped his way erect, and staggered on. He no longer knew where he was nor in what direction he was going, but he bared his teeth in a hideous grimace and cursed the storm and the frozen wilderness, and dared it to do its worst, and at last the blizzard howled past him and he was able to see again.

But he was very weak. And when he had floundered about at the foot of that ledge he had lost his axe and the pack containing his food. He touched his hand to his face, and found that it was frozen. Mechanically he reached for a handful of snow to rub on his face, but he stopped with the gesture half completed. What difference would it make? he thought dully. But then he fancied he heard again that derisive whisper in the spruces, and it acted on him like a spur to a jaded horse. He raised his head and laughed, a mirthless cackle, jerky from the pain in his groin, but a laugh, nevertheless. And the departing storm, as if in anger at the man's obstinacy, gave a last fierce shriek and hurled a gust of those steel-pointed flakes into his grinning face.

At that, the man stopped laughing, but he did not cease to stagger ahead. But he was very weak, and that last spiteful blast had blinded him. One of his snowshoes caught on a stub and he fell in a heap in the snow. He made an instinctive movement to get up, but he was too tired and too weak. He did not even know that he had staggered out of the woods onto the frozen surface of a lake, a glistening white island dropped in the midst of a sea of snow-covered evergreens.

He would have died there, if the remembrance that he was fighting and that he must not give up had not flamed up in his dimming consciousness. By some miracle of reserve strength he rose to his knees, and very slowly he came at last to his feet, though he swayed like a drunken man. The white blankness of the lake hurt his eyes, and he turned his head to avoid it — and less than a hundred feet away he saw a log cabin, with smoke pouring in a dense black column from a stovepipe in the roof. The man stiffened on his snowshoes and looked and looked, his frozen face immobile beneath his frosty beard. Then suddenly he began to laugh, a loud, meaningless laugh that never stopped. He hobbled toward the cabin, his hot breath congealing in the cold air as it left his mouth.

That was my cabin, over across this lake, at the mouth of Moose Brook, and when I heard that insane laughter, I opened the door and looked out. The man saw me.

"I won," he croaked through his split lips. "I beat the white death!"

Then he laughed, crazy as a loon. But over the white, frozen lake there came a little breeze that rustled past us with a note of jeering mockery . . .

"Ain't he some storyteller?" Vern said to me the next day as we spoke of Nash's stirring tale. "I wish I had his gift of gab. Stonewall Jackson is another just like him. Say, did you ever go back and git that story about Major Whitcomb from him?"

"No, I never did."

"You'd better not forget it. It's a rattling good story, especially the way Stonewall tells it, with all the little details and everything."

"Yes, but how much of it is true?"

"It's *all* true. Stonewall is a sort of descendant of the major, on his mother's side, and he's looked it all up in history books and everywhere. He'll give you all the facts and what's more he knows how to dress 'em up in pleasing verbiage."

FOURTEEN

Romantic Interlude

T HE INHABITANTS of the North Country do not spend all
of their time in hunting and fishing. A real adventure,
even if it was a small one, befell me one night while I
was sojourning in Island Pond and shows another facet of life
along the border.

I had tramped down the old roller coaster road from Norton
Mills, and as I came into town I saw a sign on a large, comfort-
able-looking house that said: Tourists Taken. So I went in and
was took.

That Saturday night, the good woman who owned the place
told me that she and her middle-aged husband were going to a
kitchen-junket, and if I'd like to go along I'd be welcome. Now
a "kitchen-junket" is not a uniquely North Country institution.
It flourishes in every rural district — at least it used to, back in
those good old days, when I believed in the brotherhood of
man and in kitchen-junkets. It is, in a word, a private dance
held in a farmhouse (supposedly in the kitchen), the music
being a violin, or sometimes a piano, an accordion, or even a

good harmonica. Young and old people alike are invited. Betwixt dances the old ones drink cider and the young ones make eyes at each other. Refreshments are always served at eleven o'clock and half an hour later everyone leaves for home.

I accepted the invitation with alacrity.

This particular junket I was whisked a dozen miles over the hills to attend was a little out of the ordinary since it was a masked affair. Everyone's face was hidden behind an ample black mask, which was to be doffed at the refreshment hour. Undoubtedly some of those present knew the identity of others, but equally beyond doubt it is that there were some whom nobody knew. Except for the hosts I was the only person present without a mask. It wasn't considered necessary in my case because I was a total stranger.

The dancing was just beginning when we arrived. The table had been taken out of the long dining room and an ancient, one-legged fiddler sat in a chair between the dining room and the kitchen (both were used to dance in) and scraped a violin with great vigor. Music for all the old square dances I ever saw he pulled out of that fiddle and at the same time he called the changes in a loud roar that shook the windows — "Sashay down the middle! Aleman left! Balance your partners! Ladies to the right and gents to the left! All hands around!" — and so on.

Kerosene lamps set in each corner of the dining room shed a yellow light over the scene. A small and feeble lamp in the kitchen was the only light in that room. The younger dancers seemed to prefer the kitchen, even though — or maybe because — there was imminent danger of backing their partners' haunches against the hot stove.

The floor, in its natural state, would not have been very good, for it was of softwood and was neither varnished nor waxed. But it was rendered surprisingly slippery by liberal applications of cornmeal scattered about from time to time by the host.

In between dances the guests sat decorously on the chairs

that lined two sides of the dining room — the men on one side, the girls on the other. It was a strange sight — the mysterious black masks, the yellow light flaming and fading as a draft came through an open window, and the mighty voice of the one-legged fiddler roaring out the changes.

Presently the fiddler started a lively waltz. Picking out the likeliest girl in the crowd — there wasn't much to judge her by except her limbs — I asked her for the waltz. She proved to be an excellent dancer, light as thistledown, with an eager, merry way of following her partner. The more I danced with her, the more curious I became to see her face. I was sure she must be pretty.

She didn't wear a wedding ring as some of the others did. At last the musician announced that at the end of the next dance there would be an "interlude," refreshments would be served — and all masks would come off.

At this announcement my mystery girl edged me into a corner of the dining room. She betrayed as much agitation as a girl can betray whose features are concealed by a black cloth mask. By which I mean that her bosom heaved at an unusual pace, her fingers twisted and dug into mine, and through the holes in her mask her eyes glowed like stars.

"You're a stranger here, aren't you?" she whispered.

"Yes, ma'am," I answered. "I don't know a soul here except the people who brought me over from Island Pond."

"Will you do something for me?" she asked suddenly.

"You bet!" I answered promptly.

My enthusiasm made her laugh, but it was a tense, nervous laugh. She squeezed my hand, and then I *knew* she must be a pretty girl. But we danced clear around the room again before she spoke what was on her mind.

"I'm a stranger here too," she murmured in my ear. "That is, I live down the road a little distance, but it's raining and it's dark and I'm afraid to go home alone. But I've got to leave, right now! Will you go with me?"

Would I go with her? I was the goingest man you ever saw!

There was a door leading from the dimly lighted kitchen out into a shed. When we had come through there earlier in the evening I had noticed a long row of old coats and frocks and overalls hanging on nails. We slipped quietly out into the shed. We were not the first who had taken this way "to get a breath of air and cool off, you know," so our departure occasioned no remark.

I struck a match and in its momentary glow picked out a man's raincoat that I handed to the girl, and an old overcoat that I draped over myself. The hats were too dubious. She shook her head.

So, bareheaded, we plunged out into the night. It was raining powerfully, and long peals of thunder made the earth tremble. But the accompanying lightning enabled us to stay between the fences. I held the skirt of my voluminous overcoat over the girl's head. It was quite as good as an umbrella. But as for myself, my face and hair were soon streaming wet. The water ran down my collar and I could feel it trickling slowly over my vertebrae. Every once in a while we'd step into a puddle up to our insteps.

We sloshed along for half a mile until we came to a large, square white house set back from the road. The girl marched up as bold as you please, produced a key, and as the lightning cut a jagged streak above our heads she opened the door. She hesitated a moment and then she said: "Won't you come in and get dry?" So I followed her in.

It was her house all right. And unlike the farmhouse we had just left, it had electric lights. She snapped one on and then I saw her face for the first time. She had taken off the mask, and to my delight she was just as pretty as I had imagined she was. She led the way into a long living room, cozily furnished, with a divan drawn up in front of a fireplace that had a fire all laid in it. A Cape Cod lighter stood on the floor, and in less than a minute we had a fire drawing up the chimney.

Then she took off her coat and looked around. She seemed embarrassed, but I didn't wait for an invitation to take off my overcoat and back up to that fire. I did it before she could say a word. She left the room and came back with a bath towel for me to dry my hair.

"Do you suppose all your folks are asleep?" I asked, just to make conversation. She was standing beside me, for the fire felt pretty good to her, too.

"No-o," she murmured. "I haven't any folks. We're all alone here."

Did that news make me feel bad? Well, would it you?

Presently our backs became warm and we began to think of our feet. She pushed the divan closer to the fire and took off her shoes and stretched out her feet to dry. There was a hole in one of her stockings and her little toe stuck out through it. I thought it was the cutest little pink toe I'd ever seen. I kept my shoes on, but I sat down beside her and likewise stretched out my feet. They got dry and I got restless.

Here I was all alone in a strange house in the middle of a dark night with the wind slapping the rain across the window-panes. All alone, that is, except for an unusually attractive girl (she might have been twenty-one or twenty-two years old) who had asked me to go home with her and who had squeezed my hand — remember? — and who was sitting beside me right now on a very comfortable divan before a very lovely fire whose flickering light cast dancing shadows about the room.

One of her hands lay on the divan. I picked it up. I even dared to squeeze it gently, and I thought I got a faint answering squeeze in return. Thus emboldened by success I actually started to put my arm about the girl. But at this she burst into tears. I withdrew my arm in haste.

"What's the matter?" I asked anxiously. "What's the matter? I won't bite you. Don't be afraid."

"I'm not afraid — boo-hoo! But what would you say if I told you I am married? Boo-hoo!"

I glanced up in alarm. "But you said we were alone here."

"We are — sniff, sniff — my husband is away."

And so, between sniffs, I got the whole story.

She hadn't been married very long. Her husband was a minister. He had been called here to preach, from their home in Boston, a week before. They had rented this house all furnished from someone who was travelling in Europe. But they had only been here a couple of days when her husband had to return to Boston on urgent business. He would be gone a week. And she had got so lonesome all alone in that big house that, having learned of the junket by rubbering on the party telephone, she had made herself a mask and walked up. But then she realized how compromising it would be for her, and especially for her husband, if it ever became known that she had gone, alone, in his absence, to such an affair. And she was afraid to walk home alone and of course she couldn't ask any of the natives to escort her. I was her only hope — and I'd behaved so nobly — up to now! Sniff sniff!

Well, maybe I did wrong, but anyway I got up and put on the raincoat and draped the other coat over my arm. I took a last look at the beautiful setting — the big shadowy room, the leaping flames behind the brass-bound screen, the pair of little pumps in the corner, the cozy davenport — the attractive girl curled up in the middle of it, her golden hair gleaming in the firelight and her blue eyes wide with doubt. I can see it today, as I write, as plainly as I see the paper before me. I wonder if her husband ever came back.

"Well," I said lamely, "I guess I'd better be going."

"Yes," she echoed. "I guess you better had."

She uncoiled from the divan and walked with me to the front door. I opened it and the rain blew in. I sighed.

"You're awfully pretty," I told her. "It's a shame I have to be so noble."

She chuckled deep down in her white throat and put her hands behind her and held up her chin like a child does to be kissed. I suppose she used to do that to make her husband smile. Anyhow, it made me smile. I bent over and kissed her, and I surely envied that minister's homecoming, for her lips stuck like glue and then she reached behind me and turned out the light.

So I sloshed back to the junket where no one seemed to have missed me and everyone was drinking cider and eating cake and sandwiches to beat three of a kind. The next day I had an awful cold in my head.

FIFTEEN

The Coming of the Law

THANKS to Vern's guidance and companionship over a period of years, I came onto a great number of happenings that shed light on North Country men and manners. One of the most bizarre took place on an August morning in the city of Berlin.

I had some business to attend to in that city, which is the largest town in the whole region, so Vern and I rode over there. He had worked for the Brown Company, which owns most of the timber on the Androscoggin watershed, and was quite as well acquainted with that part of the country as he was with his own side of the mountains.

It was, I remember, a Saturday forenoon. As we came into the outskirts of Berlin, Vern pointed to a large house beside the street.

"Big Alf Halvorson lives up there," he said. "I know him well. Let's go up and see him a minute." We drove into the yard. Big Alf* occupied the second floor of the house. We learned that a French family named Dumas (pronounced locally "Demass") lived beneath him.

While we were talking with Alf, a truck came into the yard and parked beside our car.

"Demass bought some furniture on the installment plan downtown," Alf explained, "but he hasn't been able to meet the payments, so the store sent up this truck to repossess the furniture. That's Axe-handle Bernier driving. He's one of our local pugilists, who occupies his peaceable moments in driving truck for the furniture store. That black fellow with him is a Canuck deputy sheriff. The other chap is just an assistant to help Axe-handle move the furniture, I guess."

"What's the sheriff for?" I inquired.

"He's for moral support," said Alf. "He doesn't have any warrant, or anything like that, but he has a badge, and it's good psychology to flash a badge at these wild Frenchmen."

"Don't look to me as if they were home," Vern said.

And in truth the curtains were drawn and the apartment seemed deserted. The visitors, however, were not deterred by that. They prowled around until they found a loose screen. They took it off and crawled in through the window — and mind you, they had no warrant or any other authority to permit them to make such an entry. But such is life in the North Country.

Having effected an entrance, they unlocked the back door, preparatory to lugging out the furniture. But the furniture was in the dining room, which was locked. So Axe-handle got a screwdriver and took off a hinge. While he was attacking the second hinge, the door sudddenly opened. The three men stepped in.

It was a great mistake on their part, for inside was the entire Demass family (all but one member) at bay. Madame Demass, a

* Alf has since gained fame as a builder of the biggest ski jump in the world, at Berlin.

formidable lady of majestic proportions, advanced upon them shrieking threats and brandishing a rifle which she seemed to have every intention in the world of discharging at their vitals. Mr. Demass, taking courage from his valiant spouse, leaped like a wildcat upon the redoubtable Axe-handle, putting him to ignominious flight.

The three invaders leaped as one man for the door — and as one man they reached it. They jammed in the doorway. The old lady poked them in the ribs with her rifle. The old man shouted wildly, dancing about and willing to strike if he had but known how. The three musketeers disentangled themselves in haste and flew out into the yard.

There, in the bright sunlight, and no longer menaced by the deadly rifle, the doughty deputy decided to make a stand. He fumbled for his pistol. But alas! At that moment there appeared from behind a lilac bush where he had been hiding, the four-teen-year-old son of the Demass Family. This fat but precocious youth was a frequenter of Wild West movies, and was accustomed to wear a .22 revolver that his father had bought for him. This weapon, loaded with blank cartridges, he now drew and began to fire at the sheriff from the rear.

It seems that our deputy had been shot at, not long before, by a jobber in the Thirteen-Mile Woods and had retained a mortal fear of gunfire — when directed at himself — ever since. At this unexpected attack, thoroughly demoralized, he turned and ran. He bounded into the truck with the agility of a jack rabbit, and one jump behind came Axe-handle and the assistant. The motor roared, the clutch was thrown in, and the truck went down the road in a cloud of dust, leaving the field — and the furniture — to the indomitable Mrs. Demass (with her empty rifle) and her sturdy son.

Alf and Vern laughed until they wept. I looked on in amazement. The *sieur* Demass strode to and fro like a fighting cock looking for fresh victims, and the old lady dusted one capable hand across the other and spat on the ground. Tableau!

217

SIXTEEN

Bears and Such

"THE DEVIL seems to be a lot more prevalent in the North Country than the good Lord," I said to Vern one Sunday as we were resting on his vine-shaded piazza. "I've seen the Devil's Slide in Stark, and you showed me the Devil's Washbowl, and I've been to a strange place called the Devil's Hopyard, way back of Mill Brook."

"Have you been there? For a young feller you really do git around. But I'll bet I can still show you a thing or two. Of course there are people who claim Old Nick ain't dead yet, but I can show you his tombstone!"

He grinned at my skeptical look.

"It's a fact," he insisted. "It's only a mile or two from here. You cross a pasture and go into the woods, and there it is."

We went that afternoon. The Devil's Tombstone is a strange thing. It is a single block of granite, eighteen feet long and ten feet high, carved as square as one could wish and standing on two small square blocks that support it at either end. At one time I imagine a man could have walked under it, but the supporting columns have sunk so low that now it is necessary to get down on hands and knees and crawl.

"You'd almost think it was put there by human hands," Vern commented after we had contemplated the great boulder for some moments. "But bless you, these woods up here are full of such — only I'll admit they ain't so big and imposing. Evidently a glacier brought them down. An odd thing about it is that no boulders came beyond this point. This is the last outpost, so to speak, and it's the biggest and the handsomest."

Vern was right. The mountainside above us was strewn with a regular avalanche of great loose rocks, but below the "tombstone" there were none.

"Have you ever seen anything like it?" he asked. "I've read of balancing rocks, but it seems to me this here is quite a novelty."

It certainly is a novelty, and it seems to be quite unknown except to the Lyman Brook natives.

"This is a glaciated region, all right," Vern said as we strolled home, "but in spite of what people may tell you to the contrary it is also volcanic. Take Monadnock Mountain, up there in front of Colebrook, the one old man Norton's gold mine is on. That was a volcano once. You climb up there on top of it and you'll see the crater plain as daylight. You can't miss it — all you got to do is follow the telegraph line. It goes right through the middle of the crater.

"Another thing," he went on. "There's a lot of valuable minerals and semiprecious stones up in these mountains, blown out of volcanoes a lot of them. It's funny more people haven't engaged in collecting 'em. I do know a man down in Gorham named Percy Leggett who works for the Brown Company and he's made a lot of money prospecting for minerals and precious stones, just as a hobby. I've often thought that when I get too old for hard work I'd go into the business myself. I know some likely places up here, where the hand of man has never set foot."

"Well," I said, "you've certainly showed me things I never dreamed of."

He laughed.

"Wait till we git home. I'll show you something I'll bet a cookie you won't know what it is. A city sport offered me fifty dollars for it once."

When we got home he went into the house and came back to the piazza carrying a slender piece of something that resembled ivory, seven inches long and slightly curved. A gold cap for protection had been put over each end.

"Well, what is it?" I asked.

"Guess!"

"It's a piece of ivory."

"No."

"Is it a bone?"

"We-e-el, in a way it is. But *what* bone?"

I remembered a trip to Alaska and an Indian war club I had seen in Juneau, made from a certain bone of the walrus, and although the disparity in size made me think that my guess was futile, I ventured it just the same:

"Is it the virile organ of some animal?"

"You've come mighty close," he said approvingly. "It's the bone from the virile organ of a bear. You know, only three or four animals have them — the bear, the coon, the sable, squirrels. That of the sable has a natural eye at its base. The Indians use it for a needle."

"But if all those animals have it, what is so rare about this one?"

"Because they are very small in the little animals, and even in bears they are seldom more than two or three inches long. I've killed and skinned more than a dozen bear and this is the only one I've seen that was big enough to be worth keeping. He was an old whopper, though, that bear was.

"A bear will fight if he's cornered," he went on, "just like any other animal, and usually a mother bear will fight if you interfere with her cubs, but not always. But ordinarily a bear is the most inoffensive critter in the woods. They're no more dangerous than a rabbit. John Locke, who was general manager of the CVL, told me that one afternoon he was sitting on a fallen tree trunk on top of a hill over in Gadwah and he saw a bear in a pasture down below him. He seemed to be working up the hill, so John sat there and waited to see how close he'd come. Well, he came poking along and the wind was right so he never scented him until he was within three feet of him. John could have reached out and patted him. Then all of a sudden he smelt him, or saw him, or both, and he gave one big squall and turned a complete backward somersault and went down that mountain like a small avalanche!

"You know a bear runs like a rabbit — his hind feet in front of his front ones, and those hind feet throw up brush and dirt like a steam shovel. There's an old riverman named Lovell Oakes — he's a farmer now like me, lives up in Columbia — and he had a bear dog that used to get so annoyed by that brush flying up in his face that he'd never run behind the bear like he should, but right along beside him. It was funny as hell to watch him."

"And you've never had any trouble with a bear?" I asked.

"No — yes, I did too. It wasn't long ago, either. I'd been over calling on Lewis Leavitt, on the Magalloway, and we'd gone out in a big pine burn to pick blueberries. There were a lot of tremendous old-growth punkin pine blown over there and a fire had swept through the section and those great tree trunks were lying just as they'd fallen.

"Well, I got off some distance from Lewis and damned if an old he-bear that was in there berrying just like me didn't rise up from behind a stump and come straight at me. I dropped my pail and fled, and I can flee when I feel like it, even at my age, believe me, but that bruin had blood in his eye, and when I saw a big hollow log in front of me I just dived straight into it, head first, and crawled up as far as I could go.

"The damn bear was a lot bigger than I am, and I figured he couldn't get at me. He couldn't, either, not quite, but he was willing to try. He crawled in after me as far as he could. I drew my feet up and he could just reach the soles of my boots with his claws. There was a little knothole in front of my nose, so I could breathe, but I guess I was never in a tighter place in all my life.

"He kept pushing and grunting and working in an inch or two more and those pats against my boots were getting mighty intimate. I couldn't push in any farther myself, so I figured my time had come and I began to think of all the low, mean, bad things I'd ever done in my life, and I tell you I felt mighty small.

"Well, finally, I got so interested in my thoughts I sort of forgot about the bear, and I asked myself: 'Vern, what is the very lowest thing you ever did in your life?' and you know, I thought, the worst thing I ever did was to vote for Roosevelt — and that made me feel so almighty small that damned if I didn't pop right out through that knothole and so I got away!"

I laughed.

"Anyway," I said, "I'm glad to know the Devil is dead and buried. Maybe the Lord will have a chance among you sinners now."

"He's got his self-appointed agents working," Vern admitted. "Just the other day I was talking with Abe Washburn up in Kidderville. 'We've got a new religion up here, now, Vern,' he says and kinda grins.

" 'That so?' I says. 'What do you call her?'

" 'She hain't no name.'

" 'Then how in hell do you know what it is?'

" 'Well, we have a name for it, but the missionaries themselves, they don't call it anything. It's something like the Seventh Daysies, but they claim it ain't got nothing to do with it.'

" 'What do *you* call it?' I asked him.

" 'We call it the Black Stocking religion,' says Abe, real serious. 'You see, the women don't believe in wearing anything but black stockings.'

" 'Great Blushing Geranium!' says I, 'You don't mean, Abe, that they just wear only stockings?'

" 'Naw!' says he. 'I mean they won't wear any stockings but what are black — and no silk ones, either. And they don't believe in having any fun or going to shows or wearing jewelry.'

" 'Sounds rather insipid,' says I. 'What *do* they do for excitement?'

" 'Well,' says Abe, 'they eat pretty regular. You see, they board at my house and preach in the church here. And they sure do enjoy putting on the feed bag. They hold meetings every night and pray and preach and sing hymns. There's two of 'em — both women.'

" 'Do they take up a collection?'

" 'No. I don't know where they get their money from,' he says, 'but somebody must pay 'em.'

"I asked him if they'd made any converts.

" 'Not right around here,' says Abe. 'I guess we're too danged sinful. But they made a lot of 'em up in Pittsburg. Jack Chapple's whole family got bit by the religious bug. They all went and joined up — old lady, kids, whole boiling of 'em, all but Jack. The danged old sinner wouldn't join. They tell me the rest of 'em kicked him out of house and home and won't let him back till he's promised to hit the sawdust trail. So he's living down at the village now, at Towle's restaurant.'

"We used to have religious revivals around here," Vern went on, "that were worth attending if you liked entertainment. I recall one time they had a meeting like that over in Wenlock that I went to. There was an old farmer came down from Island Pond. His name was Baxter. The audience would get to praying and singing, you know, and then the power would come on them and they'd speak in strange tongues, and roll on the ground, and jump, and jerk — well, as I was saying, Baxter got up and said that evening:

" 'Brethren and sistern, I want to tell you that this morning I was splitting wood and my axe slipped and cut this thumb of mine clear off, but the power of the Lord came onto me and I put the thumb back on, and here you see it, just as sound as it ever was! Praise the Lord!' And everyone shouted: 'Praise the Lord!'

"Well, the next night Baxter was back again, and he got up and said contritely: 'Brethren and sistern, many of you heard me last night when I told you how I'd cut off my thumb with an axe, and I want to tell you that truly I did exaggerate, and when I got home I felt so bad to think I had exaggerated, I shed enough tears to float a bateau all the way from Island Pond down to this church!' "

Vern laughed. "I was to a Holy Roller meeting one night in a schoolhouse over near Rangeley," he said. "The power came onto one man and he got up and shouted, 'O Lord, come down to us! Come right through the roof, I'll pay for the shingles!'

"Lumberjacks and rivermen always went to those meetings if they were handy because they were amusing and instructive. One spring the drive was held up for some days at Fitzdale and a feller came with a sort of a carnival act and set up in a hall there for a few nights and part of his propaganda was promising to give prizes to local kids. It was a come-on, of course. Something always happened so no kid ever got anything. Roaring Bert and me and some of the boys went over there one evening and there was one little girl about ten years old who was a cripple and she was in line for a prize. She didn't get it, so Bert went up to the manager after the show and told him that the next night we'd all be there and we damned well wanted to see that girl get the prize.

" 'And if she doesn't git it,' says Bert, 'may God have mercy on you!' "

"Did she get it?" I asked.

"What do *you* think?" he answered dryly.

Before I had time to reply, a long, red touring car drove into

the yard and stopped with a quick, staccato blast of its horn —
two long plus two short toots, to be exact.

"I know who that is," Vern said placidly, without turning around. "He used to work on the railroad, and he always
gives that warning toot-a-toot-toot like engineers do at grade
crossings."

We got up and went to greet the newcomers. In the front seat
of the car sat a man and woman about Vern's age, with a half-
grown girl between them. Vern boomed a welcome.

We learned that the family had been out for a Sunday ride.
They had gone to Bethlehem and Cherry Valley and Berlin and
up through the Thirteen-Mile Woods and Dixville Notch and
were now on their last lap toward home.

"I couldn't go by Lyman Brook without stopping to see you,
Vern," said Ida.

She was a portly, kind-faced woman.

"Will and Mary Ellen said they wouldn't mind seeing you,
too," she added, smiling.

Her husband was a small, ruddy-faced man with the hard,
knotted hands of a farmer, and the sharpest gray eyes I ever
saw. They both looked at the child, a slim, leggy girl of thirteen
or so. It was plain they were enormously proud of her. She
came straight to Vern, who picked her up under the elbows,
like a doll, and kissed her heartily.

"I brought you something, Uncle Vern," she cried, and ran
back to the car, while Vern introduced me and we settled down
again on the piazza.

"Vern has told me about you," said the keen-eyed Will.

His thin, hard mouth relaxed in a brief smile. "If he says
you'll do, I guess you will," he added.

I thought of the many people who had told me the same
thing in one way or another, as I made some commonplace
reply.

"We were just talking about bears and such," Vern said. "Do
you know any good bear stories?"

Will settled back in the rocker and laughed. For a small man with a hard face he had a deep laugh, sympathetic and infectious.

"You came to the right man on the right day," he answered. "When we drove through Bethelehem Junction this morning I saw a man I know, a little red-headed Irishman named Tim Gannon, working on his lawn. Well, back about 1902 I was firing on the White Mountain Division of the Boston & Maine. The road ended at Fabyans, at the foot of Mount Washington. There was a roundhouse there, and a formidable Irish woman named Mrs. Hadlock ran a boarding house for the railroad men.

"Tim was baggagemaster there at Fabyans. He was a good fellow, but kind of nervous. One day he was showing me a new gold watch when Danforth, my engineer, picked up a small, harmless green snake which he draped over Tim's arm. Tim let out a howl and hurled the watch into the bushes and ran for shelter.

"Mrs. Hadlock had a crew of girls who waited on table, did the dishes, cleaned up the house, and so on. There was always a lot to do, and if the boarders came down to breakfast late (breakfast was at seven) it put the girls behind in their work. All of the men except Tim had to be out to work early anyway, but he didn't, and he loved to stay in bed. Mrs. Hadlock would shout up the stairs to him to get up, but he'd pretend he didn't hear and keep right on snoring.

"One morning while we were all sitting at the breakfast table an Italian came to the kitchen door leading a tame bear and begged for breakfast. In those days it wasn't too uncommon to see an Italian leading a muzzled bear around. He'd play a violin or an accordion, or even a mouth organ, and the bear would dance and the man would pass around his hat and the spectators would drop in a few quarters.

"Mrs. Hadlock was busy and was about to order him on his way when she was struck with a bright idea.

" 'I'll tell you what,' she said. 'You just lend me that critter of yours for five minutes, and I'll give both you and him something to eat!'

"The Italian wasn't too hot for it, but he was hungry, so finally he consented. She hollered up the stairs: 'Tim! Tim! It's time to get up!'

"Only a snore answered her. She seized the bear's chain and went up the stairs, dragging the animal behind her. She pushed Tim's door open and walked in. He was lying in a big, four-posted bed, with his back to her. He heard her, but he just snored on. She took a half-hitch with that long chain around one of the posts at the foot of the bed, and went out, locking the door. Tim snored on.

"After a while the bear got curious at that snoring, and walked up and snuffed in his face. Tim opened one eye, and when he saw that bear he let out an unearthly yell — "Whurr-r-oo-oo! woo! — woo!' and flew out of the bed as if he had been shot out of a cannon. He reached the door in about one jump, but it was locked! There was a window in the room, open at the bottom, and outside, just below it, was the narrow, V-shaped roof over the ktichen steps. Tim let out one more frantic yell and sailed out the window, over the roof, and landed on all fours.

"Mrs. Hadlock had figured he'd do that, and she had all her girls out there armed with long, heavy dish towels they'd soaked in cold water and twisted up a little. They chased him twice around the house at full speed, batting him with those wet towels, while the rest of us were doubled up with laughter.

"She never had to call Tim twice to breakfast again."

After the family had departed down river I asked Vern about his friend's antecedents.

"He ain't much to look at," he answered, "but I learned a long time ago you can't tell by the looks of a frog how far he can jump. You meet that feller in a crowd and it wouldn't be long before you'd be noticing him. He's been first selectmen of his

227

town for years, and that's the most important position his feller citizens can elect him to. He and I drove team for Van Dyke years ago. He's one of the very best men with hosses I ever saw. I love hosses myself, and that's how we got chummy, I guess. Someday I'll tell you how I seen him cure a balky hoss once, but now it's time to go milk. Come on!"

SEVENTEEN

Gem Hunter

I KNEW A man in Berlin named Frank Everding, who was Traffic Manager for the Brown Company, and one day when I was in his office a bald-headed young man with sharp features and a pleasant smile came in to talk with him. Frank introduced me:

"This is Percy Leggett — he works in the company yard office."

"I've heard about you," I said as we shook hands. "A man named Vern Davison told me you are quite a quaint character."

He laughed. "That's real praise," he said. "Old Vern reserves that epithet for people who are somehow out of the ordinary. I hadn't realized I was so different."

"He told me you took up the hobby of trapping wild animals and the first year you took more fur than any professional trapper in the state?"

"Yes, I guess I did, but there wasn't anything extraordinary about that. Anyone else could have done it."

"But," asked Frank, "how did you do it?"

"I went at it intelligently," said Mr. Leggett. "I got all the information I could from libraries, practical trappers, the Fish and Game Commission. I learned where the animals were — or ought to be — and how to catch them. Then I went there and caught them. That's all."

"But you've always been a good woodsman and hunter," said Frank. "I doubt if a neophyte would have been so successful."

"Vern told me you're the foremost authority on semiprecious stones in the North Country," said I. "How did you become that?"

"Well, a few years ago I was over near Newry, in Maine, and I happened onto an old gem collector who was chipping schist away from a tourmaline pocket. I'd never seen such a thing before, and I stopped to see what I could learn. I've been learning ever since. If I deserve Vern's encomium it's probably because I don't have any competition."

"I'm woefully ignorant on the subject," I said. "I'd appreciate to hear how one goes about gem hunting. I take it you don't just start off into the woods looking for something to sparkle?"

Mr. Leggett reflected. "Maybe it's this way," he said. "Many citizens up here spend a lot of time out in the woods, hunting and fishing. They know the terrain pretty well. They wouldn't get lost. Most of them have probably heard vaguely of gems, semiprecious stones, but most of them wouldn't know one unless they saw it in a jewelry store. And certainly wouldn't know the most likely places to go looking for some. That's just the way I was, myself."

"What did you do?"

"I joined gem societies. I subscribed to trade magazines. I studied official reports on the geology of northern New Hampshire. I corresponded with enthusiasts in other parts of the country and swapped items with them . . . ."

"Come down to my house next Saturday morning," he

230

added. "If you're a friend of Old Vern's and of Frank here I'll be glad to show you my tools and collection."

So I went. He lived with his wife in a neat little house near a railroad station. First he showed me samples of his gems — both cut and rough. He had amethysts, topazes, opals, garnets, tourmalines, aquamarines (which are younger brothers of emeralds), and some amazing quartz crystals. One was a ninety-two-pound white quartz, the largest ever found in New England.

"I darned near broke my back, lugging it out of the woods," said Percy.

"You see," he went on, as he took me into another room to show me his 'equipment,' "the first thing a gem hunter does is to go out and find some gems. Next, being well bitten by the 'gembug,' he proceeds to buy cutting and polishing tools and amuses himself by improving on nature. Of course, incidentally, he can sell his product, whether cut or rough. I've sold a good many pieces to the Harvard Geological Museum, and then there's always a ready market for knebelite, pollusite, and other rare minerals, some of which are found only here in the North Country."

Percy's cutting and polishing equipment consisted of a "hub," a "lap," and a diamond saw. The first faintly resembles the coaster brake of a bicycle, but is pierced at certain points with holes into which a lever is put that regulates the cutting of the facets.

The "lap" (lapidary) is a jeweler's version of a small grindstone: it is a metal disk covered with an abrasive powder, and it sits flat. The diamond saw is a circular steel disk into the edge of which diamond dust has been pounded. Everyone knows that "only a diamond can cut a diamond." Most of the stones Percy had to work with could cut through steel as steel cuts through butter, and were only a trifle softer than diamonds themselves.

"There doesn't exist any printed manual on gem cutting," he told me. "I've been thinking of writing one myself. I had to

Percy Leggett with a great set of amethyst crystals set in a quartz base that he found in Stark, New Hampshire, and (right) *holding the largest rock crystal ever found in New Hampshire — it weighed ninety-four pounds.*

learn by the trial and error method. The ordinary trade gem has fifty-four facets, but I'll show you some here I've cut as many as eighty onto."

Whereat he handed me a superb amethyst he had just cut, and a magnifying glass. It had, indeed, eighty facets.

Then he showed me two tremendous white rocks, the end of each being stuck full of long, blue crystals, like a porcupine's tail is stuck full of quills. One, darker and dirtier than the other, was amethyst just as he had found it in a ledge. The other, its twin, had been washed with oxalic acid, which cleaned it and made it sparkle.

He showed me also a black, dirty piece of rock resting on a piece of photographic film.

"This," he said, "is pitchblende. You know, the mineral that contains radium. I found it one day up on Cate's Hill. Maybe there's a uranium deposit up there — who knows? Anyway, this piece contains enough active radium so that simply by lying on the film it has taken its own picture, as you can see.

"I'm going out gemming this afternoon," he told me. "Maybe you'd like to go with me, just to see how it's done?"

Impelled by a vague dream of getting rich overnight, so to speak, and also by curiosity, I accepted the invitation. A twelve-year-old neighbor boy named Don was with us.

As we drove north out of Gorham, Percy pointed to a deserted, sinister-looking house, its black clapboards swinging loosely in the wind.

"Your friend Vern tells a story about that house," he said. "It's said to be haunted, and that's why nobody lives in it. Well, some years ago there was a dentist lived up in Berlin by the name of Doc Gifford. He was a shiftless old reprobate and spent a lot of his time in saloons. One day, so Vern tells the story, the boys were talking about ghosts, and Doc lifts his chin from his egg-spattered vest and says, "You fellers know there ain't no such thing as a ghost!'

" 'But Doc,' they say, 'how about that house down by the

Gorham bridge? You know as well as we do that the last three families who tried to live there had to move out on account of the phantom.'

" 'Yes,' says Doc, 'I know they moved out, but there wasn't no ghost had anything to do with it!'

"Finally they bet him ten dollars he wouldn't dare to stay all alone in that house all night, with no light, or matches, or firearms. He agreed, and that same night — it was a Saturday — one of the boys took him down just at midnight, searched him, and watched him go into the house. They'd come back at daylight and pick him up. He didn't know Vern had hidden himself upstairs earlier in the night.

"So Doc goes in and it was a cool night with a thunderstorm coming up fast, and of course that old house was bare as a bone and dark as two yards up a black bear's behind, as Vern would say. Doc feels his way in and finally gets into the old dining room, where he pulls out a bottle of cough syrup from his hip pocket, takes a good snort, mutters to himself 'there ain't no ghosts!' wraps himself up in a blanket he'd brought along, and goes to sleep on the floor, confident of winning his ten bucks in the morning.

But along comes the thunder and makes the house rattle, and Doc wakes up. It's kind of eerie in there, and he's just taking another pull of cough syrup when he hears steps coming down the stairs just outside the door. They come slow and heavy — one — two . . . Doc's hackles begin to rise. He thinks he hears the door open and there comes a terrific crack of thunder and a flash of lightning enough to blind you and sure enough, there in the door is a ghost, and the ghost doesn't have any head! Doc is so paralyzed he can't even moan.

There comes another flash, and the ghost comes over toward him, stepping slow and heavy. Then it speaks. 'Am I alone tonight?' it asks in deep, sepulchral tones. 'Am I alone tonight?'

"At that, Doc regains his powers of speech. 'No!' he quavers, 'you ain't! But you damn soon will be!'

"And in the next flash of lightning, Vern says, 'I seen him sail out of his blanket and right through the nearest window (never stopping to open it) and away into the night!' "

We went over the height of land into the Upper Ammonoosuc valley in the village of Stark, where an eight-hundred-foot cliff appropriately called the Devil's Slide rears its mighty head.*

Presently Percy stopped his car and we proceeded on foot three miles up a mountain, through dense forest.

We came out of the woods at last to a great series of broken granite ledges. Down the middle of them a slide of broken rock and rubble offered a path up.

"This," said Mr. Leggett, "is the kind of thing we look for first. I mean the ledges. And if there is such a slide on it, all the better."

He knelt down and showed me a pocket. "See this? That's what we hunt for. Pockets are of all sizes. This one isn't three inches long, but you can see the tiny white quartz crystals in it.

"It's hot gas that blows the pockets out. Then crystals form in them — sometimes. All this rubble comes from a huge pocket up at the top of these ledges. And right where you are standing is where I found that ninety-two-pound white quartz."

We scrambled up the steep slide. My guide pointed to a hole beneath the roots of an overturned spruce. "There," said he, "is where I dug out those big amethyst crystals."

I began to be interested. "Do you suppose there are any more around here?" I asked.

"Sure. Every rain brings out more. You don't even have to dig for them."

He bent over and scanned the ground closely, grunted, and picked up a small blue amethyst chip.

* Stark, with its white church and covered bridge, is almost as photogenic as Lower Waterford, Vermont, which is said to be the most photographed village in the United States. Pictures of both places frequently adorn "popular" magazines. At Christmas, in 1959, a huge mural enlargement of a photo of the latter village hung in Grand Central Station in New York.

Came a shout from Don. He ran down the slide, holding up a piece of gleaming blue stone for us to see. Percy took it and held it up to the sun.

"No cracks or flaws," he pronounced. "That'll cut a nice stone for you, worth around ten dollars."

I got down on my knees and pawed over the shale and crawled into crevices. Like a true novice I found numerous rocks that looked wonderful to me but which Percy classified as "nothing much." Finally I did find a piece of blue amethyst about as large as Don's and a small chip of a deep purple crystal.

"That's a royal purple amethyst," said Percy. "If you can find a bigger piece you will be very fortunate." (I didn't find one.)

At the top, where the slide became bare cliff, the gem hunter pointed out a gigantic pocket, blown out aeons ago, and cracked open by rain and frost to fall down the mountain, all save its great concave back.

"There are a lot more gems down in that rubble," Percy said, surveying the course of the slide, "but I don't know how we'll get them. Some of those boulders are as big as a bungalow."

He took a long rope that he had packed over his shoulder, and fastened one end to a scrub spruce growing from a crack in the solid rock above the pocket. He strung it along the face of the pocket and fastened the other end. Then he looked at me and grinned.

"See anything worthwhile?" he asked.

I surveyed the pocket's face with professional acumen. "No," I said. "No amethysts in sight."

He climbed up onto the rope and balanced himself, hammer in hand. In front of him, in the face of the gray granite pocket, was a streak or layer of darker rock.

"This," he said, tapping it with his hammer, "is knebelite, and it's worth $4 a pound, if you can get it in chunks. I'll try to make an honest dollar here."

He pecked patiently away with his hammer, while Don and I climbed to the top of the ledge and admired the magnificent view. "Another of the advantages of my hobby," said Percy, when, having made his honest dollar, he joined us there.

After he had smoked his pipe and rested, he led us to another pocket, where he got some very handsome smoky quartz crystals with "double terminations." I am not quite sure what the significance of a "double termination" is, but I know it means quite a lot to a gem collector.

"Put one of these on the stove and heat it," he told me, "and it will turn a clear yellow color."

He pointed to a mountainside across the valley: "In those ledges over there are a lot of pockets where topazes were formed. One day I picked up forty fine topaz crystals in less than an hour — and I sold ten of them for ten dollars apiece.

"The old *History of Coos County*," he added, as we prepared to go home, "states that a lot of labradorite is found in Stark and nowhere else in these parts. Labradorite is a mineral, a variety of feldspar, that is beautifully colored. So far I've not found any, but I will some day. It's one of the pleasant anticipations that make gem hunting a fine hobby."

"I've read that history," said I. "There's a story in it about a deposit of pure silver over near Tinker Brook, in Berlin. Have you ever looked for that?"

"Of course. But I've made up my mind that the man who wrote the story was deliberately lying about the location. Personally I think it's over on the other side of the Androscoggin. I nearly got killed over there one day. I'd found a little low cave and I'd crawled into it and was pecking away with my hammer when the roof fell in. It just missed me. At least it taught me to be more careful. You know silver and lead go together. That silver deposit is doubtless merely an extension of the formation the Gorham lead mine is in. They took a solid square chunk of pure lead weighing twenty-four hundred pounds out of that mine and sent it to the Crystal Palace exhibition in London some years ago."

"I know where there's an abandoned copper mine in Concord, Vermont," I said.

"Yes, and in Franconia they used to have a big iron mine industry. And up on Monadnock Mountain is a gold mine. Nobody really has any idea of what mineral wealth may be buried up here in the mountains. Lumbering is all they've ever thought about. But in a few years they'll have cut all the trees off and then maybe more people will be interested in minerals and such things."

"What makes you think they'll cut all the trees off? I've heard people say there's more lumber here now than there was sixty years ago."

"Nonsense! Thirty-five years ago, all the hills in this North Country were black with spruce. Already the lumber companies have stopped building log camps for their lumberjacks. Why? For the good reason that there aren't any more trees big enough to make a log camp. Thirty-five years from now this country will be as denuded of trees as China. They don't have a tree in that whole country, and they've killed off all the wild game except rats and crows. Had to, to eat. We'll be the same way."

John Hinman, the genial chairman of the board of the International Paper Company, and an old North Stratford boy, recently sent me a copy of a handsome book put out in 1961 by his firm, in which Percy's gloomy prediction seems to be refuted by the new lumber company principle of "sustained yield."

I hope John is right and Percy was wrong, but in either case I am pretty sure that if, as Old Vern once suggested, when I retire I choose to pass my time hunting for gems, I'll find a lot more daylight in the North Country swamps than there is now.

EIGHTEEN

The Atavist

I F YOU want to get the story of old Chief Metallak," Vern said to me one day, "you want to tackle Lewis Leavitt, the old guide I've told you about, over on the Magalloway. His grandfather knew Metallak well. They saved each other's lives once or twice."

"Would you like to go over with me?"

"Don't care if I do! As usual, my business ain't very rushing."

So we slid up through the Notch and down Clear Stream to Errol ("More woodsmen have gone through that town than any other town in the world," Vern said), followed the Androscoggin to where the Magalloway joins it, and then kept up the Magalloway.

Mr. Leavitt lives just across the state line, in Maine. We found him raking hay with a horse rake, but he turned the vehicle over to a hired man and went with us to the house, where we sat on the piazza and talked.

Lewis was then in his eightieth year, but still sound in wind and limb. He recounted to us the life of the ancient chieftain and how he died in Stewartstown at the age of 120, blind, friendless, and alone, having once been sought as a friend by governors, officers, and statesmen.*

"And that, my boy," he terminated his story, "is the history of Metallak. They say one can perceive a moral in the lives of great men. I don't know what moral there is in Metallak's, so maybe he wasn't a great man."

"The moral," said Vern decisively, "is that you don't want to outlive your usefulness. A man's a lot better off to die at the peak, than to live to see himself slipping down the other side."

"Maybe," said Mr. Leavitt smiling. "Maybe. I suppose you don't feel that you're that old, do you, Vern?"

"Not by a damned sight! When I do, I'll go out and shoot myself!"

Leavitt chuckled. "I'll bet you will at that," he said. "By the way," he went on, in a different tone, "the dam at Parmachenee went out this spring . . . "

He and Vern looked at each other intently.

"I expect," Vern said at last, "that you're going to tell me you saw that ghost girl again?"

"There's more than that to it," the old man answered earnestly. "There's a good deal more than that. There's a queer case of atavism mixed up in it. Quite a story, in fact."

"I know what an atavist is," said Vern. "You can't scare me with any big word like that. But let's hear the story."

"Here it is," said the old guide. "It's all about a young man named Willets."

It was when he put his canoe down into Chain of Ponds after the portage from the Kennebec that Willets had felt it first. A curious sensation that irritated him because of its very elusive-

* There is an interesting relic of the old chief in the Paris Hill (Maine) library. It is a birchbark map of the Rangeley Lake country that he drew for Vice-President Hannibal Hamlin.

240

ness. It could not be explained or analyzed, but all day long it stayed with him and bothered him.

It wasn't fear. It wasn't even uneasiness, though a man might have had reason to feel uneasy at being alone in those wild forests of northern Maine.

"It seems to me I've been here before," he muttered to himself as his flashing paddle drove him northward up the lakes. "And yet, God knows I never have. But when I hit that old Indian trail I could have sworn I'd seen it a hundred times before."

That baffling sense of familiarity of his wild surroundings stayed with him all that day, and when, at six o'clock, he thrust his boat gently up onto the shale at the head of Chain of Ponds and stared at the black opening in the thick spruce that marked the beginning of the long carry to Parmachenee Lake, it had begun to affect him physically. His head was feeling light — not the lightness caused by fever or fatigue, but a kind of reckless exaltation that had no sense or reason behind its origin.

"It must be the weather," Willets thought. "I've never seen such a hot day in April. Not this far north."

A brief smile lighted up his lean, dark face.

"That's a good one," he muttered. "This far north! And last summer was the first time I was ever up here."

He sat in the canoe for a moment, his eyes fixed on the old trail that led up the steep bank, but in his mind he was reconstructing a scene with his father that had taken place a few days before.

The old man stood in front of him, tall, lean, sloe-eyed, his heavy hair as black as a crow's wing in spite of his eighty winters.

"Last summer," the aged professor had said, "you were up in Quebec and northern Maine. I do not understand why that country should attract you so. I have never been there myself, of course. And though I have never told you before, when you first began to display these Daniel Boone tendencies of yours,

241

your grandfather Nathaniel was very insistent that I let you go anywhere *except* up there. But your grandfather is dead, and you are old enough to know your own mind. So I made no objection last summer, nor do I now."

"I wonder what made Gramp feel that way?" Willets asked curiously.

The professor shrugged. "I asked him, and he would not say. I know that years ago, before I was born, he had been up there himself. But what he did or saw there, I do not know. Only it must have been a very wild country then."

Willets laughed. "It's still a wild country, Dad," he assured him lightly. "Of course I came through only a little piece of it last summer when I came down from St. Augustin with Flint in his canoe, but I can tell you it hasn't changed."

Willets remembered that conversation as he sat there in his canoe at the head of Chain of Ponds. And in his hip pocket he fingered the letter from Flint, with whom he had paddled down Parmachenee and the Magalloway the year before. Flint wrote that the squaretails were biting, and that Willets would be welcome to come up and stay at his camp on Long Pond.

So here he was. Only, instead of having chosen the sensible road — up the Magalloway as far as there was any road, and proceeding from there by canoe — some strange quirk, some atavistic desire for adventure, had inspired him to go around by Chain of Ponds.

He was twenty-five years old, was young Willets, lean, sinewy, and a trifle saturnine. From his boyhood days he had possessed a marvelous facility for picking up wilderness lore. That fact had never been so plain to him as it had the preceding summer, and the discovery had pleased him.

That was one reason he had chosen to come by this roundabout route — just to prove that he could do it without any guide or any other help. And he had done very well — so far — he told himself as he sat in the stern of his canoe and stared at the opening of the overgrown and little-used portage.

Not many men (even woodsmen) who were unused to the country could have driven their canoe straight as an arrow to that old portage, he told himself.

But he had done it, as easily as if a lighthouse had been there on the shore to beckon him. It was youthful pride in his success, combined with the heady intoxication brought on by the unseasonable weather, that urged him on to the folly that he now committed.

For by rights he should have made camp there at the head of Chain of Ponds, and waited until morning before starting the seven-mile carry to Parmachenee. But now he decided to push on and get to Flint's camp that night. He could reach Parmachenee by eight o'clock, or nine at the most, and he knew the way from there. He had been over it only once, but for Willets, once was enough.

He put one hand on the gunwhale and half rose to his feet, only to sink back again as that eerie feeling that had oppressed him all day long suddenly pressed upon him like something palpable.

"Damnation!" he said aloud. "I'd swear I've stepped out of a canoe here a hundred times before!"

He shook his head impatiently and looked at the sky to see whether any danger threatened there. Little white clouds were slowly dragging their soft bellies over the spruce-clad border mountains, but there was no storm brewing anywhere. An unusual hush hovered over all the forest; but if that seemed a little unnatural, Willets told himself that there was nothing ominous about it.

He swung the sixteen-foot canoe onto his padded shoulders, and started briskly up the trail, looking like an immense green beetle stalking along on two legs. The dense spruces swallowed him up.

He found the trail in bad condition, almost impassable in places. It was overgrown with brush, full of mud holes and slippery stones, and about halfway he came to a steep rise up

243

which he sweated and scrambled for what seemed to be miles before he finally reached the crest.

There was no breeze in the silent forest, and when he reached the top of the divide hot and panting, he sat down on a fallen tree trunk, to rest his weary muscles. Before he started on again, the last red edge of the sun had sunk out of sight to the west.

Then, as always in those latitudes, came a period of twilight, but though Willets put his best foot forward, the trail was so bad that he did not reach the lake until night had quite fallen. Night, a warm curtain of black velvet shot through by a million pulsating stars.

Willets did not know that the dam at Little Boy Falls at the foot of Parmachenee Lake had gone out with the ice that spring. He knew only that he was in a hurry to get to Flint's camp, so he came paddling down the center of the narrow lake in the starshot darkness, paddling fast, intent on getting to his destination.

He was still half a mile above the falls when he noticed a small campfire on a long point of land that stuck out into the lake like a crooked finger, its tip crowned by the black outline of an immense pine tree.

"Indian Point," thought Willets, "and what can a man be doing in such a remote place?"

But he was in a hurry. Indeed, he was in such a hurry that he had not even stopped to eat since noon, and when his darkly gleaming paddle had driven him swiftly past the fire, he promptly forgot about it.

A few hundred yards farther on he was surprised to feel the speed of his canoe suddenly increase. Thinking his senses were playing him a trick, he held his paddle suspended in the air for a moment.

There was no doubt about it. He was being drawn ahead by an invisible force. Willets looked up and around him, then, a little frightened and more than a little puzzled. To his surprise, the shores of the lake had narrowed in on him; he was already in the river above the dam, a few bends away. But it was impossible, he told himself, for any such current to exist there.

Then in the starlight he saw the first of the white water, and he knew that something was wrong, though even yet he did not guess what it was. But he knew that the dam must be just ahead, and he decided to chance the rapids as far as the carry.

He drove on his paddle to give the canoe steerageway and was about to enter the flurry of white, rock-toothed water when, to his astonished vision, another canoe appeared just in front of his own. It was a birch bark, and in its center knelt a woman — an Indian, Willets guessed her, by her clothing and the two long glossy braids of black hair that hung down her back.

The woman, if woman it was, turned the upper half of her body so she faced him, and held up her left hand in a mute but imperious warning to come no farther. Then, before his startled eyes her frail craft shot down into the white smother and vanished.

Automatically obeying her gestured command, Willets drove his canoe over against the right bank just in time to escape being sucked down into a raging quarter-mile of rapids that he had never seen before.

"Dam went out," he muttered blankly, understanding at last. "But that woman — in God's name, it must have been a ghost!"

The cold sweat of fear came out all over the man's body and he trembled violently. He thought for an instant of searching for the woman, but he realized that such a hunt would be futile. Indeed, it would be impossible until daylight. He thought of the long carry ahead of him, and then he remembered the fire on Indian Point.

Numbly, his mind still filled with wonder at his miraculous escape, Willets turned and went back up the lake. A dozen feet from the foot of the huge pine tree the small fire still flamed, reflected from a large boulder that acted as a backlog. Willets, shoving his canoe's nose silently up onto the sand, let out a hail.

"Come on in, son," a large voice invited him, and Willets came.

Though he had never been introduced to him, he recognized the ancient man who advanced to meet him. Forty years before, "Old Man" Leavitt had been dubbed "Maine's best guide," and if someone else now held the title, it was because (close to eighty years old now) the old man had retired from competition.

"I'm on my way to Flint's," said Willets, "but if you don't mind, I'll camp here tonight with you. I just saw a ghost," he finished, laughing shortly.

Instantly, the old man was all attention. "What do you mean, a ghost?" he demanded. "This is April . . . What kind of a ghost and where did you see it?"

Willets told his story. Then the old man spoke, as if to himself:

"The dam," he said, "went out with the ice this spring. I always said that if that dam went out, she'd come back, but she's never been seen except in October, and this is April . . . "

Willets looked at him in wonder. "Do you mean?" he began weakly, "do you mean that it wasn't because I'm tired and empty? Do you mean that I actually did see — see something down there?"

"I'll say you did," said Old Man Leavitt.

The two men, seated on water-washed rocks on opposite sides of the campfire, stared at each other.

"This here is called Indian Point," the old man said at last. "Maybe you'd like to hear a true ghost story — about the Indian it's named after?"

Willets nodded without speaking. He was conscious of a strange feeling of familiarity with this place. He seemed to have been here before, to have heard this story before . . . but he knew it was not so. He had never seen Indian Point but once,

246

when Charlie Flint had pointed it out to him last summer, and as for a story, he had never even heard of one. It was just a part of this queer day, he told himself — the queer weather, the queer feeling he had had all day, the ghost, and now this. He shook his head as if to clear cobwebs from his mind, and listened.

"It was sixty-five years ago," began Old Man Leavitt. "I remember it, for I was fifteen years old that spring. My father and I had come up here to trap. It was in October, and there was a full moon. We were camped up the lake about a quarter of a mile above here, on that little point you can see" — and he waved a hand toward the north. "We had had supper and we were lying there under a lean-to before the fire, looking out onto the lake. This same pine tree was here, and pretty near as big as it is now.

"My father had told me when we came by in the afternoon that this was called Indian Point, and now I asked him why it had that name. He told me that some years before a white man had come up here, a sort of missionary, who stayed with the Indians who were camped at the upper end of the lake.

"One of the young squaws was a pretty girl and this man and she fell in love with each other. He went away after a couple of months, but he promised the girl he'd come back the next Hunting Moon — October — and marry her. But he didn't come back in October.

"At night the girl used to come down here to this point and watch for him. Her tribe wandered off somewheres, like they are always doing, but she stayed. She couldn't have lived very high, but anyway she stuck it out for another year.

"October came and went, and when her man didn't show up, the girl figured there wasn't any use in waiting longer. One night after she'd stood here a long time, looking down the lake, she got into her canoe and paddled down to the outlet.

"There was no dam then, of course, and there was a darned sight more water than there is nowadays. The minute you left

247

the lake the current sucked down over rocks and rapids that you couldn't shoot a canoe over. She drove her canoe straight down into it — and never came out. But every October at the full of the moon, she can be seen coming down the lake . . .

"No, we didn't see her that time, but maybe it was because we didn't stay awake to watch. We were tired so we went to sleep. But I know three men, whose word I'd take on anything, that have seen her. And the year afterward they built down at the outlet and nobody saw her after that."

The ancient guide sat silent for several long moments, his eyes fixed on the dying fire, buried in old memories. Then he added:

"But I always said that if that dam should go out, she'd come back."

Willets listened as if in a dream. That strange sense of familiarity with this setting and this story bore down upon him like an intangible weight. And suddenly many things were clear to him. Abruptly he stood up, and his black eyes stabbed like twin daggers at Old Man Leavitt, and the breath whistled through his nostrils.

"But the baby," he demanded hoarsely, "what became of the baby?"

The old man looked up at him, and his eyes widened as he saw the emotion under which the boy was laboring.

"Did I mention a baby?" he asked. "Indeed, and there was one. A boy. Its father came back the next year and took it away from the Indians. He was never seen up here afterwards. His name? I remember it well. It was Nat Willets."

When Old Man Leavitt finished his story, Vern looked at him and seemed to be on the point of saying something, but he didn't. Instead, he turned to me.

"Do you believe that story, Bob?" he asked.

"If Mr. Leavitt says it's true, I'm willing to believe it. It could be true. You say yourself it's the exception that proves the rule. Anyway, it's a good story."

Vern laughed, and turned to Mr. Leavitt.

"I heard they nicked you for takin' beaver out of season," he said. "A man of your ability ought to be ashamed."

"I am, too," the old man declared. "Ashamed I was caught and ashamed I was mixed up in such a scrape, too. But I paid my fine, so I guess we're even now."

"I heard it cost you nine hundred dollars," said Vern, presuming more on old acquaintance than I had ever known him to before.

"Yes, I guess it did. But there was others that it cost four or five thousand. That storekeeper over in Colebrook was going to commit suicide."

"I heard something about it," Vern said. "Let's have the whole story. Or don't you want to tell it?"

"Don't want to tell it to you?" The old man chuckled. "Why, Vern, I'd tell you anything. Didn't I tell you about the brass cannon? Well now, let's see . . . "

And he began.

NINETEEN

Beaver

I T WASN'T that I needed the money," said Old Man Leavitt. "But I like to hunt and trap, and I knew other fellows were getting beaver, and I thought I might as well get my share. But I did it just for fun. I'd get a few here and a few there as it happened and thought nothing of it.

"But it appears that some of those gentlemen up in Pittsburg — you'd know all of 'em if I should name 'em — went in for beaver trapping on a big scale. The head of the Izaak Walton League, which is supposed to conserve game, was one of the worst offenders.

"Now it ain't much of a trick to catch a beaver. Put a little scent around and you'll get him every time. But it's a trick to dispose of the skin, when you live in a state where there ain't any open season on the animal. They got that fellow over in Colebrook to be the middleman. They'd take the pelts across the line and then ship 'em down to him as if he was buying them, and he'd dispose of 'em. Of course they're worth a lot more here than they would be in Canada.

"The scheme looked pretty good, and for a while it *was* pretty good. They pretty near exterminated the beaver on the Diamonds and on Indian Stream and a lot of other places. But they reckoned without old Uncle Sam. You see, beaver pelts shipped from Canada into the States must be stamped with a government stamp, or seal, and this stamp has perforations in it. The stamp the beaver poachers used wasn't just quite letter-perfect, and one day an inspector took it into his head to look at a lot of beaver pelts with a microscope.

"That was the beginning. They traced the shipment back to one of the boys that lives here on the Magalloway and when they put the screws on him, he talked. They descended on the storekeeper in Colebrook, and the condinged fool had a note-book with all the names of the poachers in it! Then came the big cleanup. We've been good boys since."

"I've trapped some beaver in my time," said Vern. "I never did it much, for it takes four hours to skin and flesh one of the critters, and it wore out my patience. But Charley Pinckney told me the way these fellers did it was to take a crowbar and a piece of iron pipe and go onto the beaver's house, in the winter. Then they'd dig a hole, stick the pipe in, and go away for a couple of days. The beaver, of course, swims away at all that noise. But he comes back and he gets used to the pipe. He sits there with his tail in the water, meditatin', and the poacher comes sneakin' back with a bottle of chloroform in his hand. He steps softly onto the house, pours down the chloroform, plugs the pipe, waits a few minutes, and then digs the beaver out. I told Charley I didn't believe a word of it. Do you?"

"Well, I never tried it myself. I have heard that same story, though. But on the whole, I don't take much stock in it."

"Why does the beaver hang his tail in the water?" I asked.

"You see," Vern explained, "they build their house from the bottom of the pond up, maybe several feet above the surface of the water. The entrance is at the bottom. Above the waterline they have a sort of nest, or shelf, where they lay down and

251

meditate. But their tail hangs over the edge of the shelf into the water, and they use it for a gauge to tell how high or how low the water is, and whether this dam is all OK."

"Also," amplified Mr. Leavitt, "that tail tells them the moment anything steps into the pond, and they can even tell whether it's a man or a moose."

"I remember the first time I ever saw a beaver dam," Vern said. "I was ten years old and I'd gone fishing with my father on Coon Brook. We stayed at an old camp overnight. Just up the brook, on a logan, was the dam. It was a grassy, swampy location, with a lot of alders beside the water, but right at the dam the ground rose, on one side, in a high dry ridge covered with small firs. It made a good place to hide and it was directly above the dam. My father said: 'We'll make a hole in that dam, and tonight I'll show you something.' So we made a hole right in the center, and let all the water out of the pond. That night we went down to watch the beaver repair it. It was better than any show.

"There was a bright moon, and we crawled down the ridge till we weren't twenty yards from the dam. They were working on it already. There was one big beaver sat on his tail at the broken place and directed operations.

" 'Just like a crew of rivermen,' whispers my father. 'He's the foreman.'

"And that's just what he was. If a beaver came swimming up with a stick and laid it in the wrong place, the foreman either waved to him to change it, or he dropped into the water and changed it himself. They all worked. Once Dad nudged me and pointed out a fat old beaver who was shirking. He had swum over to a corner of the dam, and there he lay, half in the water, half on the sticks, trying hard to keep out of sight and appear unconcerned at the same time. He was so human I almost burst out laughing. But he didn't stay there long. That big foreman snarled something at him, and we could just see him heave a big sigh of regret as he slipped into the water and back to work."

"That lazy one," said Mr. Leavitt, "was sort of on the way to become a bank beaver. You know," he went on, in answer to my unspoken question, "some beaver, instead of building houses, live in holes in a bank, and they are called bank beaver. Some people try to claim that they are a different sort than the house beaver. But bless you, those bank beaver are nothing but old bachelors that were too lazy to work, and the others drove them out of the colony. So they go off and dig a hole and live in it. That's all there is to a bank beaver.

"A farmer named Sam Brungot, down in Milan, found a baby beaver and he kept it in the house for a pet. One day the maid went out and left the water running into the washing machine, and it ran all over the floor. When she came back, that beaver had gnawed all the legs off the tables and chairs and tried to build a dam to stop the water."

"That's right," Vern affirmed. "I saw something of the same sort myself when I was cruising timber for the company on the Madeleine River, on the Gaspé. There was an old man named Tom Masters, a trapper, had a cabin on a lake way-to-hell-and-gone up near the headwaters. He'd been in there for years, but he was getting too old to be alone. He was way past eighty.

"He had a granddaughter named Etta, who was eighteen or nineteen years old, and she came to sort of look after him. Used to help him with his trap line, too. Their nearest neighbor was a Canuck named Joe Dubey, and he was a sight to behold. One time in his interestin' career a wildcat had taken a swipe at him and removed his left eye and clawed one side of his face so it was permanently twisted. He looked a good deal like a rat whose mother had been scared by a weasel, and his disposition matched his looks. Damned if that specimen of God's carelessness didn't have the nerve to ask Etta to marry him! Old Tom would have kicked him out of the house, only Dubey was their nearest neighbor, living only six miles away, and he feared reprisals.

"Well, one day Etta found a little baby beaver and she took it home and fed it on goat's milk, from an eyedropper, and made a pet of it. She named him Grumpy because he was always grumbling to himself, and she and old Tom taught him tricks.

"Dubey hadn't been around for months, pretty near a year, I guess, but along just before spring he showed up one afternoon about dark, with a hound dog he'd been out hunting with, and asked could he stay the night. Etta had answered the door when he knocked, and even if she didn't like him, she knew you can't refuse a man shelter in the woods, so she said, 'Come in.'

"Just then young Grumpy came swaying up the path from the lake. Joe's hound saw him, and yelped, and Joe sicked the dog onto him. He knocked him over, but the beaver came up onto his hind legs like a boxer, snapping his teeth and too damn mad to be scared.

"Etta started to run down and get the dog, but Joe grabbed her by the arm and held her back. But Grumpy didn't need any help. The next time the hound rushed him, those teeth of his, sharp and hard as an axe blade, snapped just once. And once was enough. He sliced a hole in the critter's throat like you'd take a bite out of an apple.

"The dog, of course, laid down and bled to death, and Joe swore and up with his rifle to shoot the beaver. But by that time old Tom had come out. He had a rifle in his hand, and it was ready for business.

" 'You shoot that beaver, Dubey,' he said, 'and I'll shoot you.'

"The Canuck turned and stalked down the path. Grumpy stood in the middle of the trail, and he had to go out into the snow to get past him.

"Well, it was the next summer and the beaver had grown big and fat and husky, when Tom came home one day to find the door shut and apparently bolted from the inside. He went around to the side and looked in a window. Grumpy was working. Tom got there just in time to see him cut the legs from the last chair in the house and drag 'em over to weave into a dam he'd constructed from all the cabin's furniture, which extended from one corner past the door, wedging the door shut.

"Grunting and whining to himself, he stuck those legs where they'd do the most good, and then he stepped back to sit on his hind legs and enjoy his handiwork. He looked so self-satisfied and human that Tom had to laugh even if his furniture was all wrecked.

"But when the old man climbed through the window and started to demolish the dam, the beaver got mad, and Tom didn't dare to touch it. Of course he could have killed or hurt him, but it was Etta's pet, and he didn't want to do that. He went back to sit on the piazza, and philosophically contemplated his nanny goat eatin' grass in the front yard until such time as his daughter came home.

"I came down the lake in a canoe and saw him there and stopped to pass the time of day, and he showed me the dam. Then Etta came home. 'Your beaver's locked me out,' says her grandpa. 'I tried to pull down his dam, and he showed fight. I didn't want my leg chewed off, so I left him alone. What are we going to do?'

" 'Nonsense!' says Etta. She climbed in the window and went up to the dam. Grumpy whined a warning, and she reached down and slapped him on the nose. I tell you, I'd as soon slapped a buzz saw. But he didn't touch her.

" 'You ought to be ashamed of yourself,' she told him, and set to work to tear down his engineering masterpiece. He didn't bother her, but Tom had had enough.

" 'Grumpy's big enough now to shift for himself,' he said. 'He's no household pet any more. And besides, as beavers get old, they get ornery. We'll just take him out and lose him.'

"And that's what they did. He'd follow Etta just like a dog. They took him over to another lake about three miles away, where there were some other beavers, and left him."

"The best way to trap a beaver," said Mr. Leavitt, "especially if you want to keep it a secret, is to set your trap near the water and tie a heavy stone to it. The beaver will drag trap and stone into the water, out of sight of passersby, such as game wardens, but the stone will hold him down and he will drown. But you, knowing where your trap was, can locate it without difficulty."

"And the best part of a beaver to eat," Vern contributed, "though you'd never think it, is his tail, roasted on hot coals."

"Is it true, what I've read," I asked, "that dam building with beaver is entirely instinct? That they don't use any reason about it?"

"Not by a damn sight!" disagreed the two sages simultaneously. "They build by instinct," went on Mr. Leavitt, "but they use their heads, too. I've seen them build a dam where engineering problems came up that no instinct in the world would ever figure out how to overcome, but they did it. You ought to go to Success Pond sometime and see the dam they built there," he added. "It's three-quarters of a mile long."

"I've been there," I assured him. "I'd like to know how old that dam is."

"I don't know," said the old man. "But I've seen beaver workings at Unknown Pond, on the height of land between Second Lake and Big Brook, that John Locke, who was Chief Forester for the CVL Company, estimated were five hundred years old. The dam there was nine feet high."

"Beavers," said Vern, "are usually friendly animals, but they can be riled up so they are dangerous. I was scaling pulpwood one winter on Island Brook, and I'd seen where a beaver had a little trail down through the deep snow, angling off from the tote road. I came along there one afternoon with my Bangor rule in my hand, and I thought it would be cute to corner him in that deep snow.

"I followed in on his trail, and there he was, and of course he was cut off from the stream. Do you suppose he tried to dash off into that snow? Or that he cried for mercy? Not much he didn't! He whined and he grunted, and he came at me with his mouth wide open and his eyes shooting sparks! One bite of those long steel-hard teeth, and a six-dollar rule would have been in two pieces. Or one very valuable leg! I jumped right out into the snow and let him pass."

"That old trapper Ervin Palmer you told me about ought to have some good beaver stories," I said. "Why don't we go up and see him, we're so close now."

"Ervin Palmer is dead," said Old Man Leavitt, before Vern could answer. "Hadn't you heard? Got his lifetime wish, too, before he died. What do I mean? Well, I'll tell you."

And this is what he told.

TWENTY

A Dream That Came True

I'M THROUGH," said Ervin Palmer to the boss of the machine shop in Berlin.

He said it not angrily, not with defiance, but with a certain finality that admitted of no argument. The boss opened his mouth to speak, but the irrevocable quality of Ervin's announcement penetrated even his insensitivity, and he said nothing at all.

So the best patternmaker the shop ever had laid down his tools and walked out. He never went back.

Ervin Palmer was thirty-one years old. He went up into the North Country, where he had lived as a boy. He went as far as there was any road, and then he went on into the woods by the trail that goes from Clear Stream to Greenough Pond and on over the height of land to the Swift Diamond.

The trail led through a deep ravine, full of ancient mossy logs, and the broken shafts of sunlight fell through the leaves to make mottled patches on the ground beneath. A bubbling brook ran through this ravine, and from the lip of a steep ledge, forty feet above the trail, another brook flashed down to join it. There Ervin Palmer halted.

On the top of the ledge, beside the flashing brooklet, he built himself a log cabin; and there he lived for more than thirty years, hunting, trapping, fishing, observing the ways of the forest creatures, and minding his own business. Almost inevitably he became known as "queer," as a "gruff, surly old cuss," as "a little cracked," and other things, all more or less opprobrious.

But it bothered him not at all. He ranged the forested solitudes from Big Diamond to the Peaks, and from Greenough to Moose Bog, and learned to know both the country and its denizens. One winter morning, down by Four-Mile Brook, he discovered a saltwater spring that would not freeze over. One afternoon, sitting before his solitary cabin, he beheld a sight that few men have witnessed — a fight to the death between a mink and a porcupine.

Especially well did the man, deeply weary of the eternal clanging of the machines, like to sit before his cabin door and watch the westering sun sink down below the dark fretwork of the evergreens that crowned the hills. As he sat there, soothed by the soft breeze in the trees and the babbling of his brook as it wound over the pebbles to the lip of the cliff; or as he sat in his snug cabin during the long winter nights and listened to the wailing of the wind and the awesome noise caused by the rubbing of the crossed limbs of the bare hardwoods, a dream came to the man, a dream that stayed with him till the day he died, and this is what it was:

He would make a violin, the like of which had never been made before. He would make it entirely from natural products of the forest, and the instrument thus conceived would be able to reproduce in their natural tones all the wonderful sounds of the forest — the singing of the brook over its pebbles, the soft sighing of the summer breeze in the pines, the rustling of the leaves, the fierce howl of the winter blizzard, the crashing of the

259

*Ervin Palmer, patternmaker, trapper, and violin maker
playing one of his fiddles in front of his cabin on Swift
Diamond Stream.*

ice as it breaks up in the spring — all these, and many more, the hermit's projected violin should reproduce.

He was in no hurry. He cut down a bird's-eye maple and rolled the log up to his cabin. He let it lie there drying for seven years before he went to work on it. He knew nothing about violins but he procured an old one for a model, and all his old skill as a master patternmaker was still with him. Carefully, correctly, without haste, he cut the wood, steamed it to make it bend, and put it in a mold. As he had foreseen, every part of the violin was made from the wild woods — bird's-eye maple, spruce, and cherry. Only the strings bothered him, and there he finally had to compromise. He made the strings from the hairs of a horse's tail!

It took a long time to do all that. And in the midst of it he was evicted from his cabin. The Coe-Pingree Lumber Company, which owned the land, kicked him out. The old man had lived there for thirty years and harmed no one, and the company owned more acres of wild land than it could count or would ever see. But they told him to get out or go to jail, and he got out. It is well for Messrs. Coe-Pingree that it was a gentle old man they jumped on so savagely. I know another lumber company that did the same thing to another trapper who was neither gentle nor old. He left the cabin, it's true, but fifteen hundred acres of the company's best spruce went up in smoke behind him.

"Old Man" Palmer, as he was now called, went over the height of land and built himself another cabin, where Four-Mile Brook falls into the Swift, and there he lived for fifteen years, until he died. Meantime his passion for the violins had grown and grown. He made four altogether, and started a fifth one, which I saw the other day behind the cabin, thrown out by the present owner. One of his four treasures was stolen, which made the old man more misanthropic than ever. The other three hung in a row on one of the cabin walls.

Game wardens, guides, fishermen, fire wardens, and hunters used to stop to see them and speak a word to "Old Man" Palmer. As a rule they found him shy and taciturn, but a few of them won his confidence. Such, for example, was young Oscar Gould, a guide from the Magalloway, who practically kept the old man alive in his last days.

The old hermit would never sell one of his violins. A city sport up there fishing once offered him $175 for one, but to no avail.

"I don't need the money," said Palmer. "They stole one from me. But they won't get any more."

"But what are you going to do with them?" asked the sport, not unreasonably.

But the old man lowered his glance and obstinately refused to answer.

Palmer cherished a great desire to have a real musician play one of his instruments, in order to prove his contention that a violin, made like these, would reproduce the myriad sounds and murmurs of the woods. But his desire was for long years doomed to disappointment, for of the few men who travelled up the remote Diamond Stream, not one was a violinist.

Then one day Oscar Gould, happening to be in Errol, fell to talking to a tourist who was having his automobile repaired at West's garage and learned that the tourist was a violinist in a great orchestra in New York City. Oscar told him of the old hermit and his dream, and the tourist said he would go and see him and his violins if Oscar would guide him to the place. That was just what Oscar wanted, and the two men drove up past Joe Hart's farm to the junction of the Swift and the Dead and from there they proceeded on foot.

They found the old man lying in his bunk, very weak and manifestly dying, but he recognized Oscar and he understood him when he introduced the violinist. Joy shone in his old eyes and for a moment he forgot his weakness and his pains as he struggled up from his bunk and hobbled to the wall.

He took down one of the violins and handed it to the stranger, who tucked it under his chin and began to play. And never, avers Oscar, was music like that drawn from a violin. All that Palmer had dreamed, had come true. All the mighty symphony of the forest, from the purling of the brook to the roar of the storm wind, was hidden in those strings and came forth at the touch of the master.

For half an hour the stranger played there in the lonely cabin; and for half an hour joy ineffable shone on the old man's haggard face.

"It does the trick, doesn't it?" he whispered hoarsely as the last notes died away.

"Yes, Mr. Palmer," said the violinist gently, and with wonder in his voice. "It does the trick."

Even as he spoke, the old man fell back in his bunk, coughing weakly, and muttered that he must sleep.

The stranger walked over to the wall and reluctantly hung up the violin in its accustomed place.

"There is magic in it," he muttered. "Outside of this place I do not believe one could get such music. But," he continued to Oscar, "the old man is very sick. You should get help for him."

The two men went away. That afternoon County Commissioner Swail, of Colebrook, sent in a horse and the old man was taken to the hospital at the Coos County Farm, at West Stewartstown, where very soon he died.

His cabin was broken into and over a hundred steel traps he owned were stolen. All his joiner's tools were stolen. Everything in the cabin, of any value, was taken.

And the violins? What became of them? Oscar Gould says Joe Hart got them at the time the old man was taken out and turned them over to Commissioner Swail at Colebrook. But where they are today is one of the many mysteries of the North Country.

TWENTY-ONE

Grandmother's Remedies

I WAS HELPING Vern tear down an old shed one morning when I ran a rusty nail into the ball of my thumb.

"I'm scared of blood poisoning," I told him. "I'm going to Colebrook and get a doctor to fix this."

"Doctors are all right when you can't do without 'em," he said, "but my old grandmother showed me a cure for blood poisoning that's never failed me yet. Come on into the house.

"Light that lamp and come down cellar with me," he ordered.

While I held the lamp he took a flat rock off the cover of a large earthenware jar and fished out a great chunk of salt pork. With a sharp butcher knife he had brought along from the kitchen he sliced off a thin piece of pork, handed it to me, recovered the rest, and we went upstairs. He laid the pork on the sink shelf, and wet it well from a bottle of turpentine.

"That'll prevent any poisoning," he said convincingly. "It's too bad," he went on, as he bound the pork over my puncture, "that more people don't know about such things. It's a funny thing that people who live outdoors and are tough and rugged are easy marks for septicemia. There was a feller named Owen Crimmins used to run the hay farm for the Brown Company on the Swift Diamond, and he died from pricking his finger with a fishhook. And I've known others who got blood poisoning easily. Must be because their blood is too clean to begin with. Just like the Injuns couldn't stand smallpox."

"I remember how you cured Hinman of pneumonia," I said, "but do you believe that story of Ginseng's about curing tonsilitis by tying a frog on your throat?"

"Of course I believe it! There's any number of those old-fashioned remedies that are mighty efficient. Some of 'em may sound like nonsense, but they work, and that's what counts. As good a cure for a boil as any doctor can give you is to take a fresh cabbage leaf and bruise it some and cover it with butter and pack it onto the boil. It'll draw it every time. If you don't have any fresh cabbage, a plain bread and milk poultice will do almost as well."

"That isn't nonsense," I protested. "The natural humidity of the cabbage, augmented by the butter, can't help "drawing" the boil. I supposed you meant those old witches' brews composed of twenty frogs and fifteen snails and a this year's pullet all boiled for eight hours and then strained and mixed with gum arabic."

"Do you think I'm a total goddamned fool?" he demanded. "I've seen these things work, sonny. I could tell you of quite a few. And if there are one or two that modern physicians would laugh at, call it mind over matter, or psychotherapy, or anything you want to. The fact remains they do the job! My own mother was cured of typhoid fever by splitting a live pigeon in two and putting it on her head. I told that to a doctor once and he said it was only a survival of witchcraft, killing an innocent animal to appease the evil spirits. Anyhow, it appeased the fever.

"When I lived in Boston I used to do a little boxing with the boys. You've probably heard of putting raw beefsteak on a bruise or on a shiner? But the best thing for a black eye is a raw scallop. It has a serum that penetrates into the tissues and exerts an effect on the flow of blood, so they tell me.

"Some years ago, before he got killed, there was a doctor down in Littleton named Beattie and he was pretty good. His prices were pretty good, too, so I've heard, but he'd studied at Vienna and I guess he had to make up for what that had cost him. Anyway, he used to come up north fishing and I got acquainted with him. One night we got into an argument over these grandmother's remedies, as he called them, and he gave me the latest medical ideas about them. He agreed some of 'em had their good points, and some of 'em he said physicians used to prescribe but don't any more.

"According to him, even first-class doctors disagree about almost everything, and about every ten years they change all their ideas about everything, so I don't know as my grandma's remedies are any more hocus-pocus than theirs."

He laughed. "Beattie told me that once he and another intern went to visit an institution for the feeble-minded and they had to stay overnight in the town. They got a room in a private house and went to bed together. It was a mighty cold winter night and they didn't think of opening the windows, but after a while the feller with him says, 'Bill, I just never can sleep with the windows closed. If you don't mind, I'll git up and open one.' 'Go ahead,' says Bill. So the feller hops out of bed in the dark and goes over and pushes up a window and crawls back into bed and sleeps like a baby. The next morning he was somewhat confused to find the room had double windows and he'd not opened the outer one at all!

"Vinegar is a useful thing in a lot of cases," Vern went on, as we went back to dismantling the shed. "For one thing, you dip a lump of sugar in it and let it dissolve in your mouth and it'll cure he-cups. Another thing about it, you rub it on a beesting and it'll stop the itching."

266

"I've heard people say you can cure hiccups by slowly drinking a glass of water while soaking a knife blade in it," I said. "Do you believe it?"

"Well, I never tried it, but I've heard of it. I told it to Doc Beattie and he said the knife blade is a symbol to 'cut the he-cup,' but he said too that since he-cups are nothing but a sudden and spasmodic contraction of the diaphragm the cure might work, because as long as a man is drinking he isn't breathing, and the resultant blocking of the diaphragm might stop the spasm."

"What about warts?"

"There's several old-fashioned ways of curing warts that I've heard different people expound," he answered. "Each feller will swear his method works. When I was a kid I had a dozen of 'em on the backs of my hands and my father cured 'em by rubbing a piece of string across each one and then tying a knot in the string for each one and burying the string in the ground. He said when the string would have rotted the warts would have disappeared."

He grinned at me. "I'm not claiming that was what cured 'em, but sure as hell they disappeared! The doctors say when a patient believes in his cure he's already two-thirds healed. Maybe I believed in it then. I was only about seven years old.

"But I can tell you something that I *do* believe in: if you git to feeling very tired, you put some cloths soaked in hot water on your wrists and the nape of your neck and lie down and you'll feel better right away."

As we worked he kept up a running fire of reminiscences of other cures he had seen or heard of, guaranteeing them with his usual vigor and conviction.

"You can cure diphtheria by drinking pineapple juice," he asserted. "It's so powerful it'll cut the membrane and make it vanish. I've seen it work more'n once. Then I know a banker up in Colebrook named Earl Wadsworth, and he told me once he'd heard of a baby being cured of diphtheria by drinking a spoonful of burnt brandy. There's a Frenchman named Frank Gochey — seein' as you're interested in such things I can tell you that his father spelled it *Gauthier* — lives down on the river, whose three-year-old daughter contracted the disease and the docs couldn't do a thing for her. They'd given her up.

"I happened to stop at his place when the child was about at her last gasp. Frank didn't have any pineapple juice, but I thought of Wadsworth's story about the brandy and there was some brandy in the house and Frank burnt a teaspoonful and made her swallow it. Damned if it didn't do the trick. Last time I saw her she was fifteen years old and healthy as a cow. Looked like one, too. I swear, you'd have thought she was smugglin' watermelons under that blouse she had on . . .

"A spiderweb is a good thing to stop a cut from bleeding," he went on, as he picked up a heavy corner-beam and heaved it aside with no apparent effort. "I remember I told Beattie that, and he agreed it has cellulose particles that help coagulation, but he said too that the dust and dirt usually found on such webs make 'em dangerous by reason of the risk of infection."

"Did you ever do any cauterizing?" I asked him.

"Only on farm animals. You remember McKelvie? He told me he'd seen a blacksmith cauterize a teamster's amputated hand with an ordinary piece of flat tire iron and then they packed it in fresh horse manure. It healed up all right. I told that to Beattie, and he said it would work but it was God's own mercy the man didn't get tetanus.

"We use glycerine for chapped hands. Every farmer has a bottle over his sink. And there's various cures for chilblains. I've seen fellers soak their feet in ice water and in hot water and others would rub butter on 'em. They all claimed they got relief. Beattie said the butter was the best of the three. It's very rich in vitamins A and D, whatever the hell those are, and those have a certain effect. In fact, he said it was all the same whether you rubbed the butter on or ate it.

268

"Then, for falling hair we used to rub egg yolk into the scalp."

"That's not an old wife's tale," I said. "Most modern shampoos have egg yolk as their base. I've heard that people used to use kerosene for the same purpose?"

"I've never known any humans that used it," Vern said, "but more'n once I've sold a pair of hosses that came out of the woods in the spring worn to the bone and I'd feed 'em molasses on their hay for a few weeks and they'd get fat as pigs and I'd have a buyer come to look at 'em and I'd rub 'em all over with kerosene that morning and they'd shine like silk."

"Did you ever try drinking water in which iron nails had been allowed to rust, in order to make you strong?"

"I never had to drink iron to make me strong. As a matter of fact, however, that's a common belief up this way. Or at least if it doesn't make you strong, it's good for anemia. Beattie said that some doctors claim the iron oxide contained in the water in which you let nails rust is transformed in the body into a colloidal solution that allows the iron to be assimilated.

"Now if you have a canker sore in your mouth, sage tea will cure it. If you don't have any homegrown sage you can get it from a druggist. Put it into a bowl and pour boiling water over it, let it steep and strain it off. When it's cold, rinse your mouth — even drink a little, if you want to. It'll git rid of the canker."

"I've heard that bee's honey is good for a lot of diseases," I said.

"Yes, I've heard that, too, but I don't know anything about it personally. Doc Beattie asked me about it, and he said it was good for bed-wetting, respiratory ailments, and insomnia."

"Everybody I ever met has a remedy for the common cold," I said. "What's yours?"

"I don't remember ever having had a cold," he answered, "but my father had 'em sometimes and he'd drink a few drops of tincture of iodine in boiling milk, and it seemed to help. I asked Beattie about that, and he said iodine's a powerful disinfectant and such a drink would certainly exert an effect on the throat. On the whole, however, I recollect he didn't seem much impressed."

"This pile of boards," he concluded, as we finished piling up the remains of the shed, "makes me think of a remedy for piles. I suffered from 'em at one time and Old Grandma Fickett — she was about a hundred years old — over in Wilson's Mills in Maine told me what to do for 'em. I tried it, and it worked, but whether it was faith on my part, or something else, I'm not prepared to say. I took a piece of red flannel and laid it on the stove and burnt it until it all turned brown. Then I took some fresh lard and mixed it with the burnt flannel until I got a soft paste. I washed the piles in good hot water and then I put on the paste. It shrunk 'em back to normal and I've never had 'em since. My pious old father advised me to try the remedy described in First Samuel, Chapter 6, but I told him I couldn't find a qualified goldsmith to make the images! Well, let's feed the hosses and we'll go have dinner!"

TWENTY-TWO

Romance

W E WERE driving through the Thirteen-Mile Woods, that strip of forest that extends without a break from Errol to Bayview (exactly thirteen miles) and from the Connecticut River to Rumford Falls (which is eighty miles, more or less). The road follows the crooked Androscoggin river and is perhaps the loveliest of all the lovely drives in the North Country.

Vern pointed to a small sawmill and camp that stood beside the road.

"One of the strangest romances you ever heard of took place right there," he said. "At least the papers called it that, at the time. But I can tell you some things the papers didn't know about.

"The man who owns that mill is named Forbush, and he had a daughter named Nancy. She was only thirteen years old, but she was a handsome piece, and big for her age. She's the heroine. The hero was an American autochthon" (Vern loved to surprise me with big words that he had picked up in his wide reading, though he often mispronounced them) "named Little-hale. His friends called him 'Bill,' though his real name was 'Nelson.' Nelson Littlehale. Now Bill was a lumberjack, but he was a tall and handsome rascal, strong in the back and fairly good-looking. He was also young. To tell the truth (and I always do when it'll do as well as a lie) he was just twenty-six.

"Now you put a handsome young male thing close to a handsome young female thing, and what do you get? Romance, of course. That's what happened when Bill met Nancy. He worked for Forbush, and he and Nancy fell in love with each other. They wanted to get married. But her mama said 'No.' Mama's reasons for saying 'No' weren't what you think they were, but they were good enough for her.

"Flaming with love — red-hot, in fact — the two youngsters decided they would elope. But where could they go? They were poor, and even love — or especially love, I've noticed — needs food to keep it red-hot. That point being decided, Bill, who was a practical sort of a Romeo, proceeded to borrow three-quar-ters of a ton of grub from his potential father-in-law, which he toted, a back load at a time, to a rude but cozy love nest he had constructed on the shore of Mud Pond, a romantic little body of water tucked away in the midst of the woods.

"But you can't expect a man who is flaming with love to remember everything — and Bill entirely forgot to ask Mr. Forbush's permission to borrow the grub from his storehouse. So Papa Forbush waxed wroth. He didn't mind that his daugh-ter had eloped with his hired man. He considered that was her business, not his. But he didn't like the abstraction of his grub.

"He notified the sheriff, and the hunt began. The doughty sheriff swore in dozens and scores of doughty deputies, and right off the bat, more by luck than by skill, they found the young lovers' hideout. I say by luck, for it would be practically impossible to find, in any other way, a man in the Thirteen-Mile Woods who is a first-class woodsman, a first-class rifle-shot, part Injun — and in love.

"One of the deputies himself told me he'd rather tackle a brace of bobcats. So they usually steered away from wherever they thought they might be.

" 'All the world loves a lover,' says the old proverb, but like most proverbs there's lots of exceptions. The young couple, driven from their home, wandered over onto the Diamonds, where they lived in peace for a while. They were in love, they had each other, and they didn't read the papers. What more bliss can one expect on this earth?

"Without any help from anyone they lived and loved and were unafraid. Nancy was a spry girl who knew how to handle a rifle or an axe, and they were as happy as that old couple we saw in the backhouse that day we were coming home from Stratford.

"But lumbermen moved into their district and they had to go. They decided to go to Canada. There's only one road — through Dixville Notch — and that road they would take. Somehow their intention became known. Bill was foolish enough to tell it to someone he thought he could trust, when he went out to Colebrook for supplies. That night the throat of the Notch, which isn't more than fifty feet wide, with sheer cliffs hundreds of feet high on either side, was filled with grim-faced deputies armed with high-powered rifles and probably a machine gun or two.

"I came through there about nine o'clock, and there were six cars, all with their headlights on, and a bunch of men armed to the teeth, all ready to catch one little schoolgirl and her feller.

" 'What in hell do you expect to do?' I asked 'em when they stopped me. 'Do you think those two are going to walk right up into these lights and let you capture them?' "

"Of course they really didn't want to catch 'em anyway, for then their pay would have stopped. As a matter of fact, Littlehale and the girl came up through the Notch and sat on a rock for half an hour, watching them. When they got tired of watching, they just turned out and slipped past them.

"But even in Canada the course of true love didn't run smooth. Bill got a job on a farm near Drummondsville, but one day a minion of the law came to seize him. Bill was working near the house. The lawman had his hand on the lover's arm, but like an eel the Injun slipped away from him and ran for the woods. Nancy, who was watchin' from the house, was a spry girl, as I said. She dashed upstairs, swept up their belongings, and raced out the back door while the sheriff was coming in the front.

"Like long-tried royal Odysseus, the lovers resumed their wanderings. In May, having been gone since the previous October, Nancy returned to the mill in the woods.

" 'Bill and I still love each other,' says she, 'but he doesn't want to cause me any more trouble. We'll wait till my mother consents, or till I'm of age.'

"Mama Forbush was a stern and unrelentin' parent till August came, when she finally gave in and bestowed her blessin'. Bill showed up like a jack-in-the-box. He must have been hidin' behind the nearest tree all the time. So on the fourteenth of August, in the Milan church, with a dozen witnesses present, the two became one.

"Then Bill went down to Berlin and gave himself up to the law. He was bound over to appear in court at a later date, but his father-in-law quashed the complaint, as a weddin' present, and now they're all livin' in that sawmill I showed you. And if that ain't romance with a capital 'R,' I'd like to know what is!"

"Yes," I agreed. "On the surface it has all the elements of a romantic true-confession story. But like most of those stories, when you strip the glamor off, you have something pretty sordid. Besides the question of how are they going to get along afterwards."

Vern spat. "With due exceptions," said he, "life is pretty much what you call sordid anywhere. When it ain't sordid, it's because the people involved have learned that a happy, or at least a contented, life is made up of give and take on both sides.

And I tell you that those two young people will get along together a hell of a lot better than a good many whose wedding pictures decorate the Sunday funny papers. There's nothing makes two people stick closer together than having gone through hard times together."

At that moment a fisherman, carrying a fly rod in his hand, slipped into the road ahead of us from the bushes between the road and the river, and jerked his thumb hopefully.

"Let's give him a ride," Vern said. "I know him. He's a Frenchman from Berlin."

So we picked him up. He was a swarthy, square-built little man about thirty years old, and he and Vern began to talk French at full speed.

"Great blushing Tomcat!" the old man exploded at last. "You know what, Bob, you were speaking of being sordid, listen to Napoleon's story — all he owned in the world was a wife and two kids and a rifle and a new sweater. He had 'em all in a little rented house there in Berlin. He works for the Brown Company in their Onco plant, and his shift foreman lives up in Milan. Poly's a good-hearted cuss and he got friendly with the foreman and often he'd invite him to stay and sleep at his house, especially when he came off the graveyard shift. It saved him that long trip to Milan. Well, the other day he had to go down to Lewiston to a funeral and when he came back damned if he didn't find his wife, his two offspring, his rifle, and worst of all his new sweater, had all migrated to Milan to live with the foreman."

"That's certainly too bad," I said sympathetically.

"Yas, by God!" said Napoleon. "That sweater was brand new, and besides, what will the priest say to me when he finds my kids are up there in Milan with that dam' Protestant?"

We let him out a mile farther on and continued on our way. Presently we had left the Thirteen-Mile Woods far behind and had travelled up Clear Stream almost to the wild gorge of Dixville Notch.

"Let's stop at the next place," said Vern. "There's a girl there you ought to know. She's a native of these parts but she went away and studied art in Paris and New York. She ain't a bad painter at all. Then her mother died, and her father, who is a sort of a country doctor, needed her at home. He ain't there much, and her old grandfather, who is 'most ninety, and pretty well bunged up, lives with them. So she gave up all her career ideas and came home and pitched in to help. She sells fir pillows and paintings and such stuff to tourists, and she's done mighty well. Also," he added, as an afterthought, "she's the prettiest girl between Maine and Vermont."

Before an old farmhouse set back from the road was a small stand, with a sign: "Balsam Pillows." I swung into the yard. Vern honked the horn and a girl came out onto the piazza. She could have been anywhere between twenty and thirty years old. She was rather small than large, with pleasing curves where curves should be, and her cheeks were the rich, healthy brown of a beechnut. Her bobbed hair was a soft lustrous brown, and when she smiled I saw that her teeth were good.

She looked at us levelly and smiled a little, though of course she did not know me, and she could not see Vern.

"Hello, Jin!" he called cheerfully as he stepped out of the coupe. "How's the 'independent woman' this morning?"

She laughed then, a pleased sort of a laugh such as women always seemed to have for the big old pirate beside me, and came forward holding out her hand.

"I'm glad to see you, Vern," she said. "Won't you come in? It's been a long time since you were here."

"This young feller here is Bob Pike," Vern said. "I'll vouch for him."

She looked at me in friendly fashion. "Anyone Vern vouches for is welcome here. Won't you both come in?"

We followed her into a large, square living room lined with loaded bookshelves. She waved us to chairs and picked up a pack of cigarettes from a table, but she put it down again.

"I almost forgot, Vern," she said. "You don't like to see women smoking cigarettes."

"Not women like you, Jin," he agreed. "If you want to show off your equality with men, for God's sake why don't you smoke a pipe?"

She offered me the cigarettes, but I shook my head.

"Has Vern been influencing you?" she asked. "For a man who swears like a preacher, he does have the funniest ideas."

An impish grin shone on her face for an instant and she went into another room. She came back bearing a whiskey bottle and glass in one hand, and a plate of fudge in the other. She set them down on the table at Vern's elbow and made him a curtsey.

Vern laughed boomingly. "You can't embarrass me, Jin," he said and reached for the candy. "I've put away a lot of rum in my time, but I never could understand why people will offer it to a guest instead of a box of chocolates. Damn it, girl, do you know that if I was forty years younger I'd ask you to marry me?"

"And if you were forty years younger, I'd take you," she answered, unsmiling.

"Why *don't* you git married, Jin?" he asked her seriously. "After all, it's a natural thing for young people to want to do."

"There was a man," she told him frankly. "I guess you know who he was. I cared for him a great deal, and I'd have married him in a minute if he'd asked me. Unfortunately — or perhaps fortunately — I made the mistake of showing him how much I cared. And so — and so he forgot to ask me to marry him."

"It's his loss, not yours," growled Vern.

"I suppose so. Still, it hurts, you know."

"Aye," said the old man. "Nobody knows better than me how much it hurts, Jinnie."

There was an awkward little pause.

"Don't you get lonesome," I asked inanely, "when you talk with all these tourists, and see them passing by?"

277

She shook her head. "I feel rather sorry for them. Going back to their lonely cities, while I have all this."

"Just what do you mean by all this?" Vern demanded.

"Sunlight," she answered slowly, "and starshine. The northern lights. Clean air. Quiet. Peace. Economic safety, too. And leisure for one's friends when they deign to come and see one."

She smiled at Vern who was obviously pleased.

"I'm glad you call me a friend, Jinnie," he said. "Personally, I think you're a mighty fine specimen of the female genus homo. I was telling Bob here how you pitched in and saved the family."

"Nonsense. I didn't do any more than most of the other women you know. You're acquainted with plenty of happy, successful families — and in every one of them there is a capable woman doing her part."

"I guess it's the truth," he agreed. "But it takes a woman like you to bring home the fact to me."

"You're a stranger up here?" she asked me.

"More or less," I confessed.

"I think," she said gravely, "that the inhabitants of this North Country have quite unconsciously developed a society that is as near being ideal as any you will find anywhere in the world. I'm one of them by birth and present status, but I was away long enough to appreciate their peculiar merits better than most of them do themselves.

"They are a self-reliant breed who face life realistically, without superstitions or illusions, and, what seems very important these days, when I think of so many other people I know, without fear of economic disaster. They are more tolerant than any people I know, and they are always ready to help their neighbors. There are none of them illiterate, and none without a sense of humor. I've mentioned the sunshine and the starlight and the other things. There is no competition here to keep up with one's neighbors. If one can't afford a car, one can always walk. It's not something to be ashamed of. We are sure of fruit and berries and vegetables and fresh meat and fish. All of us are sure of those things."

"Unless they're too lazy to raise 'em or go after 'em," put in Vern dryly.

We clasped her small firm hand in farewell and went on through the last and most magnificent of the White Mountain Notches — Dixville. Through the throat of the gorge, with Table Rock, six hundred feet high and twenty-five feet square, towering on our left. Ahead, nestled in the woods at the western entrance of the Notch, lay lovely Lake Gloriette, backed by the forested slopes of Mount Abenaki.

"So you think," I said to Vern, "that what we call romance is usually sordid, in real life?"

"There's exceptions, there's exceptions. In fact I can show you one. It's a bit out of our way, but you ain't in any hurry, are you? I'd kinda like to go over there again."

"At your service. Just tell me where to go."

A few miles below the Notch he directed me to the right, on a dirt road. A sawmill stood beside a dam in the fork of the road.

"Abe Washburn owns that mill," said Vern. "He's quite a quaint character. They call him 'Honest Abe,' and he *is* honest. Also he looks a good deal like Lincoln, except his hair and whiskers are red. He's uncle to Bill Bacon. When he was a little boy there was a potato whiskey factory here on the Mohawk and he used to go down for a jugful about every day. Finally the manager noticed this ten-year-old boy was coming in pretty frequent, and he says to him: 'You come after whiskey pretty often, don't you, sonny?' 'Well,' says Abe, 'what else can you do when there's six kids in the house and no cow in the barn?' "

After we had passed the sawmill, we twisted and turned to the north and east over a maze of steep, stony roads. At last, we crawled over the crest of a high bare ridge. The shallow ditches were hemmed with golden buttercups and blue forget-me-nots. A hundred feet to the north stood a solitary, gigantic

279

maple tree that must have been five feet in diameter. An iron fence surrounded the tree.

"This is Hardscrabble Hill," said Vern. "Let's git out."

We walked over to the iron fence. "It's to keep cattle out." Vern explained. "All Hardscrabble Hill is pasture land now."

Inside the iron fence, at the foot of the great maple, were three graves. One was old. The other two were more recent. The first one was covered with a marvelous bed of pink and white trailing arbutus, the most fragrant flower in all the North Country, and one of the rarest. There was some on the grave to the left, also. None on the newest one, to the right. There were no markers.

Vern did not look at me. He stared at the graves. "I expect you are wondering," he said at last, "what these graves are doing up here all alone in a cow pasture?"

"I think I understand that," I said, as I looked over the panorama of forested mountains that extended for miles in every direction. "But I do not understand about the arbutus."

"There's a story about the arbutus," he said. "I'll tell it to you. Many years ago — maybe forty-five — there was a farmhouse down in that valley." He pointed down the far side of the ridge. "A boy lived there. His father was very poor. The other children in the neighborhood made fun of him because of his ragged clothes, and he was a sort of lonely little feller.

"But there was one girl, a pretty girl with hair as black as midnight and eyes that shone like stars on a winter evening, who liked him. In fact, she loved him, and she had faith in him. When he was eighteen and she was seventeen, his father died. He left him a thousand dollars. He and the girl, whose name was Mary Hilliard, came up here to this old tree one afternoon in May. There was a natural bed of arbutus at the foot of the tree in those days . . . "

Vern stopped. I did not understand, so I waited in silence, and presently he went on, his long arms folded across his chest as he continued to stare at the graves.

280

"The boy said he was going away, that he would make his fortune, and then he would come back and marry the girl. It was a bright, windy afternoon, one to make you glad you are alive, but the girl was not glad. She wanted to cry. To hide her tears she bent down and picked a fragrant spray of the arbutus. She kissed it and then she held it to his lips. So they sealed the agreement between them.

"Ten years later the boy had become a man and was well on the road to success. He had met a man who was an inventor and had helped to finance him. They became partners and made much money. In all that time he never wrote to the girl but once, but he had told her he would not write until he had made good, so she was not worried, though sometimes she was so lonesome she used to cry herself to sleep. Her father was a farmer. When he died, she carried on the farm alone. She was a hell of a handsome woman, capable, strong, jolly — and a good many men asked her to marry them. But she had faith in — in her lover, and she refused.

"Then one day she saw an item in a newspaper announcing the man's marriage to a girl in Chicago, where he was living. There was a picture of the bride, a tall, dark-haired woman — beautiful. The girl read the item twice. Then she fainted. Afterwards she wanted to die, and she prayed for death to take her, but she was too strong. She thought she would never smile again. But she lived and learned to smile. But her heart was dead in her breast, and it stayed dead for twenty-five years.

"Then one day a car drove up to her house. It was a long, shining car. The chauffeur got out and asked for Mary Hilliard, and when she said she was Mary Hilliard, a woman got out of the car and came to her. Mary knew who she was, though she had never seen her. She was still beautiful, because she had never had to do any work, nor bear any sorrow. But grief had come to her lately, for her eyes were sunk in her head and circled underneath with black. And she was very nervous.

"But she came and looked Mary in the eyes, long, very

long, as if searching for something, and finally she whispered:

" 'It's the pure faith in you, Mary Hilliard; that's what you had that I lacked,' and she began to cry as if her heart would break. And though Mary felt that she should hate her, she took her in her arms and tried to comfort her. And at last she told Mary that he was dead, and dying he had told her that all his life he had loved the girl Mary Hilliard, and why he had married *her* he did not know, but being married, he had kept his marriage vows.

"But now he was dying and he would tell the truth, and he asked her to bring his dead body back and bury it at the foot of the big maple tree — 'Mary'll tell you where,'" he whispered. Toward the end he was delirious, and as his soul went fluttering out between his lips with his last breath, he murmured: 'How fragrant the arbutus is, Mary,' and then he died.

"He had told his wife to give Mary half of all he owned, and though he had made no such provisions in his will, she told Mary she was going to do it, because — because she, too, loved the man. Mary would take nothing, but she brought up the arbutus that she gathered here and there in places that she knew, and planted it on his grave, for she knew he would like it so.

"A couple of years or so later the woman wrote that she was dying, and if only she might lie beside the man, then she would rest in peace, and she asked Mary to grant her that favor — for Mary owned the land and had given only enough for his one grave. And she would not have granted it, for she had made up her mind that if she could not have him in life, she should lie beside him in death, and she alone. But at the end of the letter, the woman wrote: 'I dare to ask it because we both loved him, Mary.'

"And when she read that, her heart softened and she wept. And that grave to the left there is hers, and Mary climbed up here to plant pink arbutus on it, just as she did on his."

Vern stopped again, and he was silent so long that I thought the story was ended, but there was that other grave.

"That?" he said. "That's Mary's, of course."

"How do you happen to know all those little details you had in that story?" I asked.

"She told 'em to me. Some of 'em the first time I asked her to marry me. Some of 'em later. Some of them on her death bed. I dug all three of those graves," he added stonily.

"And she kept the faith all those years," I murmured. "That sounds more to me like romance with a capital 'R!' "

"At least," and the old man's fierce eyes softened for a moment, "there wasn't anything sordid about it."

"But you," I said, "you seem to have been pretty faithful yourself."

"Which only shows," he answered gruffly, "that I'm a damn fool."

Envoi

ALL THESE things that I have written here, and many others, flashed through my memory as I sat looking at the scissor-toothed man. And now Old Vern had got married!

"Do you suppose," I asked the man, "that they'll have any children?"

He meditated for a few moments. Then he spat his chaw of tobacco into the palm of his hand and rolled it to and fro, in the good old-fashioned way. At last he spoke:

"Nope," he said gravely, as a man who has pondered a problem and finally arrived at an irrevocable conclusion. "He won't have any children. It wouldn't be accordin' to nature. They broke the mould when they made Old Vern. There'll never be any more like him. He's the last of his kind."

Glossary

barroom: not a saloon, but the bunk-room, or sleeping quarters, of the lumberjacks.

besom: broom made of twigs.

bateau: the double-ended (*i.e.*, both ends are alike) boat used by rivermen on log drives.

bobsled: not a rig for frolicsome folks to coast down hills on, but a short heavy sled used to haul logs. The butt end of the logs are placed on the bunk (the connecting portion between the two runners), while the tips of the logs drag behind on the ground.

boom: a line of logs, connected at the ends, used to confine saw-logs, pulpwood, etc., in the water; also, the enclosed area.

bunk: cf. bobsled.

cant dog: "cant dog" (or "cant hook"), while technically not quite the same instrument as a "peavey," is a term used in the North Country to designate a peavey. *cf.* peavey in the glossary.

cut: term applied to the emasculating of farm animals.

draw-tub: a large metal or wooden tub placed on a sled and into which the farmer empties maple sap as he gathers it from the trees to take to the sugarhouse.

drive: the logs or pulpwood that are floated (or "driven") down the rivers from the woods to the mills. This takes place in the spring, as soon as the ice goes out, because then there is plenty of water and the logs do not get stranded on rocks and shoals.

dry kye: driftwood and dead trees in the water at the edge of a pond or lake.

height-of-land line: a height of land is the top, crest, or highest point of land between two watersheds. Logs may not be hauled uphill, so the height of land where a lumbering operation is going on is marked by a spotted line (*i.e.,* a blazed trail) so the loggers will not cut over the top. To distinguish it from other spotted lines, the spots are often painted red.

landing: a collection of logs brought out of the woods and "landed" on a river, or river bank, to be ready for the spring drive; such a collection in the woods, where it is loaded onto sleds to be transported to the river, or mill.

martingale: a strap fastened to a horse's girth, passing between his forelegs, and fastened to the bit, intended to hold down the head of the horse and prevent him from rearing.

oats: (to feel one's) to be full of high animal spirits, as a horse that has been fed on oats.

peavey: a stout wooden lever armed with a strong steel spike at the end, and with an adjustable steel hook. Used for turning logs. (Named after Joseph Peavey, a Maine blacksmith who invented it.)

powder: dynamite.

pulp (wood): four-foot bolts of wood, formerly only softwood, used to make pulp paper.

rear: the tail-end of a log drive. The main drive goes on as fast as it is able. The crew on the rear take time to pick up all the stranded logs that are left behind.

rollway: about the same thing as a "landing," *q.v.*, but the latter may be right on top of the river ice, whence it goes downstream when the ice breaks up in the spring, whereas the rollway is on the bank, whence the logs have to be rolled into the water.

scaler: man who measures ("scales") logs.

scarf: the notch a lumberjack makes in a tree when he cuts it down.

sheer boom: a boom, *q.v.,* strung so as to keep floating logs sheered away from obstructions in the river.

sluiced: a team is said to be sluiced when it accidentally goes off the road and piles up.

snath: the handle of a scythe.

spotted line: cf. height-of-land line.

stumpage-inspector: a lumber company will sell "stumpage," *i.e.,* standing timber, and when the buyer cuts it, the company provides an inspector to see that the buyer does not cut trees that are too small or too large.

tote road: the road going into the woods to a logging camp along which supplies are hauled ("toted") from outside.

two-sled road: this does not mean a road where two sleds can pass, but is a main logging road down which loads of logs are drawn from the woods on a "two-sled" rig, which is, in effect, two bobsleds, one behind the other and connected by an adjustable piece of timber called a "reach."

turkey: the small personal outfit belonging to a lumberjack or riverman. It can often be contained in a large handkerchief.

walking boss: a lumber company's head man in the woods. Theoretically, he "walks" from one camp to another.

wanigan: the outfit — wagons, tents, blankets, cooking equipment, etc. — of rivermen on drive; also the company store at a logging camp.

YANKEE • CLASSICS

IN THIS exciting new series, Yankee Books
brings back into print rare classics of
New England literature that previously
have commanded the highest prices as rare
books if and when they could be found.
The editors have selected only those titles
that are as lively and enthralling to today's
reading audience as they were to that of
a generation ago.